MIND FIST

BOOKS PREVIOUSLY PUBLISHED

by Dr. Haha Lung

The Ancient Art of Strangulation (1995)
Assassin! Secrets of the Cult of Assassins (1997)
The Ninja Craft (1997)
Knights of Darkness (1998)
Lost Fighting Art of Vietnam (2006)
Mind Control (2006)

Written with Christopher B. Prowant

Shadowhand: Secrets of Ninja Taisavaki (2000)
The Black Science: Ancient and Modern Techniques of Ninja
  Mind Manipulation (2001)

Written as "Ralf Dean Omar"

Death on Your Doorstep: 101 Weapons in the Home (1993)
Prison Killing Techniques: Blade, Bludgeon & Bomb (2001)

Written as "Dirk Skinner"

Street Ninja: Ancient Secrets for Mastering Today's Mean Streets (1995)
X-Treme Boxing: Secrets of the Savage Street Boxer (2002)
  with Christopher B. Prowant

MIND
FIST

The Asian Art of the Ninja Masters

DR. HAHA LUNG

CITADEL PRESS
Kensington Publishing Corp.
www.kensingtonbooks.com

CITADEL PRESS BOOKS are published by

Kensington Publishing Corp.
850 Third Avenue
New York, NY 10022

All Kensington titles, imprints, and distributed lines are available at special quantity
discounts for bulk purchases for sales promotions, premiums, fund-raising, educational,
or institutional use. Special book excerpts or customized printings can also be created
to fit specific needs. For details, write or phone the office of the Kensington special sales
manager: Kensington Publishing Corp., 850 Third Avenue, New York, NY 10022,
attn: Special Sales Department; phone 1-800-221-2647.

First printing: December 2008

10   9   8   7   6   5   4   3   2   1

Printed in the United States of America

Library of Congress Control Number: 2008932336

ISBN-13: 978-0-8065-3062-8
ISBN-10: 0-8065-3062-6

To Amber Nikole Shifferly

and

Jamerrion ("Pooter") Feagin

CONTENTS

CONTENTS

CONTENTS

TIGER CLAWS: WINNING THE PHYSICAL GAME   131

CONTENTS

MIND FIST

INTRODUCTION:
"Bully Kung-fu"

"He who by causing pain to others wishes to
obtain happiness for himself, he,
entangled in the bonds of hatred,
will never be free from hatred."
—Babbit (1936:0)

Bullies created kung-fu. To be more precise, bullies caused kung-fu to be created—out of necessity.

The short version (discussed in more detail later in this book) is that back in the sixth century A.D. the peaceful monks of the Shaolin temple in Hunan province, China (think David Carradine in the 1970's hit TV series *Kung-fu),* were constantly being bullied and beaten every time they ventured out of their temple by bands of cutthroats and highwaymen.

No matter how much these monks tried talking these thugs into changing their evil ways, the brigands continued to bully the monks. That is, until the arrival of a monk master from India named Bodhidharma (called Tamo by the Chinese and Daruma in Japan).

Bodhidharma had come from a military background before giving up his sword in favor of a monk's begging bowl, so he was no stranger to violence.

The weathered scrolls all tell how Bodhidharma first taught the Shaolin brothers "yogalike exercises" designed to strengthen them for their long hours of meditation. What a surprise these peaceful "yoga"

1

exercises just happened to double as kick-ass kung-fu* fighting techniques!

Needless to say, soon after learning Bodhidharma's exercises, the Shaolin monks (and, as we will see later, nuns, too!) were making short work of any attackers who dared cross their path. Thus was born the legend of the unbeatable Shaolin kung-fu fighting arts, from which nearly all Asian martial arts schools claim some lineage.

That's the simple version of the story. Later, we'll examine the legend in more depth to see what truths and techniques we can glean from it for our use today. Because, whether we're talking about fourteen hundred years ago, or today's mean streets, bullies are still bullies.

The Shaolin monks found an appropriate response that allowed them to effectively fight back against the bullies of their day. That's what we're looking for as well, with the operative phrases being "appropriate response" and "effectively fight back." And that's why we're going to borrow as many tried-and-true tactics and techniques as we can from "back in the day," always with an eye to tailoring these tactics and techniques into our own effective response, all geared to the realities of our own modern-day bullies.

All you need to know about the Shaolin monks is that they were bothered and besieged by bullies back then and that they did something about it. After that, the Shaolin brothers were pretty much left alone. Reputation spills less blood. Bullies pick the weakest-looking targets.

So you see, there's not much difference between the bullies back then, always lurking in the neighborhood of the Shaolin temple, and the bullies prowling in your neighborhood today.

We run into bullies every day, from the playground to the battleground, and from the bedroom to the boardroom. In the workplace. In all walks of life.

We all want things to go our way in life. Most of us are intelligent enough—or at least scared enough!—not to cross those boundaries of legality or just plain decency just to get our way. True, sometimes we all push the envelope.

---

*The Chinese term "kung-fu," sometimes written "gung-fu," more correctly means "perfect" and "hard work," implying that one is a master of his craft, such as a kung-fu carpenter. However, here we use the term as it has become more commonly known in the West to refer to Chinese-based martial arts overall. In general, Chinese martial arts are more correctly referred to as "wu shu."

On the other hand, bullies, shred—fold, spindle and mutilate!—that envelope. All of us have been—or will be—bullied sometime in our lives. Chances are we've bullied someone ourselves . . . or will to get our way.

There's a myth that "all bullies are cowards." Not true. What's true is that all bullies "pick their shots" by sizing up their victims and picking on those who show the least likelihood for resistance. Also true is that, like all criminals, bullies are an opportunistic lot. They are predators waiting for their prey to make a mistake, to drop their guard, so they can more easily separate their intended victim from the rest of the herd.

Bullies have something else in common: They learned their bullying ways early on in life, perhaps on the playground, maybe even before they started kindergarten. (More on this in a future chapter.)

The bully lesson learned early on in life—"If I threaten or hit people enough they will give me their stuff!"—is a lesson kids carry with them on into their teen years, and then on into adulthood.

It's human nature: When something works, we stick with it.

Kids watch. They listen. They take notes. They imitate.

Sure, some of it's the parents' fault for not taking time to teach kids the difference between video game fantasy and harsh reality.

Think your kids won't listen to you? Oh, they are listening, hanging on your every word—your every cussword, that is.

You have to catch bullies early on, before they become older bullies, before they get a "taste" of the bully life.

As we will learn in later chapters, you'll find out that bullies think differently than you and I, that their brains actually process information differently than nonbullying normal folk. What you and I might see as a dangerous and threatening situation and process in our brains as fear, a bully sees the same encounter as excitement.

Crime may not pay, but bullying certainly does, at least from the bully's point of view. A bully gets rewarded for his bullying by receiving the "Three A's":

1. Adrenaline. When faced with a threatening situation, the body floods us with flight-or-fight chemicals. Those of us nonbullies sometimes find ourselves literally paralyzed by this natural chemical response to danger taking place in our body. On the other hand, bullies actually get high on the feelings of excitement and power literally coursing through their veins.

2. Acceptance. Early on, many children figure out it's better to be a

bully than to be the one being bullied. That's why so many kids eagerly join gangs of bullies where, instead of being picked on, they are now accepted and admired by their fellow bullies. By out-bullying their fellow gang members, these new recruits can rise through the ranks, to the top of the heap, maybe even to become the leader of the pack, the alpha dog. Bullying can also put the bully on the fast track to adulthood, granting teenaged bullies admiration and acceptance into more adult circles and activities.

There are degrees of bullying. Some types of bullying are even rewarded by a greedy society strangled by political correctness that all too often tolerates—and even encourages—bullying under myopically convenient phrases such as "youthful enthusiasm" or even "team spirit":

- Sports superstars who get a slap on the wrist for spitting in the referee's face or for leaping into the stands to assault fans.
- In-your-face rappers who threateningly wave automatic weapons and flash gang signs at the video camera, glorifying "the thug life."
- Common street thugs—bullies all—all given their fifteen minutes of fame by the media, just enough time to threaten the few honest citizens left in their neighborhood to "stop snitching or else."*

3. Awe. In his book *The Prince,* Niccolò Machiavelli (1469–1527) tells us it is better (i.e., safer) to be feared than loved. Fear—another name for awe—lends us a certain amount of safety.

Remember that bullies always follow the path of least resistance, picking their victims wisely. How you carry yourself when you walk down the street matters. If you have a reputation as someone who can handle himself, then there's a better chance bullies will leave you alone. Remember those Shaolin monks? Remember: "Reputation spills less blood."

So bullies are "adrenaline junkies," but they're also "acceptance junkies" as well as "awe junkies." (In later chapters, we'll look at some of the psychological underpinnings that many bullies have that are fed by acts of bullying.)

For parents, teachers, concerned relatives, and community activists, the time to talk to your kids about bullying—in order to prevent there being more adult bullies in the future—is before your kids get a heady—often satisfying—experience of being a bully themselves.

---

*If you're an honest citizen, trying to do right, trying to raise your family right, it's your job to "snitch"—it's called Neighborhood Watch!

The time to talk to your kids about sex or about drugs is before they've tasted the forbidden fruit. Once they get a taste, your job becomes twice as hard. The same holds true for bullying.

Anytime we experience anything novel, we open a new, permanent "file" in our brain, a place to reference that experience and where we then store future, similar events.

Simply put, if we've never actually used a certain drug, or actually had a pleasurable sensation associated with specific actions, then we don't know what we're missing—literally, our brain has no reference point—no file to access—with which to compare our lack of that drug or pleasure.

Kids begin bullying at an early age and, unless interdicted at an early age, they carry these behaviors—this way of dealing with life's problems— into adulthood.

In the same way, unless we mentally and physically train ourselves (i.e., acquire experience) in responding to bullying, we will have no reference point to access when facing an actual bullying situation.

This same learn-by-experience principle applies whether we're trying to psych ourselves into standing up to a street thug or just finally face down the office bully, or whether we're teaching our kids—often through example—how to stand up to the playground bully.

How do we learn to do this?

We watch and listen. We take notes, and we imitate, not just those Shaolin monks, but also anyone and everyone who has ever successfully stood up to a bully, from the classroom, to the poolroom, to the boardroom.

WHAT YOU WILL LEARN FROM THIS BOOK

This book teaches only one thing: better communication. That's because better communication equals more options, more options to survive and prosper.

All too often, we don't realize what negative—potentially damaging— personal information we're communicating to others, in the form of inadvertent voice cues and by our unconscious body language.

Astute poker players (as well as alert police officers) call these twitches and itches "tells," unconscious slips of the tongue and stumbles of the foot that betray our doubt and indecision, our fears and fluctuations of spirit.

It's been estimated that 90 percent of all human communication is nonverbal. This is information we give out unconsciously through changes in our volume and tone of voice, the clearing of our throat, and those ever-annoying—and telling—Freudian slips. We also give ourselves away nonverbally by how we stand, how we sit, how we walk, and by every unmindful gesture and glance of our eye.

What kind of signals do we inadvertently give off when walking down the street that scream to predators: "Dinner's ready, come and get it?"

Our only mistake is in thinking that we're not sending similarly transparent "screw me over" signals to the office bully.

The master medieval Japanese swordsman Miyamoto Musashi, the author of *A Book of Five Rings,* taught his students to carry themselves on the battlefield the same way they carried themselves while in their homes, and vice versa. In other words, the same "prey" signals we give off that mark us as easy pickings for the office bully are the same signs a street thug looks for when deciding whether or not to try bullying us out of our ATM pin number.

Just as important, what subtle sounds and signals do we give off that our kids pick up on instantly? Remember, they really are little sponges.

This book teaches us better communication skills by showing us to become more aware of how we carry ourselves, stop sending out unconscious "pick on me" signals and to learn to deliberately carry and conduct ourselves in such a way that we dissuade a predator from ever mistaking us for his supper.

Twenty-five hundred years ago, the Chinese general Sun Tzu, arguably the greatest strategist who ever lived, taught that the key to victory in all endeavors of life depends on three things: knowing ourselves, knowing our enemy, and knowing our environment. According to Sun Tzu, the more we know these "Three Knows," the more assured is our victory.

What will learning to communicate better via Sun Tzu's "Three Knows" bring us? More options. The more tools in your toolbox (or the more weapons in your arsenal, if you prefer), the more options you will have to work with in any given situation.

Verbally disarming a bully (whether a street thug or your office manager) through reasoning with him is, of course, preferable. But to only arm yourself with words alone is to risk the possibility of finding yourself up the creek without a paddle.*

*Japan's greatest swordsman, Miyamoto Musashi, got to be Japan's greatest swordsman by killing the previous title holder, not with a sword, but with a rowboat paddle! This is the best "don't get caught up a creek without a paddle" example ever!

Increasing our options allows us to choose between *reactive* and *proactive* responses. Recall that our goal is to master "appropriate responses" that will allow is to "effectively fight back" against the bullies of the world.

At the very least, we need more than one way to deal with the bullying problems that beset us.

As we will see in a later chapter, many child development experts believe that the earlier and better a child is taught that he can choose from many different ways of reacting to a situation—that bullying is not the answer to all of life's problems—the less likely that child will develop into an adult bully.

By the way, Sun Tzu's highest praise was reserved for those generals who won battles without fighting, by becoming aware of a potentially threatening situation before it fully manifested and immediately taking actions to prevent that situation from ever getting out of hand.

Likewise, the Shaolin monks—even after they learned to kung-fu kick major bully booty—still taught new students the following mantra: "Avoid rather than block. Block rather than strike. Strike rather than maim. Maim rather than kill."

At one point in time, it was forbidden for a Shaolin monk to teach kung-fu to anyone other than another Buddhist monk because only monks (who had taken an oath not to harm others) were thought to be of sufficient character and restraint not to be tempted to use kung-fu to settle petty scores.

Luckily for us today, eventually those kung-fu techniques eventually made it over the wall of the Shaolin temple to be shared with the rest of us.

Still, we could do a lot worse than take to heart this Shaolin kung-fu mantra as we search for our own ways to combat the bullies in our lives.

Please note that at no time does this book teach that violence is the answer to all the world's problems.

Chronic (constant, long-term) world problems, like the chronic problems in our individual lives, demand dedication, determination, and long-term sweat to resolve. By contrast, acute (immediate) problems (e.g., threats) *are* sometimes settled face-to-face, mano-o-mano. Would that it were not so. Yet reality would have it otherwise.

As much as we might admire those who dedicated (and in many cases literally gave) their lives to complete nonviolence—the Gandhis and Martin Luther King Jrs. of the world—there are situations where a shovel cannot do the work required of the hammer.

The bullies of the world are a wide and varied lot. Regardless, all bullies—from the first-grade strong-arm artist with a sucker punch hidden in his pocket, to the religious nut with a suicide vest hidden under his coat—bullies all rule by fear.

Fear cloaks itself in ignorance and rules in the darkness. Knowledge is light.

From the bullying boss who knows "you can't do anything about it" because he holds your job in his hands, to some punk with pistols rampaging around campus, to those fanatic bullies blocking the cockpit door . . . the truth remains that some bullies can't be reasoned with.

At such times, we need to be able to exercise more options than only paralyzing fear, only lemminglike compliance to evil. This book will give you options.

I

The Bully Game: Then and Now

It's hard for some people to equate what they see as "harmless" even "playful" bullying on the kindergarten playground with some vicious street thug berating and beating down a little old lady for her Social Security check or with your horny boss trying to cop a feel every time he catches you at the copier. But it's all bullying.

First and foremost, bullying is about invading another's personal space—from snatching your lunch money with a sucker punch to the gut, to coughing up a degrading off-color racist or sexist punch line every time you happen to walk by, to pouncing on you at your local ATM.

Right off, we can see that bullying varies in its level of sophistication and its level of intrusion. So whether it's the kindergarten bully yanking on the little girl's pigtails, or your boss patting your behind, it's still an invasion of your personal space.

As in war so in bullying. First comes "the invasion" of personal space (often hand in hand with varying degrees of violence), then comes "the domination" (of both your mind and body) as more and more of your day—and life—is taken up with you trying to avoid the bully in your life and/or to please and placate him even as he becomes emboldened in direct proportion to your diminishing escape options.

Remember that bullies feed on fear and hesitation. For every step back you take trying to avoid trouble, trouble takes two giant steps forward.

What do you do?

First, take a deep breath and remind yourself that you have more in common with your bully than you might at first suspect—or be ready to accept.

The odds are you were both introduced to the "Bully Game" early on in your lives—if not as bullied children in your own home, then in school. Early on, before we learned to tie our shoes, some of us learned to be bullies and some of us learned to be victims.

Take another deep breath and relax, and remind yourself that in the same way we learned to be bullies, or learned to be victims, that we can unlearn to be bullies, or unlearn to be victims.

We begin to do this by giving the monster a name, by defining exactly what we consider to be "bullying" and what actions clearly label another person "a bully."

By taking this preliminary step, that is, focusing our attention on the problem by clearly defining the parameters of that problem, we, in effect, draw a line in the sand—that beyond this point of common decency and civility, thoughtless or intentionally hurtful words and actions that clearly qualify by anyone's definition as "bullying" will no longer be tolerated!

Thus, following Sun Tzu's advice, we'll dedicate ourselves to stopping little problems before they become big problems. We'll accomplish this by getting a handle on where the bully came from and figuring out what motivates the bully mentality in general and our bully's three pounds of tainted gray matter in particular.

Finally, rounding out our study, we'll study how the "Bully Game" we first encounter on the playground all too often follows us up through our troubled teen years, into adulthood—bullying us from cradle to grave. And through our study we will learn to finally take responsibility for our own safety of body and peace of mind. The buck—and the bullying—stops here!

WHO YOU CALLIN' A BULLY?

"Let no man think lightly of evil, saying in his heart, It will not come nigh unto me. Even by the falling of water-drops a water-pot is filled; the fool becomes full of evil, even if he gather it little by little."
—Babbit (1936)

"There was something mean about this boy. Troubled kids get drunk and jump off buildings. It was the meanness that bothered me." That's how

Cho Seung-hui's Virginia Tech poetry teacher described him, elaborating on her initial assessment that Cho was "a bully" (Gibbs, 2007:42). "He was very intimidating to my other students," explained another Virginia Tech teacher.

"A bully" and "intimidating" indeed. Cho's April 16, 2007 rampage across the peaceful Virginia Tech campus left thirty-two of his fellow students and teachers dead, before the madman turned the gun on himself.

And he was a "madman" by anyone's definition: angry "mad" at the world for what he saw as its refusal to recognize his genius, "mad" in the more clinical sense of the word—his fevered brow dripping beads of schizophrenic sweat.

But was he a bully in the traditional definition of the word?

We know now that, within his own mind, Cho saw himself, not as a "bully," but as a "victim," bullied (or at least ignored) by his fellow students, or else shunned by them for his bizarre mutterings and bouts of acting-out.

Counterbalancing his contention that the world—or at least his fellow students—were shunning him are numerous examples of both students and staff at Virginia Tech who tried reaching out to Cho long before that tragic April day.

And there were warning signs. Two years before, campus police had investigated Cho for "annoying" a female student. Here was a disturbed soul with a documented history of mental illness who, at one point, had been temporarily confined to a psychiatric facility by a judge's order, an order that warned in part that Cho was "an eminent danger" to himself and others (Gibbs, 2007).

But was he "a bully"?

As already noted, Cho saw himself as the victim of bullies—the "rich kid" bullies on campus who shunned him—and who knows what other real or imagined "bullies" bounced off the padded walls inside his skull.

Cho's solution to these perceived slights turned out to be eerily similar to the twisted answer arrived at by the Columbine killers (who also saw themselves as victims, "bullied" by school jocks): to become the ultimate bully himself. It seems easy to bully a whole campus when you're waving around guns!

Yes, the bully game is alive and well—and undoubtedly will be for some time to come—because we all help perpetuate bullying in one way or another, either by actively contributing to it, or else by passively turning a blind eye to such abuse. Oftentimes, society even encourages and rewards bullying, accepting "a little heavy-handedness," a little "running roughshod over the troops," so long as the job gets done.

Some of the more renown go-getters in history have been accused of being bullies—and not just bad guys.

For instance, General George Patton (1885–1945) was accused of bullying his men; he was nearly court-martialed for slapping an enlisted man he thought was showing signs of cowardice.

Likewise, the author Bob Deans says of Captain John Smith (1580–1631), "He was a bully, a braggart and a rebel with a big chip on his shoulder." (2007:61)

Deans's contribution of "braggart" and "big chip on his shoulder" to our bully definition segues well with the *Merriam-Webster Dictionary* definition of a bully as: "A blustering fellow oppressive to others weaker than himself." *Merriam-Webster* goes on to define blustering as "to talk or act with noisy swaggering threats."

The *American Heritage Dictionary* defines bully as "one who is habitually cruel to smaller or weaker people."

Ironically, our modern English word "bully" comes from the Middle Dutch word "broeder," meaning "brother," and is linked to the Middle Dutch "boele," meaning, of all things, "sweetheart."

Notice the word "weaker" keeps cropping up in any definition of bully? That's because bullies "pick their shots" by carefully choosing their targets with an eye toward those who *appear* weaker, and the bullying itself often stems from the bully's fear of appearing weak himself, thus he must mask his own weakness from others—lest he appear to other bullies as a target.

Michael Martin and Cynthia Waltman-Greenwood, in *Solve Your Child's School-Related Problems,* give a brilliantly succinct definition of childhood bullying, which just happens to also apply to all other types of bullying as well: "A child is bullying when he fairly often oppresses or harasses someone else, either physically or verbally." (1995)

It's not hard to see how this definition can fit every bully in your life, from the annoying playground Bart Simpson* to the boss who can't keep his horny hands to himself, to the street thug lurking in the shadows.

---

*Actually Nelson, the Bartman's own playground nemesis, is *The Simpsons* resident misunderstood and lonely bully.

For the purposes of this study, the word "bullies" is defined as "those individuals, situations, and sundry forces who besiege, belittle, and/or batter us on a regular basis." This could be a stranger, your boss, your spouse, or another troublesome family member.

And here's something even worse to consider: If your personality is such that you tolerate one bully in one aspect of your life, there's a pretty good chance you have—or will soon have—more than one bully in your life.

Relax. The same principles you can teach your kid to effectively deal with playground bullies will also work for you when having to deal with an overbearing boss or some intimidating punk in the street.

> *"Whether it's a grade school threat of 'Give me your lunch money*
> *or I'll give you a wedgie!' or 'Mess with me and mine and*
> *we'll nuke your whole friggin' country!' the playground to the*
> *battleground, the 'Bully Game' is alive and well."*
> —Lung (2006:51)

TYPES OF BULLYING

In *Mind Control* (2006), I describe two types of bullies: mental bullies and physical bullies, with much overlap between the two.

Mental Bullies

Mental bullies first use the threat of intimidation (personal space invasion, verbal threats, etc.) to get their way.

> "You'd be surprised to learn just how many psychological
> 'bully ploy,' some subtle, some more overt, are aimed at you
> every day." (Lung, 2006:52)

These include everything from the news media terrorizing us with on-the-spot atrocities, to ad campaigns using ploys such as "limited time offer" and targeting specifically to our age, gender, and any and all other identifications we may have.

These kinds of socially acceptable instances of bullying rely on the same type of threats as do cults who threaten us to hurry and get on board before

"The Big Payback" at the end of time. How is this any different (beyond the obvious delusions of grandeur!) from the playground bully threatening to punch your lights out at recess, or your boss threatening to fire you if you don't "play ball"?

Physical Bullies

G. Gordan Liddy understood the equation: "When you have them by their balls, their hearts and mind will follow." In other words, "where the *threat* of force fails, there's always the *force* of force" (1997:56).

Either way, being bullied is painful—whether mentally (anxiety-wise) or actually physically knuckle-to-eye painful.

Pain is classified as either acute or chronic. Acute pain is a sharp, stabbing pain, like stepping barefoot onto a piece of glass, or the instant, intense pain we feel when breaking a bone—our bones, not the other guy's bones.* This kind of pain soon passes. On the other bruised hand, chronic pain stays with us. The pain of an impacted tooth when we're unable to get to the dentist, or the type of pain someone with a spinal injury might experience. Dull, throbbing, keep-you-awake-at-night pain.

Bullying can also be classified as being either acute or chronic—with much overlap.

Acute Bullying

When a gang of street thugs crosses over to your side of the street, surrounds you, and "asks" if you have any change to spare . . . that's acute bullying: an immediate threat to your person (registered as anxiety). A sudden barroom confrontation, that is acute bullying. Like the sudden, sharp, and stabbing acute pain, so, too, acute bullying manifests as situations and encounters that are often brief.

Chronic Bullying

Chronic bullying has duration. Having to worry about being beaten up and having to go without lunch day after day for an entire school year, that's chronic bullying. Enduring years of spousal abuse (rent the movie *Sleeping*

---

*For a complete training course on how to break the other guy's bones, see Haha Lung's *Koppo-Jitsu: The Forbidden Art of Bone-Breaking* (publication pending).

with the Enemy), that's also chronic bullying. A boss harassing and belittling you day in day out, that, too, qualifies as chronic bullying.

Of course, all acute bullying has the potential to become chronic bullying. After all, chronic bullying is just a repeating cycle of acute bullying incidents.

Girls and Bullying

Lest you get to thinking our study of bullies is in any way sexist, rest assured that, time and again, longitudinal studies (studies following the development of children sometimes across more than a twenty-year span) have collected data proving that girls are just as capable of becoming bullies as are boys.* Martin and Waltman-Greenwood (1995:59) point to the fact that, while boys are still in the majority when it comes to bullying, girls also do their share of bullying.

Likewise, Daniel Goleman, in *Emotional Intelligence,* calls our attention to the slippery slope leading from childhood bullying, through teenaged delinquency, predictably into adult manifestations of bullying. Goleman refers to it as a "trajectory," as if a missile—or bullet—once set on course, has little likelihood of being diverted:

> "A telling difference emerges in this trajectory between boys and girls. A study of fourth-grade girls who were 'bad'—getting in trouble with their peers—found that 40 percent had a child by the time they finished the high school years. That was three times the average pregnancy rate for girls in their school. In other words, antisocial teenage girls don't get violent—they get pregnant." (1995:237)

Also sadly predictable is the fact that, just as aggressive little boys raised by arbitrary and harshly punitive parents all too often grow up to be arbitrary and harshly punitive fathers in their own right, it's not surprising to find aggressive little girls, raised by the same type of parents, becoming those parents when they become adults (ibid. 196).

---

*See Alexander Thomas et al., "Longitudinal Study of Negative Emotional States and Adjustments from Early Childhood through Adolescence" *(Child Development,* vol. 59, September 1988).

It is to society's credit that it is finally beginning to recognize—and seek solutions for—bullying by the "gentler sex."

In May 2007 the PBS program *State of Ohio* (WVIZ-PBS, May 11, 2007) reported on a statewide "Conflict Management Week" symposium, part of Ohio's "Safe School Summit," held the previous month.

One of the main focuses of this summit was addressing the growing problem of bullying, by first establishing a working (legal) definition of bullying (they settled on "persistent intimidation"), while addressing understandable concerns for what a school and school administrators can be held (legally) accountable for in instances of bullying. Discussions covered not just student-on-student bullying but also the rising incidence of student-on-teacher bullying.

Students bully teachers in a variety of ways, and not just with physical threats to their person, on and off campus, though there is admittedly a high incidence of these kinds of threats. Student-on-teacher bullying can also include threats to involve teachers in scandal, with allegations ranging from racial prejudice to attempted rape.

Student motivations for bullying teachers range from students who simply take pleasure in discomfiting authority figures (perhaps acting out behavior and/or anger displacement against an abusive home situation) to students attempting to intimidate teachers into giving them good grades and/or passing them to the next grade level.

Many teachers admit to having been so intimidated by a student that they purposely gave the student good grades to ensure that the troublesome student would be passed to the next grade level and therefore would not pose the same threat the following year.

Meanwhile, back at the Ohio symposium, timely twenty-first-century issues of concerns included "cyber bullying," for example, where students bash and belittle classmates (and increasingly teachers) on gossipy Web sites such as Myspace.com.

One of the symposium's topics dealt specifically with "Girls and Bullying," a growing concern that is all too often overlooked.*

---

*Columbus, Ohio: "The State Board of Education adopted a model anti-bullying policy after deciding it should not specifically reference students' religion or sexual orientation. . . . The policy recommends banning threats, taunts and intimidation through words or gestures. It is intended to help local school districts draft their own guidelines" *(USA Today,* July 12, 2007:8A).

As will become even clearer in the following sections, when we look at whether bullies are born bullies or beaten into becoming bullies, and where we examine the motivations of bullies, you'll realize how our observations (and hopefully solutions as well) can be easily applied to girls who, like their male counterparts, all too often grow into adult bullies.

BAD SEED OR BAD PARENTING?

"All the progressive parenting classes in the world
won't change the fact that, when all else fails, Mommy and Daddy
have the power to administer some 'violence' to your backside."
—Lung (2006b:57)

Are bullies just "born evil"? Or does something (or a whole lotta some-things) happen during their childhood to turn the "sweet and innocent" to the "Dark Side"? In other words, is being a bully born into them, or is it beaten into them through a succession of childhood dramas and traumas? Are they the victims of skewed genes or just screwed up parents?

Of all the specters of speculation that haunt the learned halls of both psychology and sociology, this has always been the big question: Nature versus nurture—are we born messed up, with inexorable destiny carved into our DNA? Or did Mommy and Daddy go out of their way to ensure we patterned ourselves after their every fear, foul up, foible, and faux pas? Simply put: Are we born bad or is it a matter of genetics gone awry?

Everyone agrees that a child has the best shot at a bully-free life if that child is provided with a safe, nurturing home life, one where punishments and rewards—positive and negative reinforcement—are clear-cut and consistent, where personal boundaries are established early on and religiously adhered to, where the consistent and civil behavior of parents acts as a daily beacon to help guide the child ever onward.

Yeah, good luck with that. The truth is many kids' home life more closely resembles Norman Bates than Norman Rockwell!

Still, we parents do the best we can, hoping to set a good example for our children, hoping they're paying attention when we say "just say 'No!' to drugs," hoping they're already asleep when we come stumbling in from that New Year's party.

Some child development experts harp on too little parental supervision—and your kid grows up to be a maniac! Others warn against too much supervision—stifling your child's natural development.

At first glance, this makes it seem as if parents are caught up in a lose-lose situation: Too lenient, children have no boundaries, so parents are asking for trouble there as well. However, harsh physical punishment teaches a child it's okay to hit:

> "Punishing a child with harsh, frequent spanking, teaches a child that it is OK for bigger people (parents) to bully smaller people (kids). Not surprisingly, children who bully usually pick on smaller, younger, or weaker children." (Martin and Waltman-Greenwood, 1995:59)

Furthermore, it's not realistic to teach children that all of life's problems can be settled with a few well-meaning words.

There really are some sadly sick and scary monsters lurking out there in the world, and we need to realistically prepare our children to meet such challenges.

As in all things in life, a balance needs to be struck: a balance between teaching our children that it's all right to hit anything anytime—thus turning our own children into bullies—to teaching our children when it's okay to take a stand against the bullies of the world.

As we will soon come to realize, the problem is not so much in teaching our children that there are clear-cut rewards and punishments in life, starting with clear-cut discipline within the home, but rather our failing lies in not being consistent with our lessons, rewards, and punishments.

THE MIND-SET AND MOTIVATIONS
OF A BULLY

"Bullies are not going to disappear,
because there will always be people with the kinds of
people problems that result in bullying personalities."
—Wright and Smye (1991:216)

Children learn to be assertive from others: parents, family, friends, and enemies at school. But there's a big difference between assertive behavior and aggressive behavior. Assertive behavior radiates from the inside out, and is a natural, positive by-product of self-esteem. On the other hand, aggression fixates on an external object, often with vague, unorganized, and chaotic attention (i.e., wrath).

While some experts still weigh in on the "nature" side of the equation, maintaining that some children have more innate tendencies toward aggression than others, no one can successfully dispute the influence parents—"nurture"—has on a child's development.

Parents pass their own aggression to their children, by word and by action, by both the way they deal with the child in particular and how the child observes the parents dealing with the world in general. Aggressive parents produce aggressive children.

According to Goleman (1995:235) the family life of such aggressive children typically involves parents who vacillate between the extremes of neglecting the child on the one hand while harshly and capriciously punishing the child on the other hand; an inconsistent pattern of punishment that all too often causes the child to see the world at large through paranoid and/or combative glasses.

Goleman goes on to track the development of such aggressive children through kindergarten, up through grade school, where they continue to use the tried-and-true bullying techniques they learned from their parents and have already used successfully on their parents.

Simply—if somewhat gloomily—put: by the time these children enter school, they have already learned in their homes a somewhat successful coercive bullying style of dealing with others. These newly minted bullies now barrel headlong down a predetermined path of childhood bullying, followed by (often violent) juvenile delinquency into, at the very least, failed social and personal relationships as adults, and as a worse case scenario, a life of criminality (see Goleman, 1995:236).

Nothing skews a child's view of the world more than the inconsistency of parents. Children are nothing if not resilient, capable of adjusting to almost any extreme, even the harshest of punishments. But there truly is something to be said for consistency.

Conversely, the hardest thing for any human being to adjust to is inconsistency, because there is no sure place to hang your hat, no clear-cut boundaries, no trustworthy referee in life.

Uncertainty breeds uncertainty, and not knowing what tomorrow—or even recess—might bring often prevents a child from developing viable and healthy coping strategies—for the day, for life.

An inability to cope effectively out in the world breeds uncertainty within the child, which, in turn, initiates a truly vicious cycle of inner doubt and outer timidity that literally paralyzes the child, preventing him from effectively dealing with the world at all.

Not surprising then that such children begin their formal schooling carrying around a battered box of broken crayons that cannot but color their world chaotic. These crayons of the mind are the failed (and in some cases frightening) coping mechanisms—inner psyche defenses—children will in all likelihood carry with them up through their teen years into adulthood.

Later, when we discuss workplace bullying, we'll see how these childhood mental defense techniques (coping mechanisms) all too easily translate into teenage angst and acting out and into adult bullying tactics.

Bully or Victim?

"The bent of mind that aggressive children take with them through life is one that almost ensures they will end up in trouble."
—**Goleman (1995)**

Many see bullies as being victims themselves who, at an early age, are exposed to and taught negative ways of perceiving, and thus responding to, what they see as a threatening world.

Yes, we are laying responsibility for this squarely in the lap of the parents. Says Robert J. Meadows in *Understanding Violence and Victimization:*

> "The evidence is clear: parents of aggressive children punish more frequently, but inconsistently and ineffectively. They also tend to negatively reinforce coercive and manipulative child behavior and fail to adequately reinforce positive, pro-social behavior." (2004:150)

Meadows's assessment is both succinct and eye-opening. Here we see a combination of factors coming together to midwife the birth of the bullying mind-set: Parents frequently punishing the child, but doing so inconsistently and ineffectively, thus negatively reinforcing coercive and manipulative child behavior. Finally, parents of aggressive children fail to adequately reinforce prosocial behavior.

Other experts then take this assessment to the next level, pointing to how messed up kids become messed up grown-ups, dragging their dysfunctional "inner child"—kicking and screaming!—with them into their adult years:

> "When it comes to bullies, knowing that your soul is being sapped because there is a Wounded Child Within, who has been unable to resolve his pain from an adult perspective, doesn't seem as significant as the immediate task of dealing with the Loathsome Adult Without." (Wright and Smye, 1996:53)

Comparisons: Bully vs. Victim

Both the bully and the victim suffer from negative self-image (NSI). The bully and the bully's victim differ only in how they attempt to (re)solve the anxiety caused by their NSI.

Martin and Waltman-Greenwood (1995) define the word "victim" well:

> "A victim is the child who, for a fairly long time, has been the focus of aggression from others, with someone often picking fights, teasing, or ridiculing him or her. This is not a one-time victim, but someone who has not learned how to be assertive enough to protect himself." (1995:60)

On the other hand, bullies turn their NSI outward:

> "Children who get more negative comments directed to them than positive ones don't feel good about themselves. Eventually they expect the world to be negative toward them, so they strike first by bullying." (ibid. 59)

Given the fact they've been taught limited options, limited responses to the stressors of everyday life, it's hardly surprising that time and again the bully should opt for a preemptive strike, hitting the world before it hits him.

Recall that Goleman (1995) blames capricious disciplining for infecting the child early on with feelings of worthlessness, helplessness, and paranoia to threats in the world at large. We find these signs and symptoms of NSI in both the bully and the victim. Indeed, in a side-to-side comparison (Figure

1), we can easily see that bullies and their victims are but two branches from the same root.

PRESOCIAL AND SOCIAL INFLUENCES
(e.g., parenting style, harsh but capricious, absentee, etc.)

BULLY	VICTIM
Low self-esteem/NSI	Low self-esteem/NSI (Martin and Whitman-Greenwood, 1995:59)
Risk-taker (self-undervalued)	Fearful, doesn't take chances (low self-expectations, less of a target to bullies)
Hypersensitive to offense (Wright and Smye, 1996:54)	Hypersensitive to giving offense.
Afraid of showing weakness	Sometimes emphasizes weakness to appear less of a (threat) target.
Suspicious/paranoid offensively	Suspicious/paranoid defensive (Higgs, 2007)
Lack of empathy (Goleman, 1995:96)	Sensitive (Martin and Whitman-Greenwood, 1995:60)
Externally oriented (extrovert)	Internally oriented (introvert)
Frustrated outward (Higgs, 2007)	Frustrated inward
"Macho" demeanor (Wright and Smye, 1996:54)	shamed, furtive (Higgs, 2007)
Faux-positive self-image (overblown, unrealistic)	Negative self-image (body dysmorphia, believes self inadequate to counter physical threats),
Attitude: sarcastic, critical, fault-finding	accomodating, conciliatory, passive
Action-oriented (restless)	Sedentary
Consciously seeks attention (negative attention acceptable) (Martin and Whitman-Greenwood, 1995:59)	Unconsciously seeks attention while giving outward appearance of being quiet, retiring, and timid.

Figure 1: Bullies vs. Victims. One-in-seven school children behaves as either a bully or as a victim. (Martin and Whitman-Greenwood, 1995:59)

Inflated (albeit fragile) self-image	Insecure (Martin and Whitman-Greenwood, 1995:60)
Manipulates (and dominates) peers (Martin and Whitman-Greenwood, 1995:59)	Avoids peer interaction (Martin and Whitman-Greenwood, 1995:60)
Manipulates adults (Meadows, 2004:150)	Overly dependent on adults (becomes resentful and further withdrawn when adults "fail" to protect them from bullies)
Poor impulse control	Overcompensates, keeps "low profile" trying to avoid notice. Sublimates urges and needs to the point of frustration and further self-loathing.
False sense of power	False sense of helplessness
Feels superior, false bravado (Martin and Whitman-Greenwood, 1995:59)	Feels inferior (worthless, inadequate to task, etc.)
Limited responses to stressors (responds with frustration, anger, acting out)	Limited responses to stressors. (responds with "overthinking," hesitation, and indecision)

As we can see, young bullies (who all too often grow up to be adult bullies) share many of the same anxieties and frustrations as their victims, differing in the main only by how the two express (or repress) these tensions.

Both the bully and the victim of bullying suffer from low self-esteem.

The bully compensates by picking on those smaller and weaker than himself, thus inflating (albeit temporarily and precariously) his own fragile ego. In other words, he builds himself up by tearing down others.

Both bully and victim are hypersensitive to their surroundings, especially to the actions and reactions of others.

The bully is ever on the alert for trespass, for someone "making fun" of him behind his back, any "chump diss'n" (i.e., disrespecting) "his space" or "cockblocking" his "game." Thus, the least trespass by the victim—the slightest mismovement of hand, a curious glance in the bully's direction, a joke the bully takes personal—can all too easily be misperceived as "disrespect" by the bully and can be just the excuse he's looking for.

Not that a bully needs an excuse to be a bully. But the bully usually enjoys watching you squirm, enjoys your discomfort and growing fear as you hopelessly try to reason your way out of his crosshairs, struggling in vain to explain the reason you—a lowly maggot—dared deliberately to trespass against his invisible and obviously arbitrary boundary lines.

The victim is also hypersensitive—he has to be in order to survive. Like the victim's nemesis, the victim can't afford to trust the world, after all the world is full of bullies!

Constantly scanning his surroundings for the approach of the bully, ever on the alert, always attuned to the bully's every nuance of word, every narrowing of the eye or sudden wave of the hand—these are all vital survival skills if the victim is going to anticipate what the unstable and protean bully might consider a "slight," a "trespass," a "dis" today.

Both the bully and his victim have a skewed sense of self. On the one hand, the bully has an overinflated view of himself as "alpha dog," "king of the roost," the "big man on campus" who others fear and who can do no wrong.

By contrast, the victim has an equally distorted self-image, albeit an underinflated one.

Whereas the bully unconsciously undervalues himself (this accounts for his risk-taking and disregard for self), the victim consciously undervalues himself by constantly reinforcing his false belief in his own inability to combat life in general and the bullies in his life in particular.

Both bully and victim seek the attention of others. The bully seeks it consciously (reveling in the fear of his victims, while basking in the awe and admiration of his fellow bullies). The victim unconsciously seeks attention from adults and others to help make his world more safe.

Sadly, because much of the victim's petitions are often unspoken pleas for help, his cry for help all too often goes unnoticed until it overtly manifests in the form of self-mutilation and or self-defeating behaviors (e.g., drug abuse, promiscuity, etc.).

Finally, the most important thing a bully and his victim share in common is that they both rely on limited responses to stressors.

For example, a boy raised with a macho ("manly man") outlook or "thug" mentality often develops into a man with limited avenues of emotional expression—save feigned stoicism, frustration, anger, and inevitable violence. That is, if his antisocial and violent mannerisms and methods allow him (and the rest of us!) to survive at all:

"Psychologists argue that raising boys to be strong and silent is promoting the outbreak of school shootings and violence, subsequently causing the smoldering climate of despair among male teenagers. In other words, American boys are reared largely in keeping with the traditional code of male toughness, which encourages boys to take action while inhibiting expressions of feeling and gestures of physical affection." (Meadows, 2004:150)

Victims also have limited responses to stressors (e.g., the bullies in their lives). Most often this is due to their undervaluing their innate ability to counter what life throws at them.

This is where awakening your Inner Tiger comes in!

Victims understandably have trust issues. Why shouldn't they? The world is constantly jumping out from behind a bush, sucker-punching them, and taking their lunch money! To make matters worse, the victim all too often feels betrayed by his own body. Just thinking (i.e., visualizing) what a bully is going to do next causes butterflies in the stomach, sweat to break out, the mouth to get dry, even his legs to begin trembling—all signals the victim incorrectly perceives as signs of his fear—his cowardice—his not being worthy to walk among "normal" and "brave" folk. Dwelling on being a coward sets up the most vicious of cycles, a downward spiral of self-doubt, leading ever lower into self-loathing and, all too often, self-destruction.

The victim must learn to trust his body, to recognize these bodily sensations as signs of preparedness, not signs of cowardice.

We will delve into this later in depth, along with numerous techniques for awakening the Tiger within. But for now a quick lesson in the kung-fu you already know:

You are suddenly attacked by someone swinging a baseball bat, trying to strike your head. What do you do? More to the question: What does your body automatically do to defend itself even before your brain has had a chance to realize what's happening?

Your natural reaction—everybody's natural reaction—is to instinctively throw both your hands up (to protect your head), while at the same ducking lower (instinctively making yourself a smaller target). (See Figure 2.)

Figure 2. Instinctive (natural) "duck-and-cover" reflex-reaction.

Now let's say you're tired of living in fear or, worse yet, tired of getting your butt kicked everyday and have, instead, decided to take up some form of self-defense training (karate, kung-fu, etc.) promising to teach you how to defend yourself against a physical attack.

First of all, any martial arts training is better than no martial arts training. If nothing else, working out on a regular basis will help you "get your wind up" in case you need to flee quickly from danger and/or exercising regularly will help strengthen your body to help you survive an ass-kicking (just in case your sensei doesn't know what he's talking about!).

That being said, you could spend time deprogramming yourself from your natural reactions to this attack before learning (programming) some new (foreign and fancy) responses into your mind, muscle, and bone—a process that could take years. Will the bullies in your life wait that long?

Or you could do what comes natural—only do it better! (See Figure 3.)

Using the natural instincts your body already possesses, you practice turning your already raised arm at a more acute angle (so as to better deflect the club rather than letting it break your arm by hitting square on).

Your other hand—also instinctively moving up to intercept the club— can be trained to strike inward into your attacker (disabling your attacker with a solid "Palm-blow" or, at the very least, forcefully pushing him away).

Figure 3. Trained crouch and counter (*see also* Figure 41).

Simultaneously, taking advantage of the automatic "duck" response nature was wise enough to wire into your DNA, you have trained yourself to lower your stance into what's known as a "Tiger squat," a firm-footed position that still makes you a smaller target while it opens up several further flight-or-fight options to you.

Keep in mind that all the physical response techniques you'll learn from this book merely build on what you already know and what your body already knows to do instinctively.

But all this will come later. Right now, let's get back to job one: Understanding the enemy. And the best way for us to understand the enemy is to understand ourselves.

> *"The body is ever with us but mysterious,*
> *an anatomical counterpart to the sociological stranger.*
> *We experience its reality while we form images of it and its*
> *possibilities. Although we may not explore its interior and cannot*
> *inspect its full surface without the aid of mirrors, we nevertheless*
> *are constantly limited by its limitations, aided by its capacities."*
> —Lyman and Scott (1989:59)

> *"Mules are good if tamed, and noble horses too,*
> *and great elephants; but he who tames himself is better still."*
> —Babbit (1936)

The Bully Payoff: Power!

> *"Power—the capacity to impose one's will*
> *upon the behavior of others."*
> —Weber (1947)

What's in it for the bully? What's he get out of bullying you? What's his goal? Is it something concrete like your lunch money, some piece of property you possess, moving into your corner office, sex? Or is your bully's agenda something more abstract, some inner, subconscious drive scratching at his spine?

The anger displacement theory says your bully has unresolved anger, probably from childhood (angry at parents, angry at the world, anger because he himself was a victim of bullying), anger issues he's probably not consciously aware of, subconscious anger issues that keep spilling over into his conscious world.

Keep in mind it's not your responsibility to psychoanalyze a bully when he is trying to beat your brains in. True, when being verbally brow-beaten by a bully, you might have the leisure time to try coming up with just the right insight into his "troubled personality" that would allow you to diffuse the situation with a few well-muttered Freudian zingers. On the other hand, should you suddenly find yourself in a physical struggle, one that requires you to fight to save your teeth and salvage your dignity, the time for putting the bully "on the couch" is over, it's time to put him on the ground!

Be that as it may, knowing what makes your bully tick could be the trick to winning confrontations the way Sun Tzu preferred: before they happen!

Like the rest of us, bullies are either internally motivated (listening to their own inner dialogue between Id, Ego, and Superego in deciding to do right or wrong), or else they are externally motivated (taking their cues from others and from their surroundings and then reacting in the best manner possible to survive).

Externally motivated bullies generally want things like money, property, or sex. Internally motivated bullies are driven by vaguer inner stirrings, warped psychological needs and necessities, most often a mystery to the bully themselves.

To complicate matters, even when a bully insults and assaults you for what seems like conscious external-concrete gain, all too often that bully is actually being motivated by subconscious inner drives that falsely tell him acquiring external objects will finally pacify his inner demons. More often than not, the acquiring of the external object is not the prime mover for the bully, it's what the external object represents that spurs the bully on. Even sexually motivated predators and racially motivated bullies fall into this category.

Dominating others gives the bully a sense of power—whether the power to give someone a wedgie on the playground, the power to force yourself on someone sexually in the bedroom, or the power to sexually harass and belittle ad naseum in the boardroom.

In the end, whether the bully is trying to dominate us physically or mentally, whether his goal appears to be external (e.g., money) or more vaguely inner-demon-driven, in the end, it all comes down to power.

The Will to Power

The philosopher Friedich Nietzsche (1844–1900) maintained that all human beings have a "will to power," an innate need to be the master of their domain, cock of the walk, to exert cunning and force and to see that cunning and force bear fruit in their life.

Later, the psychologist Alfred Adler (1870–1937) would adapt the same idea, that man has an innate drive to influence, that is, gain power over himself and his environment.

At first glance, this Adlerian will to power theory seems to directly challenge the will to pleasure theory put forth by Sigmund Freud (1856–1939), that man is first and foremost a pleasure-seeking animal. But the two need not be mutually exclusive.

When bullies lord over those weaker than themselves—when they arbitrarily wield power—it does, indeed, bring them pleasure.

Whereas other normal folk might feel sorry for, and/or identify with the suffering of another, one of the hallmarks of the bully mentality is that the bully lacks empathy for his victim.

Lack of empathy in abused children has been well documented.* Goleman points to such a lack of empathy as the jumping off point for a child's— and eventually the adult's—descent into bullyism, if not out-and-out criminality:

> "This failure to register another's feelings is a major deficit in emotional intelligence, and a tragic failing in what it means to be human. For all rapport, the root of caring, stems from emotional attunement, from the capacity for empathy. . . . That capacity—the ability to know how another feels— comes into play in a vast array of life arenas, from sales and management to romance and parenting, to compassion and political action. The absence of empathy is also telling. This lack is seen in criminal psychopaths, rapists, and child molesters."

---

*For research and findings on abused day-care children and empathy, see Mary Main and Carol George's "Responses of Abused and Disadvantaged Toddlers to Distress in Age Mates: A Study in the Day-Care Setting" (*Developmental Psychology*, vol. 21, no. 3, 1985). For similar research on preschoolers, see Bonnie Limes-Dougan and Janet Kistner, "Physically Abused Preschoolers' Response to Peers' Distress" (*Developmental Psychology*, vol. 26, 1990).

Some psychologists see this natural quest for power in our lives as part of our reaching for self-actualization—an innate need to fulfill ourselves, to live up to our true potential, to engender within ourselves positive feelings of self-worth and efficacy. So, consciously or unconsciously, we all do seek power in our lives.

Merriam-Webster defines power as "the ability or capacity to perform or act effectively . . . strength or force exerted or capable of being exerted; might."

Of course, ideally in a perfect world, this power should not come through the belittling and battering of weaker individuals. Thus, sometimes it falls to us to point out to the bully that he's looking for power in all the wrong places. This is never as easy as it sounds, because the bully associates power with safety and security.

This is called the caveman theory of aggression. Back at the dawn of man, when small tribes were living in caves barely managing to stay alive, the most aggressive hunters ate first and ate best. Back then, aggression was rewarded—and still is to a great degree in the modern world: during wartime, in sports, in politics, and when negotiating with Donald Trump. The best bullies back then got the best cuts of meat . . . and the best women. So I guess not much has changed. Add to that the fact that your best and strongest hunters were never the first chosen to have their heart cut out with a flint knife in order to appease the angry thunder god, and you can see how power (strength and status) came to equate safety in the primitive mind.

It's still pretty much the same in the primitive mind of today's bully. Better to be a bully (higher up on the food chain) than to be the one being bullied.

Perhaps the most disturbing of theories ever suggested to explain man's aggression (and bullying) is the Milgram theory. Based on the oh-so contro-versial experiments done by Stanley Milgram (1933–1984), this theory proved that, under the right (or wrong?) circumstances, we are all capable of unspeakable cruelty—even torture—toward our fellow human beings (so long as some authority figure is footing the bill). At the very least, the major-ity of us can rationalize turning our eyes the other way at the most conven-ient time *not* to get involved in the troubles, travails, and—yes—even torture of another. Does Abu Grab ring a bell? Rodney King?

Not surprising then that the more the bully can make you squirm, the better (safer and more powerful) he feels. Also not surprising is that one short stumble beyond Milgram we run into the sadism theory.

Sadism

Stanford M. Lyman and Marvin B. Scott define sadism as simply "the pleasure felt from the observed modifications of the external world produced by the will of the observer" (1989:193).

On the surface, this sounds a lot like Nietzsche's (and Adler's) will to power; the need we have to feel we have some kind of control, or at least influence, over our lives. This need to feel in control is inherent in all people and is akin to Abraham Maslow's "survival and safety needs."

Abraham Maslow (1908–1970) is best known for his "Hierarchy of Needs" pyramid, which postulates that man seeks to satisfy, in ascending order, first his "physiological needs," then his "safety needs," before then pursuing higher goals such as "love and belongingness needs," "self-esteem needs," and, finally the capstone of the pyramid, "self-actualization needs."

Self-actualization means different things to different people, although a general definition should include those thoughts and activities that give us feelings of self-worth and even "spiritual" transcendence above the mundane by allowing us to realize and utilize our full potential as human beings.

Whatever you've heard about the Marquis de Sade (1740–1814), there's a darn good chance it wasn't anything good! After all, the man did spend thirty years of his life in prison, including the final thirteen years of his life. And all he's got to show for it are a bunch of writings—mostly incredibly pornographic!—and the fact his name has become synonymous with whips, chains, and Helga the Dominatrix.

Yet, beyond the obvious titillation (or is that curiosity?) and prurient snickers, lies a serious—albeit uncomfortable—insight into the nature of human thought and interaction. According to the Marquis (at least give him credit for being an astute observer of human frailty), the sadistic urge (need) is natural, man's most basic instinct.

But there's more to sadism than just that twinkle in Helga's eye. There are two important distinctions (or degrees if you will) to sadism proper: the more passive schadenfreude and the decidedly more aggressive algolagnia.

Schadenfreude is the sense of joy and/or excitement we get when we watch others suffering pain and unhappiness. But while we enjoy this other person's pain and discomfort, we are not the ones directly (actively) responsible for their misfortune and suffering (Lyman and Scott, 1989:193).

Before you start protesting that you personally could never take pleasure in the discomfort—let alone pain—of a fellow human being, ask yourself:

Have you ever laughed at *America's Funniest Videos?* Someone slipping on the banana peel? A Three Stooges movie? This is technically a harmless (socially acceptable) form of schadenfreude sadism, as is every practical joke ever played.

On a more serious side, we also take joy when bad things happen to bad people, when an evil enemy such as Adolf Hitler or Osama bin Laden gets what he got coming. Thus, like it or not, our sense of "justice," "karma," and "fate" all qualify as sadism.

To make you feel a little less uncomfortable, there are two categories of schadenfreude: benign and belligerent. Benign is when we see something happen to someone (that stranger slipping on a banana peel) and we laugh. Belligerent schadenfreude is when we see the banana peel lying there and can warn the approaching stranger, but choose not to . . . just to see what happens. Thus, we err—sadistically speaking—through our in-action.

By contrast, algolagnia encompasses the whips and chains part of sadism. Algolagnia is defined as the pleasure (including sexual pleasure) you get from deliberately and actively inflicting pain on others.

This is pure bully territory. Unlike schradenfreude, algolagnica is active, not passive.

To recap, schadenfreude comes in two types: the passive kind, where merely observing others' discomfort and suffering brings us pleasure, though we are not the direct cause. The second type of schadenfreude occurs where we allow someone to suffer through our in-action and/or lies of omission. Algolagnia is more aggressive. Pleasure comes from being directly responsible for another's suffering.

It's not hard to spot in the overall mentality of the bully elements of both types of sadism: the more overt algolagnia type, and the more subtle "B-type" schadenfreude (where a bully, such as your boss) allows you to be discomfited when it is in his power to prevent or stop it.

Dominance

Just as society accepts—and even encourages—certain types of aggressiveness—such as in war, sports, and business dealings—so, too, society perpetuates certain types of traditional dominance that the bully can take full advantage of and take to the extreme.

Despite great strides made in the past few decades toward age and gender parity, society still has unwritten, untalked about traditions that give (or at least imply) dominance of one segment of the population over another and different operating rules and special privileges. For example, men are still given dominance over women, and adults dominance over children.

In addition, certain recognized and accepted forms of authority also automatically (by virtue of their position) hold dominance over others. As already mentioned, men are still perceived as having dominance over women. This is reinforced by legal authority that recognizes the dominance of the husband over his wife (or wives, as the culture may be).

Legal status and authority also give dominance of judicial and law enforcement personnel over the rest of us—up to and including the right to execute. There is also bureaucratic authority dominance (e.g., elected officials, school principals, and your boss). Add to this the fact we all too often voluntarily give various pseudo-qualified individuals dominance over us (e.g., religious leaders and politicians).*

Growing up, the bully is surrounded by these traditional (and often arbitrary) examples (e.g., parental examples of kowtowing to others, perhaps spousal abuse, etc.). He sees how one segment of the population has the right to lord over another segment of the other. It's understandable the blossoming bully should want his piece of the domination pie, whether following his inner drives of will to power or some vestigial caveman urge to secure his place in the world's harsh pecking order.

Bully Benefits

> *"Fools of little understanding are their own greatest enemies,*
> *for they do evil deeds which must bear bitter fruits."*
> **—Babbit (1936)**

The bully benefits (at least in his mind) from his actions. There are benefits (or by-products, if you will) from the power the bully acquires (review Figure 1). These feelings of power inevitably lead to feelings of superiority as the bully begins benefiting from his actions in the form of a pliable and playable reputation that wins him the fear of his peers and all too often causes even adults to either cater to him or else avoid him altogether because he's too much of a bother, too much of a "problem child."

---

*See "How to Be an Instant Expert" in Haha Lung's *Total Mind Penetration* (2007).

Attention-Getting Behaviors. The bully first receives attention in the form of fear and obedience from his peers. Reputation—of being a tough (or at the very least unpredictable) character—works as well for the modern bully as it did for the caveman by providing him status with his cohorts and a modicum of safety within the larger "tribe" (at least until a new, bigger bully comes along).

Of course, being left alone can all too soon become loneliness.

A bully's peer support network is fragile. He is supported either out of fear or else because other bullies have banded around him for their mutual gain. Thus, even the densest of bullies intuitively seems to realize how shaky his position of power really is. And so paranoia and a constant testing of loyalties is the norm in bully cliques, crews, and gangs. So it is with cults as well, those led by bullying, paranoid leaders.*

To the bully, it matters not if the attention he's basking in is positive or negative. In fact, being "singled out" or "picked on" by an authority simply reinforces in the bully's mind (and in the mind of some of his slavish cohorts) that the bully is "important" or "a threat"—a much valued status in bully land.

Thus, the bully enjoys even the negative attention he receives from adults, the admonition he gets from authority figures who might otherwise be ignoring him—for love-starved children (and adults!), negative attention is better than no attention at all (see Martin and Waltman-Greenwood, 1995:59).

In a curious extrapolation of the Stockholm syndrome (where kidnap victims and hostages begin identifying with their captives), among long-term torture victims, such as prisoners of war subjected to long periods of isolation and solitary confinement, some of these victims admit to actually beginning to look forward to regular interrogation and torture sessions. For these prisoners, overt torture is preferable to mind-numbing isolation from their fellow human beings—no matter how cruel those other human beings are (see Lung and Prowart, 2003).

Feelings of Superiority. Between physically menacing his fellows and the attention being given him by concerned (or placating) adults, the bully inevitably develops feelings of invincibility and superiority:

---

*See "How to Start Your Own Cult" in Haha Lung's *Total Mind Penetration* (2007).

"Picking on others also makes them feel superior, and they get plenty of attention for it." (Martin and Waltman-Greenwood, 1995:59)

This creates a vicious cycle: Getting attention makes the bully feel superior (see Figure 4).

Feeling superior, bullies act out more against rules that "don't apply to them." As a result, they inevitably get more attention.

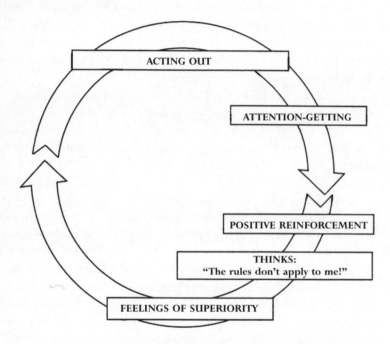

Figure 4. The vicious cycle of bully reinforcement.

Feelings of superiority are positively reinforced even more by the effect the bully has on the adults in his life.

This is called the "Blowback Effect," where the child in the home, and later the bully in the school, successfully turns the tables on the adults around him. In effect, the inmate becomes the warden.

This blowback effect begins in the home when parents capitulate to the demands of a stubborn child:*

"This occurs when parents reinforce coercive child behavior and are inadvertently negatively reinforced themselves—by giving in to their coercive child. In other words, children learn that aggressive behavior often leads to parents giving them what they want." (Meadows, 2004:150)

Having used these methods successfully on his parents and other senior family members, the bully will later use these same manipulation methods on teachers, in student-on-teacher bullying incidents. In fact, such methods, which have been tested and honed in the home, up through high school, will remain the bully's mainstay for dealing with adult problems.

METHODS OF BULLIES

"Let a man overcome anger by mildness, let him overcome evil by good; let him overcome the niggard by liberality, the liar by truth."
—Babbit (1936)

In their book *Corporate Abuse,* Lesley Wright and Marti Smye describe the typical workplace bully: "A bully's stock in trade is sniffing out vulnerabilities and capitalizing on weaknesses. That's why they strut and shout and broadcast messages like 'If you can't stand the heat get out of the kitchen.' This makes us feel ashamed to admit we cannot cope. We are afraid of confrontation, so we avert our eyes and let them get away with it. So they do. And the bullying goes on" (1996:54).†

Of course, Wright and Smye's description could all too easily be used to describe bullying across the board: from childhood and teenager classroom bullying, to adult relationship abuse.

---

*This is the subject of every episode of the reality TV series *Supernanny!*

†Ironically, as this is being written, one of the most popular TV shows airing on the FOX network is a so-called reality show called *Hell's Kitchen,* featuring a loud, obnoxious, cursing, and bullying "superchef" with an anger-management problem who takes sadistic delight in berating and belittling his novice, wannabe chef trainees.

Sniffing out our vulnerabilities allows the bully to get inside our head. Understanding your enemy's—or, in the bully's case, your victim's—mind is the first step in controlling and overcoming that enemy.

The much feared ninja warriors of medieval Japan called this Kiai-Shin-Jutsu, tactics and techniques (Jutsu) that directly attack the intended victim psychologically by "shouting" (Kiai) into his mind (Shin).*

Within Kiai-Shin-Jutsu, ninja developed many subcrafts, each designed to sniff out and then take advantage of not only weaknesses specific to targeted individuals but also potentially fatal chinks in the mental and emotional armor we all share.

Because peoples' emotions have changed little since medieval times, and because people are pretty much the same everywhere, it's not surprising that, while he may not call them by the same name, or even take time to categorize them, the tactics and techniques used so ruthlessly by our modern bully have much in common with those medieval Japanese mind-slayers, method-wise.

Weaknesses and Warning FLAGS

The Japanese mind-manipulation art of Gojo-Goyoku derives from an even more ancient Chinese mind-control art called Wu-Hsing. In the West we refer to the Gojo-Goyoku as the "Five Warning Flags," with FLAGS being a handy mnemonic.

According to Gojo-Goyoku, in all people at all times, one of five distinct feelings (emotions) dominate: fear (kyosha), lust (kisha), anger (dosha), greed (rakusha), and sympathy (aisha). During the course of any given day, all of these five emotions can manifest in us naturally.

However, according to Gojo-Goyoku theory, each of us is dominated, personality-wise, by one of these emotions. For example, those quick to anger are dominated by anger: whereas for others greed or lust might be the fishhook in their nose (or other body part as the case may be!) that reels them in. Likewise, those exhibiting too much sympathy, no matter how well intentioned, can all too easily be led astray by the unscrupulous.

While our bully can goad us into anger, and even play on our sympathy

---

*For a complete course in kiai-shin-jutsu, see Haha Lung and Christopher Prowant's *Mind Manipulation: Ancient and Modern Ninja Techniques* (2002).

(e.g., to help a friend get out from under the bully's thumb) by and large the bully relies 99 percent on the emotion of fear to herd us like frightened sheep in the direction he desires.

Not by coincidence is fear the first and foremost of the Five Warning Flags. The book of *Dune* warns us that "fear is the mind killer, the little death that brings total oblivion."

The modern-day self-help mantra of breaking fear down into the acronym False Evidence Appearing Real is all fine and dandy but is quickly forgotten when you find out that your bully's knuckles are all too real and the red evidence dripping from your nose!

It is not that the foe is so fearsome . . . it is that we are so fearful! Fear is the bully's friend. And we think (incorrectly) that fear is our enemy.

The bully knows this, so he uses our natural fear (our body's recognition of a bodily threat) of his ability to hurt us. But, more important, he counts on our misinterpretation of our body's readiness as fear to convince us we are cowards.

We've touched on this subject already, and we will deal with it at length later in this book, where we will give you proven techniques for mastering your fear (see Liddy, 1997).

How do you overcome your fear? By recognizing that fear is your friend! And don't let that bully convince you otherwise.

The Six Killer B's

"Bully" is one of the six Killer B's that can be used to deliberately manipulate people. So it's not surprising that these six Killer B's should find their way into your bully's bag of tricks.

The six Killer B's are: blind, blood ties, bribery and blackmail, brainwashing, bully, and bury (see Lung, 2006b, 2007). Briefly, "blind" are attempts to confuse you. "Blood ties" play on your connections to others and/or on knowledge of your misdeeds someone is holding over your head (as in "I know what you did last summer!" and "What happened in Vegas ain't stayin' in Vegas!"). "Bribery and blackmail" are the twin sides of a self-explanatory Janus coin. "Brainwashing" may sound a little too Fu Manchu to you but when you start believing your bully is invincible and all-knowing, that there is nothing you can do to combat him (mentally or physically), then he's already succeeded in brainwashing you.

Then, if your bully can't do what he does best, bully, he can always bury you—literally. (But relax, most bullies aren't killers, they're punks and predators—both looking to separate the weakest from the herd. And you are far from the weakest in the herd, otherwise you'd never have picked up this book, seeking solutions.

In the end, from our standpoint of learning to combat bullies, all six Killer B's come down to some sort of bullying, if not physically, then at least mentally.

Mental Bullies

Before you punch them in the head, punch them in the mind. Buddha once said, "Your greatest weapon is in your enemy's mind." And, while he's the furthest thing from being a Buddhist, the bully still somehow knows this. (Maybe he beat the hell out of a Buddhist monk or something in his past life?)

Before that actual punch to the gut after school comes, you spend all day waiting, waiting, and more waiting—dreading—the punch to the gut after school.

Waiting and dreading what's going to happen is often worse than the actual event, whether it's eye-balling the clock on the classroom wall, dreading your pending rendezvous with a right hook come recess, or dear old Mom wagging a finger and saying, "You just wait till your father gets home!"

Here's an important rule that will come in handy later, when we're learning how to diffuse a bully: "Anticipation breeds visualization." The bully knows threatening you causes you to create all kinds of crazy scenarios in your mind till, eventually, ideally (for the bully) your anxiety paralyzes you and you give in to the bully's demands.

With training, you can not only learn to control your mental pictures, your visualizing, but also you can turn this into a valuable tool that will help you turn the tables on your tormentor.

Everybody from Madison Avenue to Manson cults use the "Bully Game" to make us hurry up and buy into their "limited time offer":

> "You'd be surprised to learn just how many psychological 'bully ploys,' some subtle, some more overt, are aimed at you every day." (Lung, 2006b:52)

Physical Bullies

The bully actually has two chances to get over on you. First, he can try to bluff you (out of your money, homework, etc.) by threatening to introduce you to a world of hurt. And, if that doesn't work, he always has a real handful of hurt on which to fall back.

Remember, when the *threat* of force fails, there's always the *force* of force:

"Let's not waste time repeating clichés like 'Violence is the last refuge of the ignorant' and 'Violence never solves anything.' Sure it does." (Lung, 2006b:56)

Down through the ages, up till this very day, the threat of physical violence, social unrest (read: violence), politically rationalized violence, and sadder still, relationship violence has successfully moved more people than extrastrength Ex-Lax!

Threats, effective ones anyway, always have to be backed up by your believability to deliver on the threat if necessary. And your believability is directly linked to your ability to deliver on that threat. (Word of advice: It helps if you have a history—or at least a reputation—for senseless, random violence in the past.)

In turn, ability equates to how much power—and what kind of power—you truly possess . . . or at least you can make your victim think you possess and are ruthlessly willing to bring to the party.

The Five Types of Power

There are five types of power available to human beings:

1. *Love and respect power:* This kind of power depends on how much we are liked by others. It is genuine power flowing from people who care, support, and follow you out of love and loyalty.
2. *Expert power:* This kind of power comes from special skills, unique abilities, or special intelligence you've collected. On the positive side, this kind of power dovetails into respect power, where people acknowledge and admire your abilities and willingly accept your expertise and follow your lead in a particular field. If manifested negatively, this kind of power demands that others kiss your ass because they are dependent on you not withholding your needed expertise like a petulant child.

3. *Position power:* This kind of power comes from your recognized and agreed on right to issue commands and to make demands of others because of a position you hold in society in general or some position you hold at a particular job (e.g., you have several people below you at work). Of course, this kind of power is all too easily and often abused.

4. *Carrot power:* Also known as "reward power," this comes from your ability to manipulate others by dispensing (or withholding) rewards.

5. *Stick power:* Also known as "coercive power," this comes from your ability (and willingness) to threaten and punish others. Stick power is the type of overtly observed power we usually associate with bullies—in others words, threats of force and the force of force.

A bully doesn't always immediately use his stick power. He might, at first feign using carrot power, by offering not to beat you if you do something for him. But be warned: Even through he is offering you a reward (carrot) make no mistake that, even if you comply, the "stick" cannot be far behind.

Bullies can also use other types of power. For example, in the workplace you might find yourself at the mercy of a bully-boss in a position of power (position power) allowing him to demote or fire you if you don't "learn to play ball."

On the same job, you might likewise find yourself being bullied by someone with expert power, some one—a slacker co-worker perhaps—who has the power to make you look bad simply by him not doing his part of the job (putting you in a position to where, more often than not, you will do his part of the job as well, just to be done with the project).

2

The Bully Playground:
Settings and Solutions

"Bad deeds and deeds harmful to ourselves are easy to do;
what is salutary and good, that is very difficult to do."
—Babbit (1936)

Inevitably, after a violent tragedy, especially a tragedy involving the young, we desperately grasp for answers. Columbine in the spring of 1999. Virginia Tech in the spring of 2007. What, if anything, could we realistically have done to prevent them from happening?

As after every such tragedy, everyone has an answer, but, sadly, nobody seems to have *the* answer. Some claim "it's the parents' fault!" Others decry violent rap music, TV, and video games. Still others demand more gun control.

It's no secret that Seung Hui Cho, the Virginia Tech killer, bought two handguns, one right after the other, within a four-week period in preparation for the terror-to-come already taking root in his tortured mind. But such purchases were perfectly legal—even for a troubled individual who, less than two years before, had been found by a court to represent a possible danger to himself and/or others because of his depression and suicidal tendencies (Rachel Johnson, 2007:3).

A better database specifically designed to flag and prevent such purchase might have helped. (Good luck getting that kind of legislation passed! Guns don't kill people . . . bullets do!)

Others argue, with some persuasiveness, that heavy calibers weren't the cause of Cho's madness, merely the brushes with which he chose to paint his bloody masterpiece.

Still others argue we should search for some catalytic event—drama or trauma—further back in the confused and chaotic childhood of such killers—in the way they were harshly raised (or just as enthusiastically ignored) by their parents.

And while we all agree parents have the right to raise their children as they see fit, sadly—sometimes tragically—what "works" in the home might not work as well out in the real world.

So could we conceivably have spotted some early inkling of Cho's mad meltdown, or Eric Harris and Dylan Klebold's mutual misery-into-massacre pact? Perhaps something in the way they established (or avoided establishing) relationships with peers and with the opposite sex?

And if Harris and Klebold hadn't turned their high school into a bloody video game, and Cho hadn't gone haywire at Virginia Tech, would we have still learned about them years later when, as adults, the same sort of frustration finally boiled over and they started shooting up their place of disappointing employment?

These kinds of questions can never be answered. Such speculation only lends itself to finger pointing, recrimination, personal guilt, and endless second guessing.

It is better that we concentrate on preventing the next Columbine, the next Virginia Tech. One way to help do this is to look for similarities between such incidents—similarities of thinking.

In both instances, and in all postmortem probes into these minds of the killers, one word appears time and again: bullying.

If, indeed, bullying is at the root of such tragedies, then jerking that wicked weed up before it has a chance to bear bitter fruit would be our most rational course of preemptive action.

In the 2002 Tom Cruise movie *Minority Report,* police in the not-too-distant future develop a method for peering even further into the future, thus preventing murders before they are committed. Wouldn't that be a handy solution.

Meanwhile, back in the real world, what we need to do is look for those similarities—similarities between how bullies operate, regardless of their age and the setting.

IN THE CLASSROOM

The good news is that the number of under-seventeen children who committed murder decreased between 1993 and 2004 (Gibbs, 2007:54). The bad news? Other research done during this same period revealed that one in seven children behaved like either a bully or a victim (Martin and Waltman-Greenwood, 1995:59). Follow-up studies have collected similarly sad statistics:

> "By 1992, in an average month, about a half million attacks, shakedowns, and robberies occurred in public secondary schools across the country. Nearly 8 percent of urban middle and high school students miss one day of school a month because they are afraid to attend." (Martin and Whitman-Greenwood, 1995:59)

Recall how the researcher Daniel Goleman tracked the trajectory (development) of the child bully mentality, from preschool, up through high school, ever deeper into antisocial and eventually outright criminal behaviors:

> "While most children, especially boys, are rambunctious in kindergarten and first grade, the more aggressive children fail to learn a modicum of self-control by second grade. Where other children have started to learn to negotiate and compromise for playground disagreements, the bullies rely more and more on force and bluster. . . . Studies that have followed children from the preschool years into the teenage ones find that up to half of the first graders who are disruptive, unable to get along with other kids, disobedient with their parents, and resistant with teachers will become delinquents in their teen years. Of course, not all such aggressive children are on the trajectory that leads to violence and criminality in later life. But of all children, these are the ones most at risk for eventually committing crimes." (1995:236)

Goleman goes on to conclude:

> "The prototypical pathway to violence and criminality starts with children who are aggressive and hard to handle in first

and second grade. . . . impulsivity in ten-year-old boys is almost three times as powerful a predictor of their later delinquency as is their IQ. . . . The bent of mind that aggressive children take with them through life is one that almost ensures they will end up in trouble." (ibid. 237)

If it begins in kindergarten and progresses up through high school (such as Columbine in 1999), why then should we be surprised to see similar strains of bullying and aggressive acting out at the college level (such as Virginia Tech in 2007). Even in the less extreme, in the college setting we see such frustrations and angers expressed in binge drinking and sexcapades—not the least of which culminates in date rape.

So now we know the problem. But what do we have in the way of realistic solutions against classroom bullying?

When it comes to classroom bullying, especially at younger ages, when our children are most vulnerable and lack any sort of adult skills for successfully dealing with bullies, it is imperative that parents and authorities (teachers and school officials) become aware and involved.

Zero Tolerance

First off, let's talk about what's not the answer! Zero tolerance.

Zero tolerance is a hip little cure-all phrase being tossed around more and more these days. But zero tolerance takes *zero* thought. It's an easy fix for something that doesn't have an easy fix.

Zero tolerance implies that all problems are alike and can therefore be solved with a single answer and that our children are all alike (and I think, we at least can agree that's not true!). Zero tolerance sounds just like what it is . . . laziness on the part of parents, school administrators, and even police to devote time and effort to job one: *keeping our children safe.*

Real problems demand a hands-on approach that is capable and willing to examine differences, nuances, and circumstances on a case-by-case basis, rather than by using a one-size-fits-all cookie-cutter solution. Banning this, restricting that, in the end only serves to further deprive children of a full measure of both education and childhood.

Whether it's complex problems such as drug use, gang violence, or bullying in the classroom, complex problems require time, effort, and money to solve. But isn't it better to spend time, effort, and money now than later? In the courtroom, in the hospital, or heaven forbid in the cemetery.

For example, numerous studies have documented the proven success of anger-management intervention classes in curbing bullying behavior (Goleman, 1995:238).

But you have to catch bullies early in life. And if you think such things take too much time and effort and are just too expensive, weigh the cost of timely intervention against the cost of a criminal trial court lawyer!

And, ask yourself, what better could we possibly spend our time, effort, and money on than on our children?

Address the Signs of Bullying Immediately

If you think something's wrong with your kid, you're probably right. If you think he's being bullied, he probably is. Trust your gut—it evolved a few million years earlier than the higher reasoning part of your brain that's going to try to convince you "you're only imagining things." Better to look stupid than to have to look for a funeral home.

Learn to Spot the Players

Parents and other concerned adults must train themselves what to look for, both in bullies and in their victims. One cannot exist without the other.

Increased observation is the key. Because job one is to safeguard the kids, the best way to go about accomplishing this task is to become adept at identifying bullies as early on as possible and then get them treatment.

Spotting bullies can be relatively easy. We're looking for signs of fighting (bruises, especially on the knuckles), and we're looking for patterns of behavior and attitude as well. For example, the bully might openly express defiance and disrespect toward others and manifest outward contempt and hostility toward authority—as we would expect of a bully.

However, a more insidious type of bully might take a different tact: being helpful and even overly polite to adults—in their presence—only to literally attack peers his own age when those same adults aren't looking. And, predictably, when allegations of bullying are leveled against "such a nice boy," there are always adults ready to come to his defense.

What about bullies as victims? Sounds somewhat counterintuitive doesn't it? But Harris and Klebold saw themselves as victims. As did Cho. This is an important clue to pick up on when talking to repressed kids, that they see themselves as victims (of injustice, imagined slights, etc.).

Because casting themselves in the role of victim is a great alibi for bullies (whether done consciously simply to mask their bullying, or whether the bullies actually believe themselves to be victims of some injustice or imagined slight), this is a great signpost for counselors and concerned parents to take note of when listening to bullies express themselves and their view of the world.

In other words, if I feel the world is treating me unfairly (because that kid over there always seems to have enough lunch money), then I may feel more justified in "setting things right" by beating the crap out of that kid and taking his money.

While it's nigh impossible (not to mention an invasion of privacy and just downright rude and nosey!) to peer over our neighbors' back fence, figuratively and literally, thus helping prevent our neighbors from inadvertently raising a bully, what we can do is spot the genesis of bullies early on as they enter the school system, where their raucous behavior can be observed and recorded and appropriate steps can be taken to intervene, breaking the bully mold before it has a chance to set into concrete.

Recall from Goleman that research has shown that fledgling bullies can be spotted as early as five years of age. For example, children younger than five are usually physical in settling disputes (grabbing, pushing, etc.). Between five and seven, normally developing kids increase their verbal skills and begin using those skills to negotiate their disputes with others (agreements to share, trading one object for another, etc.). However, if by this time children are still physically settling disputes, research shows them beginning to separate into the sheep and the wolves: those who begin giving in (acquiescing) more and those who have already figured out they can get what they want, not through negotiation, but through bullying.

Something more important even than identifying the bully is identifying—and saving—the victim.

How do we identify a victim? Michael Martin and Cynthia Whitman-Greenwood's succinct definition bears repeating:

> "A victim is the child who, for a fairly long time, has been
> the focus of aggression from others, with someone often

picking fights, teasing, or ridiculing him or her. This is not a
one-time victim, but someone who has not learned how to be
assertive enough to protect himself." (1995:60)

Martin and Whitman-Greenwood go on to explain how victims of bullies seem to give off unconscious signals to others that they are insecure and
that they probably won't fight back if insulted or physically attacked. Such
victims may actually appear physically weak, making them more inviting targets to bullies.

These children may also be, or at least appear to be, emotionally weaker.
These children may complain or otherwise seek attention from their peers
and/or curry the favor of adults in ways (e.g., tattling) that ensure the jeal-
ousy and wrath of their peers (review Figure 1).

One major indicator that your child is being picked on is "bully dodging." Bully dodging (avoidance) includes, but is not limited to, truancy. Your
child doesn't want to go to school (which is normal), but he also doesn't
want to go outside to play (which is suspicious). Perhaps you discover your
child walking to and from school by alternate routes?

FYI: As you will see in the following section on bullying in the boardroom, bully dodging is not just found in children. In fact, Lesley Wright and
Marti Smye (1996) mention adults at work using this same tactic.

A child should have a regular, agreed on route for walking to and from
school. This makes it easier for a parent to backtrack the child in case of an
emergency. Likewise, neighborhood safe houses should be clearly established
(and rehearsed) by you and your child. Safe houses are homes of known and
trusted neighbors and/or businesses along the child's route to and from
school that the child can safely stop by (or run to) in case of an emergency.

Being a victim of bullying may also be at the root of your child having
body issues, for example, where he sees himself as a "wimp" or refers to himself as ugly or stupid. If your child ever taunts a younger sibling with such
slurs, or with physical actions for that matter, such words and actions could be
a sign he is displacing anger from having been (or still being) bullied.

If a child's property (clothing, books, or bike) is missing or damaged,
this could be a sign that property has been stolen or damaged by a bully.
Missing property can also be a sign said property has been used to buy off a
bully.

If you discover your child stealing money from you, don't automatically assume he is using it to by drugs. He could be paying extortion to a bully.

And if your child refuses to talk about a large part of his day, that, too, could be a sign he's hiding something—perhaps he's being bullied, perhaps he is the one doing the bullying.

Establish Dialogue

Do whatever it takes to establish a dialogue with your child, the children your child interacts with (or avoids interacting with) on a regular basis, other parents, and school administrators. Bullies breed in silence.

Make it easy for your child to tell you, or someone else, if he has problems. Often, a child will confide in an extended family member or family friend before telling a parent.

Don't be so quick to interrupt or judge your child. Listen to what your kid's *not* saying, those obviously missing pieces in his narrative.

Play "The Friend and the Bully Game."

Don't ask your child directly if he's being bullied. Sometimes, his fear and shame keep him silent. Instead, tell your child about "a friend of yours" who lives on the other side of the city—the farther away the better—who has a kid that goes to a completely different school who just so happens to be having a problem with bullies. Ask your kid for advice. What should that other parent look for?

This subtle approach then leads into you asking your child, "Do you know of any kids being bullied at your school?" If the child tells you he "thinks" there might be some kids at his school being bullied, ask him for their names and/or the names of any bullies bullying those "other kids" at his school.

Quiz your kids' friends. Do they show similar signs of physical and emotional bullying?

Contact your child's friends' parents who might not be as perceptive as you, and whose children you might be able to "grill" into spilling the beans about what's happening to your kid.

"Bullies are just mirror images of the fears we all have inside."
—Higgs (1997)

Involve the Authorities

Involve school authorities. Remind them that, despite what they might think, their responsibility (and liability) doesn't necessarily end when the school day does. Remind them how if a bartender callously gives an obviously drunk customer more drinks, doesn't take his keys, and allows that obviously drunk person to get behind the wheel, the bartender can still be held liable.

In the same way, teachers and administrators who allow "an atmosphere" of bullying to fester in their school can still be called to answer for it when that bullying spills over into off-campus, after-school activities.

Involve the Parent and Teachers Association (PTA). Convince it to empower a committee to investigate complaints of bullying. Sift through data collected to determine if any specific grade level or specific segments of the school population is being targeted for bullying because of race, gender, religion, or sexual orientation, or if your child's school has developed a toxic "jocks vs. wimps" culture—the kind that reportedly contributed to the 1999 Columbine massacre.

If race is involved—involve race. If it's a choice between "playing the race card" to get attention for your child's problem . . . deal 'em up and deal off the bottom if you have to. Better for you to be hated, than for your child to be beaten.

The Japanese have a term "masakatsu," which can be roughly translated as "do what is necessary" or, if you prefer, "by any means necessary." When it comes to the safety and sanity of our children, *masakatsu!*

Involve the police. And this doesn't have to be your last resort. Many police districts have trained personnel, social workers, and speakers who will help bring you—and the PTA—up to speed on the latest efforts to combat gangs and other juvenile problems in your area. (You get instant attention to your problem when you show up at the quarterly PTA meeting in the company of a police officer!)

Involve the media. The last thing a principal wants to see when arriving at his school is a media van parked across the street.

Beware "The Snitch Factor"

When doing a James Bond into your child's life, be determined but discreet. Use a little sensitivity when "investigating" your child being a victim of bullying.

Keep in mind that your kid *has* to get along with other kids. It will not help your child in the long run to be labeled as a "snitch" or a "rat" by the other kids, further undermining his self-image, perhaps further alienating him from his peers.

By the way, it's okay to "spy" on your children. It's part of your job description as a parent. But, like any good spying assignment, this sort of domestic spying works best when the kid doesn't know you're spying on him.

"Like its politicians and its wars,
society has the teenagers it deserves."
—J. B. Priestly (1894–1984)

Teach Your Kids to Defend Themselves

"And in truth bullies aren't important,
they're just predators trying to add a little strength to
their insecurity by feeding off you. But the seemingly all
powerful bully soon disappears when you develop yourself
internally and start changing thoughts that belittle into thoughts
that build you up. Bullies and victims attract each other.
When you kill the victim inside, you kill the attraction too."
—Higgs (2007)

We must teach our children to fight back. I know that scares you. It scares most parents. Ideally, we will teach our children verbal coping skills that will help them diffuse potential bully situations before they turn into actual physical struggles.

But we must not be so naive as to hope we can wish away every physical bully danger to our child.

Sometimes a bully doesn't engage you—or your child—in threatening conversation before resorting to violence. Some bullies say "hello" with a right hook to the head. Teaching your child to respect others' physical boundaries—their space—is all part of helping our children become good human beings. But, hand in hand with teaching our children to respect others' boundaries is teaching our children to defend their own boundaries.

Any course (regular routine) of physical exercise is good for your child.

Obvious health benefits aside, a regular routine of vigorous activity helps bolster the self-esteem of a child (or a couch-potato adult for that matter).

And if you're going to involve your child in an exercise routine, nothing could be better than enrolling him in a traditional martial arts school. Even that bully-to-be you're raising can benefit from such study. Though it may sound counterintuitive, formal martial arts training has been shown to help aggressive kids (i.e., potential bullies) to elevate some of their pent-up aggression and anger while engendering in them feelings of true self-worth as well as increasing their empathy and respect for others.

This is especially true of traditionally structured Asian-inspired martial arts studios, where the students literally step into another world, one requiring them to wear a traditional karate GI or kung-fu uniform, bow and speak respectfully, perhaps even help clean the practice dojo at the end of class. Some classes also teach meditation.

The setting of a well-managed martial arts school provides not only positive and consistent adult role-models (which may be lacking in the home) but it also forces the child to interact with a wider range of age-mates, some of whom, while physically smaller and appearing physically weaker, may actually excel the "bully" in physical ability, which is an often cautionary eye-opening and humbling experience for any potential bully.

Finally, a well-structured class, with clearly established goals (e.g., achieving belt rankings and tournaments) provides a needed focus in a child's life and engenders genuine feelings of self-worth.

Overprotected by parents, children often fail to develop viable coping skills. On the other hand, negligent children often lack restraint. And, while the dojo is not a babysitter, its structured, consistent environment can help instill needed social references and values—including self-value—that might have been too cursorily passed over or, sadder still, not provided in the home.

We teach by example. We now know we should never use physical restraints or corporal punishment on our children. Hitting the little people only teaches the little people that it's okay to hit, okay to dominate those at your mercy.

Use common sense when punishing your kids.

A good technique is to ask them what they think would be an appropriate punishment for whatever infraction they may have committed. Then use their suggestions to gauge your children's understanding of cause and consequence, and of their growing social consciousness.

When it comes to physical punishment, the body learns quicker than the mind. The downside of this is that we carry childhood physical trauma around with us, physically fretting and flinching for the rest of our lives. The upside of this is that, when studying to physically defend yourself, while your fear-filled mind's still trying to convince you "there's no way you can hurt that big bully," your body is already raring to go, having already flooded your system with the adrenaline needed to get the job done via flight (sometimes the better part of valor) or fight (sometimes unavoidable).

> "As a victim you've been playing a role. It's learned behavior. The positive thing about this is you can unlearn it." (Higgs, 1997)

Would some statistics help convince you to teach your child martial arts?

According to records kept by the National Center for Missing and Exploited Children, nearly 450 attempted abductions of children were foiled when the targeted child victims did one of the following:

- 12% got help from an adult
- 32% walked or ran away from kidnapper
- 56% yelled, kicked, or pulled away from their would-be abductor. (*USA Today,* May 18–20, 2007:A1)

Tricks-into-Techniques: The Classroom

Well-mastered tricks are called techniques. Half-learned techniques are merely tricks.

While your child is busy studying at a good martial arts school—increasing his self-esteem (not to mention his chances of surviving a violent encounter)—here are a few quick tricks-into-techniques you can put into play to help even the playing field and to help turn the hunter (the bully) into the hunted.

Mark your child. For example, record the serial number of any dollar bills you give him. That way, if his money is ever stolen or otherwise bullied away from him, any subsequent search by school officials or police of the bully's person, locker at school, or his home will turn up the marked bills and serve as evidence of his bullying and theft.

Identify coins by either scratching a small mark on them or else by using a colored marker to dot them.

Do the same thing with your child's clothing, backpack, bike, anything that might be stolen or snatched by a bully. (You don't have to tell your child you've marked his stuff.)

Provide younger children with an emergency whistle, because drawing attention can be useful, provided you train the child to use it only in cases of duress and danger. Attach this whistle somewhere onto his clothing (or a necklace), where it won't be lost.

In the same vein, teach your child to carry a crayon or permanent marker in his pocket in case, God forbid, he should ever be abducted. He can make marks inside a car, inside a car's trunk, and so on, leaving evidence he has been there and helping searchers to find him.

Play the "Indian Tracker Game" with your kids. Teach them to leave signs for others to follow, small Indian signs such as deliberately pressing their shoeprint into soft ground, breaking small branches when being led through wooded areas, dropping small scraps of paper or small items of clothing, and so on.

Create your own "Family Emergency ID Kit." Take small samples of your child's hair (for DNA), his fingerprints, routinely updated full face and side-view face photo, as well as copies of other pertinent birth, medical, and dental records. Keep these in a safe place, such as a fire-proofbox lock box in the home or a safety deposit box at your bank.

Cautionary note: This is personal information about your child and need not (some experts warn should not) be given to authorities (school, police, or the FBI) except in a dire emergency. If, on becoming an adult, your child chooses to voluntarily provide the proper authorities with this vital information, that will still be his choice to make.

Record this information about your child with the prayer that there will never come a day when, or a reason why the government should need—or demand—such personal information from one—or all—of its citizens. Bullies come in all shapes and sizes.

Go hi-tech. Take full advantage of all the latest hi-tech electronics, anything that might help your child stay safe (while you're secretly keeping an eye on him twenty-four-seven). Get your kid an emergency cell phone, one you can program with restricted emergency numbers (in case you're worried your kid will be running up the bill and/or be yakking on the telephone while in class).

If your child has a cell phone capable of taking pictures, encourage him to take pictures of the bully the next time the bully confronts him. Teach your kid to take pictures of any suspicious strangers (their cars, license plates, etc.) he might see cruising the neighborhood.

Consider this scenario: A suspicious car pulls up to the curb as your child is passing on the sidewalk. The driver calls to your child, asking for directions, perhaps flashing a picture of his "lost" puppy.

Immediately, your child pulls out his picture phone and snaps a picture of the "nice" man in the car, presses "send," and the picture has just been sent to Mom.

Now, if this stranger is truly an upstanding citizen looking for his lost puppy, it's doubtful he'll mind having his picture taken. If, on the other hand . . .

I think you get the picture.

Or how about one of those nifty hand-held GPS trackers that come with small "bugs" you can easily, secretly, sew into your child's coat. These are invaluable for tracking him in an emergency.

Recorder pens, which look like a normal ballpoint pen, are perfect for helping your child secretly record threats made against him. Your child can do the same thing by using speed-dial on his cell phone (so you can listen in).

"Insanity is hereditary; you can get it from your children."
—Sam Levenson (1911–1980)

IN THE BEDROOM: RELATIONSHIP BULLYING

"The bedroom is the room in which most people tell a lie."
—Keith Beardon (2001)

Isn't it ironic how the Middle Dutch word "boele," meaning "sweetheart," shifted to our modern English word for "bully"? And yet, it is sadly apropos to our immediate focus: relationship bullying.

Relationship violence is sometimes called "spousal abuse," "domestic violence," and, the more clinical and technical "intimate partner violence."

As previously pointed out, longitudinal studies of children from age eight to thirty have shown that childhood bullies continue to use the same bully tactics they've learned and have been rewarded (i.e., positively reinforced) for using, up into adult life. Not surprising then that these bullying bastards should use their successful tactics and techniques on those supposedly nearest and dearest to them.

It's been pointed out that the average person's home life more closely resembles that of Norman Bates than Norman Rockwell!

Bullies "pick their shots," picking—and then picking on—those they perceive as being weaker—emotionally and physically.

Giving Away the Bride

"My wife and I were happy for twenty years. Then we met."
—**Rodney Dangerfield (1921–2004)**

Men everywhere, regardless of time and clime, have perceived women as "the weaker sex." Societies in general, and religious cultural "traditions" in particular, help institutionalize this misperception with a thing called "marriage."

Consider: We still "give the bride away," as if she is property. We still emphasize that she must be "untouched" and "pure," in itself implying that for her to be otherwise is to "devalue" her exchange rate as "damaged goods." In many societies, dowries are still required—a trade of equal value, if you will, for money or livestock.

In Old Testament times, a man could get away with rape simply by paying the offended virgin's family fifty shekels of silver . . . and he got to *keep* the raped woman (Numbers 22:16 and Deuteronomy 22:28)!*

In some societies, men are still permitted to have more than one wife. Despite protestations from these lands that "we treat our women as equals!" have we ever heard these "enlightened" societies extending the same "you can have five husbands" right to a woman?

For instance, in Iran a man is limited to having only four "permanent" wives (some Islamic countries permit five), but he may have as many "temporary" wives (segheh) as he wants.

Segheh marriages are temporary unions between a man and a woman, the length of which are agreed on by the couple. The man then has to pay a

---

*Keep in mind that, back in the good old days, a woman's menstrual period was seen as a "sickness" (Leviticus 20:18).

dowry. While, theoretically, these segheh marriages can be contracted to last for ninety years, these temporary marriages can be negotiated for as short as one hour! Some Muslims regard this practice as no better than prostitution because a man can pay for a "wife" for as little as an hour. One respected Islamic scholar finds no fault with the practice and even invokes the name of Muhammad to justify the practice: "The Prophet brought in this law of 'temporary marriage' to canalize the sex instinct in sound channels" *(The Week,* June 15, 2007:11). Keep in mind this is the same theocracy that, in 1980, banned contraception and encouraged women to go forth and raise suicide martyrs.

In most societies, men still control the money and the means of livelihood; thus, they control the relationship.

Men's absolute economic control over women has changed somewhat in the West over the past few decades, as evidenced by rising divorce rates, divorce rates that reflect the rising independence of women overall—that is, women's lessened economic dependence on men and their rising expectations. Still, worldwide, nine out of ten heterosexual adults marry. And even of those who divorce, three out of four remarry (Myers, 2005:131).

It seems that establishing and maintaining a viable relationship is never easy to get right, but we keep trying:

> "The bond is most satisfying and enduring when marked by a similarity of interests and values, a sharing of emotional and intimate self-disclosure. Marriage bonds are also likely to last when couples marry after age 20 and are well educated."
> (Myers, 2005:131)

When a marriage works, everybody benefits. Neighborhoods with high marriage rates typically have low rates of "social pathologies: crime, delinquency, emotional disorders among children" (Myers, 2005:131). It seems that when it's good, marriage is really good. But when it's bad, it's often homicide.

In extremis, East or West, for some insecure sadistic SOBs, a marriage license literally becomes a license to kill.

As with all bullies, relationship bullies literally use the one-two punches of emotional (psychological) abuse and physical violence to cower their victims into compliance. Perhaps answering to the subconscious demon echoes of their own childhood abuse, striking out for real or imagined and manufactured slights, these bullies feel free to "punish" their wives and girlfriends, rationalizing and justifying that "she brought it on herself."

In this way, the relationship violence bully exercises Godlike power over his woman, his possession, often with the blessing of religious and cultural tradition.

Forewarned Is Forearmed

People often speak of "the institution of marriage," meaning, of course, tradition. However, there's an interesting—and somewhat frightening—comparison that can be made between the institution of marriage and other institutions—a prison perhaps?

What starts out as a good idea, or even seems ideal, can all too easily go catiwhompus when the seemingly carefree—albeit practiced—personalities of courtship are traded in for the real and more serious faces of married life.

Like any other institution, within the institution of marriage we all too often find both cowering prisoners and bullying wardens. Perhaps you recall from Psych 101 Philip Zimbardo's (1972) examination of a 1970s college experiment where volunteer male college students were randomly divided up into "guards" and "prisoners" before taking their place in a makeshift "cellblock" that was set up in the basement of a campus building.

The experiment had to be called off after only six days. In short order, both the "guards" and their "prisoners" began showing abnormal signs of stress and abnormal behavior. Given "absolute power" over their charges, the "guards" had become overbearing, bullying, and outright sadistic. Some of the prisoners became rebellious, but just as many became "passively resigned" to their fate and withdrew within themselves. In other words, in only a few days, the participants had divided into "bullies" and "victims"!

> *"The normal reaction to an abnormal situation*
> *is abnormal behavior."*
> **—Waller (2002)**

We find something frighteningly similar to the Zimbardo experiment in relationships where the bullying husband acts as "warden" by imposing impossible restrictions and demands on his passive "prisoner" wife/victim.

Consider: In less than a week, Zimbardo's subjects were acting like sadistic bullies on the one hand, and passive victims on the other. How much more so might such abnormal symptoms manifest with couples married for years, especially with the tacit "blessing" of authorities who all too often look the other way when it comes to "domestic disputes."

That's why women need to train themselves to look for warning signs before marriage.

Glance ahead to the next section where we reveal "Ten Ways to Recognize a Bully." Though these were originally drawn up for the workplace, they can just as easily be applied to the home.

Do any of them sound familiar? If so, odds are you (or someone you know) is trapped in an abusive relationship. (Oh yeah, that black eye could be a clue as well!)

The following are some signs to look for:

- Is he a "control freak"? Does he control all the money in the relationship? Is he a tightwad? Does he also control the car keys, controlling when you travel?
- Does he monitor you constantly?
- What do you really have in common? Sure he's a nice guy, wining and dining you, catering to your every desire while dating. The whole flowers and chocolates spiel. But what appears "cavalier" and "charming" when he "insists" on treating you "like a lady" while dating may be a prelude to him "keeping you in your place," "barefoot and pregnant" once you've been "given" to him in marriage. Before marriage, you have to ask yourself, what do you and your significant other really have in common? Despite what you might see in the movies, or read about in the romance novels, opposites don't attract, nor do they stay together, except by force.
- Does he show signs of paranoia?
- Does he have a history of mental illness?
- Does he have a history of family violence? The fruit doesn't fall far from the tree . . . and that fruit might just beat you with a branch from that tree!
- Is he a misogynist? Forgive my French, but many men love pussy but hate what it's attached to. They lust, but once that lust is satisfied

they resent the control women have over them, the "weakness" they feel, along with self-loathing for having exposed their "need," the self-hatred that flashes the bully back to an earlier (childhood) time when he was the one without any power, perhaps picked on and abused himself.

"Needing" what a woman has makes the misogynist feel "weak." Abusing the woman afterward makes the bully-misogynist feel falsely powerful, in control again. Sometimes, this kind of bully just splits the difference and you wind up on the receiving end of date rape and relationship rape. In extremis, misogynist serial killers prey on prostitutes; satisfying their lust for sex and power, and then killing the very "thing" they desire.

We find this same attitude among "straight" men who operate on "the down low" (i.e., who have clandestine gay liaisons but who still consider themselves straight). Such men often resent the attraction (i.e., "hold" gay sex has over them) and thus resort to bullying and abusing their partners in order to "get their manhood back."

The serial killer John Wayne Gacy, who was executed for killing thirty-three young men and boys he'd had sex with, is an extreme example of this. Unable to come to grips with his own homosexuality, yet lusting for gay sex, he felt compelled to destroy the object of his "weakness." Even more telling is the fact that, after killing his gay lovers, Gacy then buried them under his house—Freud would have a field day with that symbolism!

We should not be surprised by such revelations, considering that "fag-bashing" has been and continues to be a popular "sport" for young bullies.

- Does he have abandoment issues? Other women have left him (is it any wonder?) and so now he is afraid you will do the same. You keep something from running away by keeping it locked up as much as possible. Someone with more of a Freudian bent might speculate that the abuser-bully was, early on, ignored or else otherwise abandoned by his mother and that's why he grew up to be such an abusive SOB. Even though childhood trauma might be used to explain adult actions, it should never be accepted as an excuse for such actions.

Women Bullies?

"Woman was God's second mistake."
—Friedrich Nietzsche (1844–1900)

Just as it's near-inconceivable to a loving parent that their darling little first-grader still in pigtails might be a bully, so, too, it's hard for a lot of us to think of women as bullies:

> "The notion that women are violent is hard for many to believe. The opposite perception is prevalent, despite the fact that women are more likely to commit child abuse and child murder than are men." (Meadows, 2004:45)

In fact, statistics show that women are more likely than men to use a weapon during a domestic dispute—it's called an "equalizer." In addition, research has shown that men are just as likely to be victims of domestic violence as women and that women kill men at approximately the same rate as men kill women (2004:45).

Women can also be bullies in the bedroom using "carrot power," by withholding sex until they get their way. More sinister, vindictive, and vengeful female bullies can be given knee-jerk benefit of the doubt when lodging allegations of sexual harassment or rape. Case in point: the infamous 2006–2007 Duke Lacrosse incident. Even when the accused men are exonerated, the whiff of scandal lingers permanently.

It is also not beneath some wifely bullies to make false allegations of child abuse against their estranged husbands, especially in custody battles. Sadly, we've seen both parents act self-centered and heartless, ruthlessly using their innocent children as pawns in divorce proceedings.

Tricks-into-techniques: The Bedroom

"A man is not just if he carries a matter by violence."
—Babbit (1936)

Stop Making Excuses for Him
Stop being your abuser's enabler, excusing him by rationalizing his abuse away: "He works so hard, he's under a lot of stress," "It's not him, it's the

booze," "If he'd only get right." But he is not going to "get right." You need to get right out of there.

Second, stop making excuese to stay.

Some women stay "for the children." But think about it: If he verbally and physically, perhaps even sexually, abuses you—even if his excuse is "an anger management problem" or drinking—what's to stop him from going after the kids next?

Other times women stay in an abusive relationship because they have no visible means of independent support for themselves and their kids, they have nowhere to go for shelter, and they worry about how to feed and clothe the children.

Power freak bullies always keep their women undereducated, unskilled, and penniless. That way, even when such a woman succeeds in getting free, she has to worry that her husband (who has a job, the family home in his name alone) will seem a better provider parent when it comes to a court granting custody.

Often, abused women have been so cowered that they just give up, passively accepting their "fate." Remember Zimbardo's passive and despondent prisoners?

Abused women can think of a dozen reasons for staying, and really there's only one good reason for leaving: You (and your kids) are not punching bags!

Leave. No, it's not easy. Just do it.

Keep a Record of Your Abuse

Take pictures of your black eyes and bruises to document the abuse. This is vital for getting criminal court convictions for assault rape and other crimes and strong evidence in family domestic court when suing for custody of the kids.

Use your digital phone to take pictures as soon as possible after the attack occurs, sending them to friends or to your pastor instantly. Disposable emergency phones cost little, so you can afford to hide one in your "bolt hole," a place where you can hide and/or barricade yourself in until help arrives.

A bolt hole is anywhere you can run to in times of emergency. Ideally, this is a police station, church shelter, or a friend's home. Other times, in extreme situations, or in situations where a family lives far out in the country, a bolt hole may be just that, a hole, a hiding place where you can hide from your abusive attacker—at the very least, until he drinks himself into a stupor.

Think of your bolt hole as your fallout shelter. As much as possible, stock it with a disposable cell phone, a bottle of water, granola bars, a flashlight, and maybe a weapon. Individual situations vary and you must give thought—and preparation—to the creation of your bolt hole beforehand.

Most important: Whenever possible, construct a bolt hole with more than one way out. Don't trap yourself with no way out unless unavoidable In such a case, prepare to securely barricade yourself inside against any possibility of break-in. Equally important: Make sure you can still get reception on your cell phone from inside your bolt hole. Remember: Land lines can too easily be cut.

All cell phones are now equipped to dial 9-1-1 whether you have a carrier or not. There have been instances where battered wives have set up secret camcorders to record abuse on videotape.

Involve Others

Involve anyone you can think of, such as personal friends, your pastor or priest, police, public shelters, and domestic abuse help groups. Involve bystanders by yelling "Fire!" . . . but you didn't hear that here.

Watch a Good Movie

- *What's Love Got to Do with It* (1993). The Buddhist angle is quite empowering. Learning to meditate helps Tina Turner finally turn the tables on Ike. (We'll teach you to meditate in the next section. Trust me, it'll help.)
- *Sleeping with the Enemy* (1991). Note how carefully Julia Roberts plans her escape, beginning with squirreling away money, culminating in her faking her death. (Of course, she still ends up having to gun down the stalking SOB at the end!)
- *Enough* (2002). Jennifer Lopez develops a well thought out escape and evade plan and ploys (disguise wigs, "trips-n-traps" for slowing pursuit, and escape vehicle parked nearby and packed with provisions at the ready) to help her get away from her stalker husband.

But when she realizes he's just going to keep coming, she finally opts to learn how to physically fight back.

This is a great training film for abused women. The self-defense information in this movie is presented realistically. And it contains both a personal empowerment message as well as a moral one when, in the end, Lopez's character shows that, despite dealing with an in-human enemy, she still manages to hang on to her own humanity.

- *The Burning Bed* (1984). This is a revolutionary movie that introduced "battered wife syndrome" to the American consciousness. The title pretty much gives away the ending to this mother-of-all "battered wife literally turns up the heat on her abusive husband" movie.

Learn Martial Arts

Or at the very least, exercise regularly to keep yourself physically fit. If nothing else, it'll help you survive your next beating. (We'll teach you what you need to know in the second half of this book.)

Train Your Daughters

Break the cycle. Refuse to allow your daughter to grow up in fear. Educate and empower her with knowledge and skills to make her self-supporting. Teach her to defend herself, verbally and physically. Insist that classes against relationship violence be taught in your school district. Forewarned is forearmed: Teach your daughters to be safe. Train them to survive.

Train Your Sons Not to Be Abusers

Break the cycle. In one of the sickest displays ever televised, *Oprah* (2007) aired an actual videotape of a husband verbally and physically abusing his wife. What made the spectacle even more horrendous was the fact the bullying husband made his teenaged son hold the videocamera during the entire ordeal—in effect, he was training the next generation of abusers!

There ain't a pit deep enough.

"The way to fight a woman is with your hat. Grab it and run!"
—John Barrymore (1882–1942)

Postscript: Outside Looking In

"Like a well-guarded fortress, with defense within and without,
so you guard yourself."
—Babbit (1936)

Ever heard of the "bystander effect"? Simply put, it's a well-documented sociological phenomenon that proves that the more people (bystanders) who witness an incident or accident, the less likely any one of them will intervene. It has something to do with people always thinking (hoping, wishing) the other guy will get involved so they won't have to.

That being said, at what point should you intervene in an obviously abusive situation between a husband and wife? And how can you do so safely?

First, when it's not your job, involve the police. Even if no one else is lifting a finger to help, at least lift your finger to help by dialing 9-1-1. Now that wasn't so hard, was it?

If you see a man abusing his wife in a public place, dial 9-1-1 and report "an attempted abduction." You are much more likely to get a quicker response if you report an abduction in progress than if you report "There's a man and a woman arguing."

Liability note: It would be very irresponsible (not to mention possibly illegal) for anyone to advise you to ever "fib" to those nice 9-1-1 people. Let your conscience be your guide. It's no surprise that first responders respond faster to "officer down!" and "Fire!" than they do to a routine domestic dispute. If a life is at stake—yours or someone else's, let your conscience be your guide.

When it is your job, always opt for verbal intervention, as opposed to possibly adding fuel to the fire by intervening physically. Use a ploy rather than direct confrontation.

You can also yell loudly, "Hey, buddy, I think that old biddy [or the owner, etc.] over there just called the cops! You better beat feet before they get here!"

When you need to stop a fight by clearing out a place (e.g., a bar), run to the door and scream, "Hey! The place across the street is on fire!"

Yelling "Fire!" always gets everyone's attention and it gets everyone involved, as opposed to "Oh my God! He's killing her. Somebody do something!"

What? They're still fighting? Well, I can't advise you to pull a fire alarm because that would be illegal, though there's a pretty good chance that if you did it to save someone's life, you'd probably get off with a slap on the wrist. Let your conscience be your guide.

Okay, so you don't beat your wife. And you're not an abused wife. Anyway, you'd never expose your children to something like that, right? However, if you can hear your neighbor beating his wife, then there's a pretty good chance your kids can hear it, too. Maybe those little rugrats are watching the drama unfold from their upstairs window?

So what are your kids learning? Are they learning it's okay to abuse? That it's okay to beat your wife or okay to be beaten if you're some jerk warden's prisoner-wife? Or are you just teaching your kids that it's okay to stand around watching a man beat unholy hell out of his wife?

They really are little sponges you know.

Let your conscience be your guide.

IN THE BOARDROOM: WORKPLACE BULLYING

"The term 'bullying' suggests children and immaturity.
We've all seen it at daycare centers and in the schoolyard,
but it can be found creating havoc in workplaces too."
—Wright and Smye (1996:51)

Lesley Wright and Marti Smye reveal in *Corporate Abuse* (1996) the five key elements that constitute someone bullying in the workplace. These include destructive behaviors such as:

* Using abusive and/or vulgar language
* Humiliating co-workers and/or employees
* Stealing ideas from co-workers and employees
* Sabotaging the work efforts of others
* Bosses failing to promote and reward diligent workers. (51)

Wright and Smye go on to give us "Ten Ways to Recognize a Bully" by describing the obnoxious and odious behavior of adult bullies in the workplace.

With just a smidgen of Freudian "reverse engineering," it's not hard to see how the adult bullying behaviors catalogued here, particularly when it comes to bullying bosses, could have easily had their genesis in childhood bullying.

Let's give the beasts a name:

- *The Burning Man* displays uncontrollable anger by flying into a rage without warning, shouting, and using abusive and vulgar language.
- *The B-Rater* enjoys berating and humiliating you in front of your co-workers. No matter how good your performance, this type of boss never gives you an A.
- *The Critic* constantly criticizes you, either directly, or via well-aimed sarcasm.
- *The Ignore-Ant* deliberately ignores and or isolates you by marginalizing you and excluding you from active participation in discussions, meeting, and so on.

    This type of elitist exclusion is a serious type of bullying, especially at the high school level. For example, that snobbish clique of high school cheerleaders who thought their pom-poms didn't stink, who took devilish delight in excluding (i.e., torturing) all the less perfect blonde girls from hanging out with them. No surprise then when exclusion by their peers subsequently contributes to those shunned girls' lack of self-esteem, perhaps opening the door to bulimia and anorexia and any number of other expressions of angst and acting out.

    Or what about the jocks? Being excluded and marginalized by Columbine's "jock culture" was one of the grievances of the Columbine killers. Likewise, Cho felt himself excluded from activities at Virginia Tech—this despite reports that several of Cho's V-Tech fellow students actively tried to involve him in extracurricular activities.
- *The Deadliner* sets impossible deadlines and changes the game plan without warning, for no other reason than to make life difficult for you and your failure inevitable.

    Remember the abusive husband in *Sleeping with the Enemy* (1991)? Perfect example. No matter what Julia Roberts' character did, she was never going to reach the bar he set impossibly high.
- *The Narcissist* is convinced the sun rises and sets in his butt. He has trouble delegating authority because he's certain no one can be trusted to do the job right except him. As a result, he's a microman-

ager, always looking over your shoulder, always second-guessing you. Paranoid, he's like the schoolyard bully who never gets the joke and so thinks everyone is laughing at him. That's why he punches your lights out, funny man (even when your joke was an honest attempt to include him in the group).

Likewise, we can speculate that a paranoid loner like Cho might have suspected "a trick," that he was somehow being "set up" for humiliation by those he (erroneously) felt had been shunning him up till that time. Remember what happened in *Carrie* (1976) when the cruel kids literally set shy Carrie up with a date to the prom?

- *The Taker* takes credit for other people's ideas but never takes his share of the blame when things go wrong. If this kind of bully is a co-worker and you're assigned to work with him, you can expect to do both your job and his job. Of course, when you still succeed in bringing the project in on time and under budget, who do you think is going to be clawing around for the lion's share of the glory? This is the same type of bully who in school made you do his homework and forced you to help him cheat on tests.

- *The Dasher* takes sadistic pleasure in dashing your hopes and trashing your plans. Like the deadliner, he changes schedules without notice, canceling your vacation—perhaps even interrupting your vacation! No reasonable request is too small for him to refuse! "If I do it for you, I'll have to do it for everyone."

This is the same bully you tried "reasoning" with in grade school and in high school. Each time your bully pretended to "think it over," right before he punched your lights out.

This kind of bully boss follows a predictable (sadistic) pattern. He pretends to listen, pretends to "think it over"— perhaps asks you to do "an exhaustive case study and present him with a perfectly bound prospectus," which he'll then "consider at length," all the while knowing he's going to turn you down.

- *The Digger* continually undermines your authority and work efforts. He shares traits with the critic.

- *The Cockblocker* keeps getting in your way, stalling your promotion and not allowing you to present your revolutionary idea further up the chain of command. This kind of bully boss is insecure, afraid you will outshine him. He's often middle management material who's already seen too many younger go-getters (like yourself) leave him in the dust, speeding ahead with their careers while he's left spinning his glazed donut wheels.

Beware of co-workers who possess these same traits. Remember Iago in *Othello?*

This kind of bully husband keeps his wife barefoot and pregnant, afraid she will outgrow him and leave.

Sadly, we often find such "toxic" bullies in our own household, those family members or friends who tell us to "aim a little lower" and "don't dream too big." Their "concern" seems motivated by not wanting to see us "get hurt" but, subconsciously, might they not just be expressing their own insecurity of our moving ahead in life . . . without them?

Bosses from Hell

"Management by terror has been a time-honored technique
because it works."
—Bing (2007)

Overbearing bosses in the movies are humorous, like the Dabney Coleman dumbass in *9-to-5* (1980), who Dolly Parton and the rest of his employees finally take revenge on. Or how about Meryl Streep's wicked witch of the Westside routine in *The Devil Wears Prada* (2006) or Glen Close in FX's *Damages* (2007)?

Of course, mentally misanthropic bosses aren't so funny when they're like Ralph Fiennes's Amon Goeth, the Nazi camp commandant in *Schindler's List* (1993) who enjoyed using his prisoners for daily target practice.

Thankfully, you probably won't have to put up with a bully boss actually taking literal potshots at you—the occasional insensitive sarcastic snipe perhaps—but, still, there's a good chance that during your life you'll run into more than your share of bizarre, brazen, and back-stabbing bosses.

In *Crazy Bosses* (2007), Stanley Bing lists "bully" as one of several types of crazy bosses we're liable to run into on any given job. Bing believes bully bosses are driven by rage, as evidenced by their frequent mood swings, aggression, and attempts at manipulation. We hear echoes of the bully types outlined by Wright and Smye in Bing's list of crazy boss types:

- *The paranoid boss,* who is motivated by fear, is highly mistrustful of others and is given to fits of hysteria.
- *The narcissistic boss* has a short attention span and is incapable of empathy. He looks right through you. Only his own needs are real.
- *The wimpy boss* is a worrier who is driven by anxiety and takes credit for others' work.
- *The "disaster hunter"* boss is driven by desire and lust. A workaholic who never listens to others, he is vindictive and vicious when he feels his position or plans are being threatened.

Together, Bing's paranoid boss and narcissistic boss exhibit all the characteristics of the narcissist bully personality we get from Wright and Smye's observations. Likewise, Bing's wimpy boss echoes the taker type.

There's not much difference between the put-down on the playground and the put-down you receive from your bullying boss in the boardroom. In the same way a criticized child internalizes such abuse—be it verbal or physical, or both—though we might deny it, as adults we also take the criticism of our superiors to heart, to the point that it can negatively impact our self esteem:

> "Bullying can throw us into a downward spiral until we start to doubt our worth and abilities. . . . This diminished sense of self, whereby a person actually comes to believe that the bully's lies and distortions are true can be extremely damaging." (Wright and Smye, 1996:52)

The thing to remember is: He's not your "superior," he's just your boss.

When You're the Boss

The thing to remember is: You're not their "superior," you're just their boss.

"Work" is a four-lettered word. "Boss" is too. Chances are you'll be uttering more than a few four-lettered words once you're put in charge.

It's not easy running the show. There's lots of stress. However, "lots of stress" can never be your excuse for treating your employees like rodent roadkill.

As boss, you catch heat from both above and below.

Always keep in mind the l-word: liability. Personal liability toward you, and/or toward a company that—despite assurances that "we got your back!"—are not going to be too happy when you get them dragged into court to answer charges of sexual harassment, age discrimination, racism, or just generally encouraging "a hostile work environment."

It really is lonely at the top, except for all the lawyers!

And you have to watch out for young and up-coming (read: hungry!) pups trying to become top dog by wresting the big bone away from you.

Some of these up-and-comers are natural schemers, whereas others are adept students of the "Black Science."* These unprincipled upstarts will play the race card, the age-discrimination card, or the sexual harassment card. They'll drop names (like their executive uncle) and they'll drop lugs (innuendo), which are subtle (and not so subtle) bullying tactics designed to get their way by getting you out of their way.

If at all possible, don't stoop to their level.

As boss, it is important that you maintain control of the job at hand while receiving your due of respect from those under you and those over you, without your having to resort to heavy-handedness. In other words, don't become a bully.

Niccolò Machiavelli (1469–1527) literally wrote the book on bosses— good and bad. In both *The Prince* (1513) and *Discourses* (1517) he gave instructions for how a prince should rule, so as to achieve maximum efficiency and production, while being sure to watch his own back.

Machiavelli's observations and insights into interpersonal dealings (and double-dealings) were so accurate that we now refer to those who are ruthless (some might argue realistic) in their business undertakings as "Machiavellian."

Machiavelli's often (mis)quoted axiom asks the question whether it is best for a prince to be feared or loved by his subjects. We need only substitute "boss" for "prince" to see how relevant Machiavelli's advice is to us today:

---

*The "Black Science" is any strategy, tactic, or technique used to undermine a person's ability to reason and respond for himself. For a complete course, read Haha Lung and Christopher B. Prowent's *The Black Science* (2001) and *Mind Manipulation* (2001), and Haha Lung's *Mind Control* (2006).

"Men are mainly moved by one of two emotions: love or fear. A boss has a choice to make himself loved or to make himself feared. In the end a boss who makes himself feared is usually better obeyed, his orders more quickly and closely followed, than a boss who depends on being loved." (*Discoures* III:2)

True, things are (thankfully) a little more benign, business-wise, than they were in Machiavelli's day. Today's business community has checks and balances to see that predatory speculators and ruthless Wall Street witches who would wickedly profit off the disenfranchisement of others are swiftly brought to justice. Just ask Martha Stewart!

But seriously, people haven't changed much since Machiavelli's time, and the key to being a good (benevolent) boss isn't so much balancing those numbers at the bottom of the page as it is learning to judge and juggle the personalities of employees, co-workers, and your own boss.

You need to learn to read what people are saying. Really saying, and, most important, what they're not saying.

This is the singular most important survival skill you will learn from this book. Whether it's surviving a bullying verbal confrontation with your dignity (and job) intact, or whether you find yourself cornered by a heavily armed disgruntled employee—where the least wrong twitch on your part could spell disaster for yourself and your fellow hostages—learning to "read" another person—his voice, his body language—can literally be a lifesaver!

Tricks-into-Techniques: The Boardroom

"I'd like to find your inner child and kick it's little ass!"
—The Eagles, "Get over It"

Recall that Wright and Smye subscribe to the "wounded child within" theory of bullying:

"Research tells us that bullies are bullies usually because of experience in infancy or childhood. If a child has been treated harshly and is profoundly affected by it, he carries the expe-

*For a broader discussion on the Machiavelli method, see Haha Lung's *Total Mind Penetration* (2007)

73

rience with him into adulthood. In his subconscious the child who experienced aggression looks for opportunities to relive the experience, but this time instead of being the victim, he becomes the powerful aggressor. The process of recognizing what happened to him as a child and resolving his pain from the perspective of an adult has never occurred, to even the score. Knowing all this is well and good. But what do you do when you are confronted with someone whose face is contorted with rage, who has the power to fire, demote, or harass you? When it comes to bullies, knowing that your soul is being sapped because there is a Wounded Child Within, who has been unable to resolve his pain from an adult perspective, doesn't seem as significant as the immediate task of dealing with the Loathsome Adult Without." (1996:53)

As tempting as it might be to feel sorry for any adult still breastfeeding his wounded child within, surviving a bully is more important than psychoanalyzing him!

Thus, we must develop viable strategies and tactics for dealing with bullies in general, and our workplace bullies in particular, whether that bullying is psychological harassment or actual physical confrontation.

Avoid Confrontation

Handle your bully harassment problem in the wrong way, a little too forcefully, and it could make you look like the bully.

You need to dot your i's and cross your t's. You don't want to end up looking like the aggressor. It's always a major propaganda coup when you can make your enemy look like the bad guy, and a definite detriment to your cause when he can turn the tables and make you look like the aggressor rather than the aggrieved.

In Japan in 1701 there was contention between Lord Kira (by all accounts an evil man, but the shogun's master of ceremonies) and his longtime foe, Lord Asano (by all accounts an upright and honorable man). Now whereas all things right seem to have weighed heavily in Lord Asano's favor, nonetheless he was ultimately defeated by the wily Kira, who successfully goaded Asano into anger, causing Asano to draw his sword while on the shogun's grounds—a capital offense that required Asano to commit seppuku (ritual suicide). Thus, evil Kira defeated good Asano simply by making the latter appear to be "the bad guy."*

Avoiding confrontation (a positive) is not the same as bully dodging (a negative). Bully dodging involves deliberately rearranging your schedule— your life—around what you think (i.e., worry) your bully is going to do, avoiding places where you think your bully is going to appear.

In the same way you used to volunteer to stay inside and clean the blackboard during recess (so you wouldn't risk running into your favorite bully out on the playground) or the way you took the long way home from school in order to avoid paying the "bully toll" for walking down his street, so, too, every day, full-grown adults resort to bully dodging by avoiding co-workers, adjusting their schedules, and inconveniencing themselves so they won't accidentally run into their bully. Some bully dodgers even go so far as calling in sick, even leaving and coming to work by the back door (see Martin and Whitman-Greenwood, 1995:59, and Wright and Syme, 2007:5)

But they're not really "full-grown adults" yet, are they? Not so long as they still use juvenile solutions to "solve" (actually, to avoid dealing with) their adult problems.

We're here to help you with that.

Keep a Record

In the same way as you would document spousal abuse, document any harassment at work. Record conversations. Use a pocket recorder, minicam-corder, and so on. (No, this isn't hard or complicated to do. Ask the guy down at Radio Shack, or look up one of those nifty spy store places on the Internet.) At the very least, write down all those "chance meetings" with your bully in the copy room and the parking garage—too many chance meetings to be coincidence. Keep copies of any harassing e-mails, notes, and memos your bully sends you. Document your abuse until you're ready to present your evidence to the proper authorities or to defend your own ac-tions when your bully tries to pull a Lord Kira on you.

---

*Lord Asano's tale has a "happy" ending, samurai-wise, when Lord Asano's forty-seven loyal knights eventually succeeded in taking revenge on Lord Kira. For a more detailed telling of this most famous of samurai tales, see *Mind Manipulation* (2002).

Find Allies

Confide in friends and family and ask their advice. Ask trusted co-workers to help you document abuse, especially those who have suffered similar abuse. If at all possible, acquire a "patron," someone higher up the corporate food chain who will come to your defense when the fecal matter finally collides with the oscillating rotor!

Complain Higher Up

There is an ancient Chinese adage that warns: "Never strike a king unless you're certain you can kill him." So while you want to get help for your bullying problem ASAP, you must likewise cover your butt, making sure you have proof that you are being bullied and, if at all possible, have already alerted a superior about what's going on.

It's important, whenever humanly possible, to go through the chain of command by alerting your immediate superior of any problems you and your bullying co-worker are having.

Of course, the chain of command goes out the window when it's your immediate superior who's the one doing the bullying! In which case, you have to go over his head.

There's also the possibility that whoever along the chain of command you contact might be the "sweep it under the rug" type rather than someone willing to take action. Should it come to this, shoving the L-word in their face is usually enough to get them to act. Make them see it's their job on the line.

Go through the chain of command as much as possible, but don't let them use the chain of command to strangle you or to hang you out to dry.

Worst case scenario: Remind those higher up that the chain of command doesn't stop at the owner or chief executive officer of a company . . . it stops at the police or, better yet, the dreaded m-word: media!

Look for Another Job

I know, you're not the one at fault, and in a perfect world you shouldn't have to be the one to move on. In a perfect world.

No matter how happy you are with your present job, it never hurts to put your name into one of those handy Internet job search sites, the ones where they send you a periodic readout of jobs you're qualified for and businesses that are actively recruiting people with your job skills.

Why should you do this? It's good for the self-esteem. No matter what kind of abuse they heap on you at your present job (i.e. "you're damn lucky to have this job!"), you know different. You know your skills are in demand.

Also, it's always good to have options. Recall that one of the theories for the existence of bullyism in the world is that baby bullies are not taught enough options for how to deal with frustration early in life. As adults, they then have fewer options to fall back on (i.e. less problem-solving ability), become easily frustrated, and opt for bullying as the easy way out.

Job options give you breathing space and stop you from imagining that your life will be over if you lose your present job. There's a time to fight and a time to fold up your tent.

Of course, that doesn't mean you can't burn your enemy's tents before retiring!

Use Black Science

Should you fight fire with fire? Match your enemy dirty trick for dirty trick? Or do you take the moral high ground?

Given the choice, always seize the high ground—be it moral high ground or actual high ground. It's always easier to piss down on your enemies than to piss up at them.

Taking the moral high ground, doing what's "right," is all good and noble, but it doesn't necessarily keep an honest man working or keep food in his fridge. Let your conscience be your guide.

There are two main types of ploys within the black science: mental ploys and physical ploys.

Mental Ploys Mental Ploys depend on distraction and reaction. You distract your bully, mad boss, or hostage-taker by talking to him and/or otherwise adapting your body language.

Calming down a mad boss or distracting a hostage-taker all rely on correctly reading and then rewriting the same basic human reactions. Granted, the consequences for failure will be more extreme with the latter.

Your bully has grievances, real or imagined. Listen to those grievances. But, more important, listen to how he expresses those grievances. Is there tension in his voice or resolve. Is he ranting incoherently or is he deathly calm and resigned to his (and your!) fate?

Become an empathetic listener. Focus your attention on him. Keep him talking. Acknowledge his feelings and sympathize with his grievances (but don't get caught patronizing).

Whenever possible, turn the battleground into a common ground. Agree with the bullies in your life . . . until you're in a more advantageous position to disagree permanently.

More on reading body language in a minute.

Ask for the other person's solution. What does he want? How does he see the situation playing out?

As long as he's still talking (even if he is ranting and raving), at least he's not throwing punches . . . or lead.

In her eye-opening book *Success with the Gentle Art of Verbal Self-Defense* (1989), Suzette Haden Elgin tells us about the three types of lies:

- Incompetent lies that don't need to be told, but people just can't seem to stop telling them. There's an old saying that a man begins by telling you what he knows but, if you allow him to keep talking, he begins to tell you what he doesn't know (or at least, tell you things he doesn't realize he's telling you). So the good news is people are constantly giving themselves away because their body language doesn't match their face, their expressions don't coordinate with their gestures, they have a waver in their voice—all of these are clues. Become a good watcher.
- Polite lies that help us get along in society: "No those pants don't make your ass look fat!"
- Survival lies that, as the name implies, help us survive. Do what you have to, to survive. Say what you have to, to survive.

If you get a vague feeling he's about to go postal, about to get violent, or start slaughtering up the whole room—*trust your gut.* Remember, your gut instincts evolved a few million years sooner than that higher reasoning part of your brain that says, "Sure, we can reason with him!"

Sometimes you can. Sometimes you can't. Like it or not, you are betting your life (and perhaps the lives of others) on your being right. Practice the verbal, prepare for the physical.

Physical Ploys

> **"All language is manipulative;**
> **all language is attempted persuasion."**
> **—Elgin (1989:86)**

There are two types of language: verbal language and body language.

It's a fact that many of us "bite our tongue" when bowing to societal pressures and protocol, thus hiding our true feelings. That's why people's true emotions do not always match up with the words coming out their mouths.

Fortunately, long before we hear someone speak, often what they are not saying is being broadcast loud and clear—by the way they walk, avoid eye contact, fidget, and wipe imaginary dust from their clothing. It's called body language, and you needn't be a psychiatrist to master this skill to read people like a book. You just need to become a good watcher.

Reading body language is literally the bread and butter of police, psychiatrists, and poker players, all of whom become masters at intuiting your feelings, indeed, your innermost thoughts, not only by listening to the tone, timbre, and tremble in your voice but also by observing every twitch of your face, every slight gesture.

All too often, the bright friendliness rushing out of a person's mouth only serves to distract us from noticing the deeper darkness lurking just inside the shadows of his eyes.

You need to become a good watcher.

First, watch your bully's body language. Be alert for any opening that might work to your advantage.

You remember: Distract a schoolyard bully by looking over his shoulder and muttering, "Is the principal coming?"—then run like hell when he turns around!

What about that drug-addict mugger or that mental patient whose holding you at knifepoint? Are his eyes glazing over, taking on a far-away look? (A sure sign he's distracted listening to the voices in his head!)

What about your hostage-taker? Is he growing tired, or sleepy, lowering the barrel of the gun toward the floor?

Second, watch your own body language. You mustn't appear threatening. You don't want to draw undue attention to yourself.

If the bully (mugger, armed robber) wants your money—give it to him. Material possessions or your life? There's no comparison.

If, on the other hand, your attacker wants you, then you're going to have to fight. Whether he's after sex or blood, or a lot of both, you're going to have to fight.

When the time comes—and Heaven forbid it does!—each person has to decide how to act and react in a dire threat situation.

The most common scenario that comes to mind is rape.

Each woman (and man) reacts differently to the prospect of being raped. No one (including this oh-so-gifted author) can tell you how to react when faced with such a potentially life-altering attack.

You may gamble that your attacker merely wants to rape you and has no problem leaving you alive to identify him later. Let's hope you guess right.

What we do know from the accounts of women (and men) who have fought back against a rapist is that, despite the damage done to their body from fending off an attacker, those who fight back seem to suffer less long-term psychological trauma. This is because their having fought back leaves them with less guilt ("I should have fought back, I should have tried harder") and with more self-esteem for having tried to fight back.

In other words, fighting back helps lessen the shame of something that, in a perfect world, a victim should never have to feel shame for in the first place.

Anytime you are facing a bully, try to remain physically calm, even when faced with a dire threat situation. (We'll teach you some techniques for doing this in chapter 3—it's called "centering.")

If at any time during a verbal confrontation you feel physically threatened or just physically ill-at-ease (remember that part about trusting your gut), find an excuse to exit the scene, and then immediately alert others.

If you can't leave the area, without getting your head beat in (or blown off!) try to move around the room as much as possible without arousing suspicion or otherwise pissing off your bully.

Maneuver toward an exit. Keep a clear line of sight and, if possible, movement, between you and any windows. In an actual hostage situation, try to maneuver the aggressor in front of a window (so a police sniper will have a clear shot!).

Take some time today to look around your home, around your place of business, around your school, looking for places you can hide—and barricade!—in case of an emergency. This is no different from our previous advice for helping an abused spouse build herself a bolt hole, a safe place to run.

Look for natural bolt holes (walk-in freezers, elevator shafts, etc.). Look for any escape routes out of a building you'd generally never consider: emergency stairs (up onto the roof, down into the basement), out a window (onto a fire escape, a ledge leading around the side of the building, onto a drain pipe, soft ground, shrubs, even into the thick canopy of a tree), air ducts, sewers lines, and so on. Don't worry about losing your dignity when Death's trying to catch up with you.

An added benefit of doing this kind of on-site assessment of potential emergency exit routes in your own home (and/or business) can alert you to possible routes burglars can use when breaking into your home.

When you can't get away, use delaying tactics.

Ask your bully if it's okay to get a cup of coffee—offer him one. (A hot cup of coffee makes a great "environmental weapon.") Any time you find yourself in a dire threat situation, fill your hand with a pen (for stabbing) or chalk dust (for blinding)—the list is endless. Outside, fill your hand with a rock, dirt, a stick, anything you can use to fight back.

Familiarize yourself with weapons, both conventional weapons (the most common being the gun and the knife), as well as environmental weapons you glean from your surroundings. We're not saying you have to become Rambo, it simply means that most untrained people have exaggerated ideas about what a gun or knife can do.

Here's a crash course on facing down a weapon:

- *Guns:* If an assailant pulls a gun on you, the chances are he won't shoot. If he does shoot, the odds are he won't hit you (of course, this is mitigated by how close your assailant is to you and what kind of weapon he has—an automatic spits out more bullets, increasing his chances of actually hitting the broad side of a barn). Even if he hits you, chances are he won't kill you (because 80 percent of the body isn't vital). Immediate first aid will staunch most bleeding, giving you enough time to get hospital care.

  By the way, learn first aid, for yourself and for your loved ones. It's a vital survival skill.
- *Knives:* Here is the martial arts rule for knives: If he can't hit you with his hand, then he can't stab you with his knife. Once you learn to block in-coming blows (which I'll teach you to do in chapter 3), because you'll have learned to block an attacker's arm, you will—by default—be able to block anything that arm is holding.

• *Other weapons:* I know you've heard the horror stories of how abusive husbands, stalkers, and other bullies have cut their victims with shards of glass, thrown acid in their victims' faces, and even run their victims over with cars.

The adage that "You can't plan for everything" still rings true, but what you can do—will do!—is put yourself in a new mind-set where you will realize *you can survive* and *you can win* against an attacker—from a bullying confrontation to a hostage situation. (Terrorists are just bullies with bigger guns.)

Here's the key: Any weapon a bully decides to pick up and use against you, such as a club, brick, and so on, is also available for your defensive use.*

In chapter 3, we'll teach you what you need to know about fighting off a bully who has a weapon, as well as bring you up to speed on the treasure trove of environmental weapons available to you at a minute's notice.

CONCLUSION

Do what you have to, to survive.

Are you worried about legal liability if you fight back tooth and nail to protect yourself and your loved ones? Remember: It's better to be judged by twelve . . . than carried by six.

We can't predict what will happen tomorrow, what violence might come to our doorstep. We can't predict, but we can prepare.

Bullies are the same everywhere, in every time and clime. Therefore, the warning signs are the same—if not at least glaringly similar—when it comes to our spotting potential trouble and dealing with it before that trouble gets the upper hand.

Sun Tzu would be proud. And, in the next chapter of this book, we will make him proud by training ourselves to be more alert and to act and react in ways that will prevent little problems from becoming big problems.

Remember: forewarned is forearmed.

Well, so far we've forewarned you, now let's get you forearmed!

---

*For a complete course on what environmental weapons are available to you in your home and/or place of business, read Ralf Dean Omar's *Death on Your Doorstep: 101 Weapons in the Home* (1993).

82

3

The Bully Battleground:
Victims Victorious!

"The past is studied for the sake of the present."
—Mao Tsze-tung (1893–1976)

"Those who do not learn from the past are condemned to repeat it."
—George Santayana (1863–1952)

No book can make you a black belt in karate, kung-fu, or any other martial art. What a book can do—what this book will do—is increase your awareness of what others are capable of, but, more important, what you are capable of when the weather goes south and your world suddenly gets a whole lot more violent.

Hopefully, we accomplished our intent in chapters 1 and 2 of this book, by making you more aware that bullies exist in all walks of life and that bullies do affect your life—if not you directly in the classroom, bedroom, or boardroom, then indirectly by targeting your friends and family.

Hopefully, we have also made you more aware of some of the theories behind what causes bullies, which, in turn will help you better spot emerging bullies and bullying situations, so as to better prepare you to intervene yourself ("bystander effect" be damned!), and/or alert the proper authorities to intervene.

Whereas the first two chapters focused primarily on nonphysical responses to bullying behavior, this chapter will focus on physical responses. "Physical" doesn't necessarily mean "violent."

Always, always, always remember that your preferred option when facing a possibly explosive, possibly violent bullying situation is to walk away. Walking away is a physical response. So, this is the first and foremost physical response I want to teach you. But then again, I don't have to teach you to flee from danger—Mother Nature has already provided you with the flight or fight response. Notice the "flight" part comes before the "fight" part? Mother Nature is no dummy.

But there are times when you can't walk away from danger. Indeed, there will be times when you are trapped and can't flee the scene. Other times, as the brave are sometimes wont to do, you will choose to stand your ground, to draw a line in the sand. Think of the passengers on Flight 93.

Martial arts is just that: "martial," meaning "war." For all the beautiful gymnastics, impressive board-breaking, and high-flying action of Hong Kong kick-flicks, at its root, martial arts comes from war. And it should prepare us for the same.

This is why the brothers of the Shaolin temple were kind of particular about who they accepted into their order—especially after they had honed Shaolin kung-fu into such a potentially deadly fighting art.

Never forget that Shaolin kung-fu did not start out as a particularly deadly fighting art.

It is true that Bodhidharma, who is credited with introducing Indian fighting exercises to China, had seen his share of bloodshed in his younger warrior days. Still, so legend maintains, he first taught exercises to his fellow monks in order to strengthen them against the rigors of the marathon meditation sessions he demanded of his students.

Only later, when the acute oppressive bullying the peaceful brothers (and sisters) of Shaolin were being constantly subjected to by local rogues and ruffians turn chronic did the Shaolin monks and nuns turn their martial arts to more martial uses.

This is the same formula we will follow in teaching you self-defense appreciation (i.e., awareness) and self-defense application; tried-and-true techniques designed to, first, strengthen your mind and body, before then giving you the physical skills to fight back against bullies—but only when absolutely necessary.

These techniques are presented to you in degrees of sophistication, beginning with what might seem like simplistic, common-sense concepts—mirroring your own growing awareness of physical defense options.

Before jumping feet-first into learning how (and where) to punch and kick, we first want to understand the mind-set of those masters who developed these arts. This is called the "Appreciation Phase."

Having attained the proper attitude—the proper respect—for the art, only then will we begin to master the dangerous, possibly lethal, self-defense techniques the Shaolin brothers so prudently guarded for all those years.

With diligent focus and commitment, you will soon begin to see how your child being "shook down" on the playground for his lunch money is not all that different from that Shaolin monk being harassed and robbed everyday when going to the market.

Or perhaps you will identify with Lady Wing Chun, threatened by a bleak future filled with spousal abuse whose life was changed by learning kung-fu from a Shaolin nun.

Or perhaps you will learn to better identify and deal with the *caibu* ("energy vampires") at work who daily drain your energies and steal your ideas.

Yes, there is much we can learn from the Shaolin brothers and sisters.

A prayer: May the regretful words "If only I had" never find a resting place on your lips.

RISE OF THE TIGERS

In the same way in which much of what we today recognize as Chinese kung-fu martial arts originated in India, so, too, China has India to thank for much of its philosophical underpinnings.

Traditional Chinese philosophy is a mixture—generally a harmonious blending—of Confucianism, Taoism, and Buddhism—the latter imported from India.

While it's not necessary to the task at hand that we undertake an in-depth study of Asian religious philosophy in general, it will benefit us to at least touch on the fact that the overall mind-set of the martial arts, and the Chinese martial arts tradition in particular, has inherited much from these three schools of thought, all of which came together to form the core philosophy of the Shaolin Order.

Taoism came to prominence in the sixth century B.C. with the writing of the *Tao Te Ching* by the Taoist patriarch Lao Tzu.

However, in keeping with the sometimes deliberate mysteriousness of Taoists, some claim Lao Tzu was a fiction created by Chang Tzu, a humble student of Lao Tzu. This is bolstered by the fact that there is no accurate birth or death dates for Lao Tzu, who, according to Taoist legend, at the end of his life disappeared into the mountains separating China from India.

Some legends go so far as to subsequently list Lao Tzu as being one of the mentors of young Siddhartha Gautama, the Indian prince who became the Buddha.

Taoism is all about living in harmony with nature. Indeed, according to Taoists, should one attain perfect harmony with nature, one will also gain immortality.

Taoists were/are world-renown alchemists and herbalists and are credited with the development of more meditative and health-oriented practices such as tai chi (also a devastatingly effective martial art by the way!) and chigong health exercises, as well as practices such as acupuncture.*

Taosist were always arguing with the followers of Confucius (551–479), who was a real person. Confucianism stresses duty to your ruler, familial fealty, and piety toward the gods.

Added to this sometimes contentious mix of Taoism and Confucianism came Buddhism, which stresses seeking a balance in all things. Brought to China by Indian missionaries over several centuries, the most important "wave" of Buddhist teachings (for our purposes) came around A.D. 520, when Daruma, aka Bodhidharma, came to teach at the (then) Taoist monastery in Hunan province.

Bodhidharma taught a fusion, a mixture if you will, of Confucianism, Taoism, and Buddhism that emphasized dhyana, an Indian word meaning simply "meditation."

Dhyana was called shan (also written ch'an) by the Chinese, which, when translated into Japanese, later became what we now know as zen.

Zen is the lynchpin of Japanese martial arts, especially where it took

---

*The Taoist discipline of acupuncture was later perverted by the Chinese ninja (aka Moshuh Nanren) into the Dim-Mak "Death Touch," capable of killing a man with a single touch. See Ralf Dean Omar's "Ninja Death Touch: The Fact and the Fiction" *(Blackbelt,* September 1989) and Haha Lung's *The Ninja Craft* (1997).

root in the hearts and minds of the samurai warrior class. It is there we see a similar blending of philosophies to Shaolin, in this case, with Buddhism and Confucianism combining with the indigenous Shintoism folk-faith of Japan:

> "The code of the samurai was a mixture of Shintoism, Buddhism, and Confucianism. Shintoism taught the warriors that they were descendants of divine beings and that upon death they, too, would become 'gods.' From Buddhism they learned to accept the transitory, fragile nature of life and view death as crossing into another plane of existence. From Confucianism came the concept of absolute loyalty to their lord." (Naito, 1989:20)

What's all this got to do with you facing down a bully in a dark alley?

First, don't take shortcuts through dark alleys! From Taoism we learn to do what comes naturally by listening to what our body is telling us. Our body knows how to survive already. Recall the lesson learned from illustrations 2 and 3, on how to turn a natural "flinch reaction" into an effective counterattack.

From Buddhism we learn to seek balance in all things, first within ourselves, then within the world.

The fear you feel is merely your mind in a state of unbalance. We will help you find your balance again.

And from Confucianism we learn that sometimes our duty to help others—family, friends, perhaps a complete stranger—overrides our fear.

Sometimes you can't walk away. Sometimes, you can't just be a bystander. Sometimes you have to fight. Remember Flight 93.

At the Master's Feet (Mental and Strategic Origins of Kung-fu)

> *"Fight only as a last resort. Let the enemy create your victory."*
> —Cao Cao (155–220)

Zizhi-Dao: The Art of Control

The Chinese term "Zizhi-dao" (pronounced "dzee-gee-dow") means "The Art of Control." Control in this instance refers to things outside ourselves that influence us, such as fate, the government, or the gods. But Zizhi-

MIND FIST

dao also applies to the amount of personal control (will) we exert over ourselves. Gaining more personal control over our lives means taking more responsibility, as well as disciplining and challenging ourselves both physically and mentally before our enemies and our environment do.

What was it Hannibal the Conqueror advised us in his "99 Truths": "Test yourself with fire and ice, sea and sand, blood and bile, before your enemies do."

In the East, better control over your physical fate in general and your physical health and safety in particular is often accomplished by mastering one of the many traditional martial arts.

In China, what we in the West call "kung-fu" is called "wu Shu" ("war art"). "Kung-fu" (sometimes written "gung-fu" or "gong-fu) can mean "hard work," "excellence," and "mastery"—implying that one has mastered a particular field of endeavor. Thus, while "kung-fu" can be applied to martial arts, it can just as rightly be used to acknowledge a person who has mastered cooking, carpentry, or some other art or craft.*

"Kung-fu" can therefore be applied to mental arts as well as martial arts—both the mental control and mastery we exhibit over ourselves, as well as the cunning (i.e., influence and force of will) we use to overcome our enemies.

It has oft been said "All battles are first fought—and won—in the mind."

Now while it might not seem like you put much prior thought (or effort) into getting sucker punched, the fact is all your prior thoughts (thus actions) you had in your life ("Should I go out, should I stay in, should I take a shortcut through that dark alley?") have brought you to the point to where you now find yourself facing down (or, in some cases, looking up at) a bully who has already decided he doesn't have to work for an honest dollar so long as he can work you over for a dishonest dollar!

To counter this attitude (to say nothing of his right hook!), we must make an effort to get inside his head.

Gancui: The Mind Fist

To successfully "get inside" your bully's head, we use what the ancient Chinese masters called "Gancui" (pronounced "gang-kway"), which literally

*The popular U.S. Marine war cry "gung-ho," meaning enthusiasm, comes from the same Chinese root.

88

means "to penetrate neatly and completely" (i.e., getting inside an enemy's head in order to discern his intentions, to instantly develop an effective counter strategy).*

Gancui ranges from techniques designed to confuse an enemy (thus making him hesitate), to tactics designed to terrorize him into never raising his hand to you (or a loved one) again. Remember that Buddha said our greatest weapon is in our enemy's mind.

The two acknowledged Chinese kung-fu masters of Gancui mind fist are Sun Tzu and his strategic successor Cao Cao.

Sun Tzu's Ping-fa

The Chinese term "ping-fa" refers to military cunning, but it is often specifically applied to a written opus of an acknowledged military strategist. The greatest such guidebook ever written is the *Ping-fa* of Sun Tzu.

Sun Tzu wrote his treaties twenty-five hundred years ago, yet his insights into human nature still ring true. He realized early on that all human beings are capable of making mistakes. It is left to us then to make our enemies make those mistakes. We can learn much from Sun Tzu.

First, we should take to heart his teaching that "all warfare is based on deception." From the immediate need we have of dealing with the bullies in our lives (and the lives of our loved ones), we can relate to this adage because deception is what our bully is trying to sell us.

Sure, he may be willing to back up his threats with physical violence (and we must always be prepared for him to go to such extremes—as well as be willing and able to go there ourselves), but half the time the bully is pure bluff. Show the least resistance, and he will seek other (weaker) prey.

Second, we must embrace Sun Tzu's "war is deception" adage as our marching orders, honing our own skills of deception by bringing them to bear as our first line of defense against bullyism.

Even after we actually fortify ourselves through better understanding of what makes a bully tick (chapter 1 of this book) and through strengthening ourselves physically to withstand and effectively counter a physical attack, we must still learn to project this new, more formidable image we have of ourselves out into the world.

---

*For a complete, in-depth course on the Gancui mind fist, see Haha Lung's *Total Mind Penetration* (2007).

Without projecting false bravado, we must show the world (and its bullies) by the way we carry ourselves and conduct our daily business that we mean business—that we are fully capable and willing to defend ourselves at whatever level the bully wants to take his bullying fantasy to.

The bully's stock and trade is intimidation. We must therefore learn to inimidate the intimidator—effectively beating the bully at his own game.

This is not as daunting a task as you might first imagine.

Remember: Bullies look for the weakest link in the chain, looking to separate the hindmost from the herd.

By projecting an image (based on fact) that we are fully capable and willing to defend ourselves (and our loved ones), the vast majority of bullies will prudently seek prey elsewhere.

This then was Sun Tzu's (and should be our) highest ideal: To defeat an enemy without having to raise our hand in violence, to end a fight before it begins, to never allow that molehill to grow into a mountain.

Cao Cao: The Martial King

"Fight only as a last resort."
—Cao Cao

Cao Cao (also written Ts'ao Ts'ao) is arguably the most famous general to have lived through China's violent Three Kingdoms Period. He lived and fought from 155 through 220, earning him the title the "Martial King" for his mastery of battlefield strategy and tactics. He eventually used these skills to become king of the kingdom of Wei and founder of the Wei dynasty.

An avid student of Sun Tzu, Cao Cao can be thanked for editing Sun Tzu's *Ping-fa* into its present thirteen chapters.

Cao Cao is also credited with creating a devastatingly effective form of unarmed fighting for his soldiers known as "Iron Wall kung-fu," which included tactics gleaned directly from his battlefield experience and incorporated many of the "Tiger style" techniques you'll be learning later in this book.

Cao Cao's main maxim was clear: "Nothing is constant in war save deception and cunning."

Already from Cao Cao we find here something we can adapt to our own modern antibully mind-set: Be prepared to think on your feet, because circumstances are constantly changing.

Embracing this concept will, in and of itself, give you a decided advantage over your bully because, by his very nature (as evidenced by his chosen "profession"), the bully is not that imaginative of a thinker. He comes to the party (or mugging, if you will) with a simple game plan. The least little thing you do—the least shifting of circumstances—and the bully's game plan is thrown out of whack.

A confused and hesitant enemy is a Godsend. Cao Cao put it this way:

> "Just as water has no constant form, so too war has no constant dynamic. As water adapts to each vase, so too those adept at war adopt an attitude of flexibility, thus adapting to flux and circumstance. So much of this cannot be known in advance but must be judged on the spot with a practiced eye."

Notice Cao Cao's use of the word "water," a common Taoist teaching metaphor. Notice, too, how Cao Cao advises us to use our "practiced eye." This means we've put some prior thought—and sweat!—into possible defensive scenarios.

Cao Cao was known—and feared—for his quick decision making and for arriving at the battlefield well in advance of his enemy. Here, then, is another lesson for us. We must train ourselves to not only make decisions, but to make them quickly. In any self-defense situation: hesitation equals death.

As will be discussed in more detail in the following section on physical reactions to threats, all too often our body hesitates when it ought to be moving—running, throwing punches.

And, no, you didn't "freeze up like a coward." This is simply a matter of your failing to recognize your body's signals for readiness to activate either flight (to safety) or else fight (tooth and nail!) and your neglecting to (re)program the proper release sequence into your mind-body system that would have allowed you to activate "flight-or-fight" automatically when needed.

We'll teach you how to do this in a minute.

According to Cao Cao, a wise general (that would be you in this case) possesses five virtues:

- *Wisdom:* Know when to stand your ground and when to run. Mother Nature has painstakingly sewn this into your genes: Flight or fight. Both are appropriate at different times. Develop the wisdom to know which works when and where. There is no "dishonor," no "cowardice" attached to running from a burning building or in "saving yourself" (in order to escape, survive, and bring back help).

- *Integrity:* Practice doing the right thing, and doing the right thing will become your practice. If you know in your heart that you are right, this will grant you strength far beyond what you think you now possess.
- *Compassion:* The Golden Rule which is found in all the world's great religions. Buddha said, "I would not do to others what I would not have done to myself." The "bystander effect" be damned, because we're all in this leaky boat together. There's an old Estonian proverb that warns, "If the Russian bear is dancing in my neighbor's yard, will not my yard be next?"
- *Courage:* True courage is not the absence of fear . . . it's doing what needs to be done in spite of being scared! Remember Flight 93.
- *Severity:* This means doing what has to be done. Shoving a pencil through an attacker's eye and into his brain beats using that same pencil to write your own obituary, or the obituary of a friend or family member.

The first four of these comes together at this point: where your wisdom to sense the severity of the situation merges with your determination—your integrity—to do what's right, a feeling bolstered by your compassion and your courage.

There is a saying from the Bhagavad-Gita, which was meant to set the warrior's mind at ease when deciding whether a cause is worth killing and possibly dying for. Krishna (God) tells Arjuna (India's greatest warrior, now despondent and hesitant to fight against former friends and allies): "Win, and you will enjoy this world. Die in this just cause and you win the approval of Heaven!"

Cao Cao admonishes us to win our battles with as little bloodshed as possible—an obvious paraphrase of Sun Tzu's ideal.

Cao Cao rejoices when "the enemy surrenders without a battle having been fought. Without engaging the enemy in battle, the wise general achieves his goal entire and intact, is victorious under Heaven, and has not subjected his troops to blood and sword."

Cao Cao accomplishes this by using the warrior's Three Knows: know yourself, know your enemy, and know your environment.

In knowing the enemy, Cao Cao advises us to dig deep into an enemy's motivations: "One must seek the subtler origins." We learned to do this in chapter 1. Cao Cao's greatest teaching is perhaps in assuring us that we—and not the enemy, not the bully—controls the situation. Ultimately, says Cao Cao, "All depends on the skill of the warrior."

Let us now move forward to acquire that skill!*

With the Masters' Hand (Physical and Tactical Origins of Kung-fu)

We cannot know the taste of the fruit until we place it in our mouth. We may appreciate its inviting shine, its fragrance, even the feel of its skin beneath our fingers, but until we truly taste it, how can we know the true taste of it?

This is an example of "appreciation" versus "application."

Likewise, it's easy to look at a masterful painting to appreciate its beauty. But how many of us are skilled enough to create such a painting ourselves? Again, this is the difference between appreciation (thinking) and practical application (doing).

So, too, with the martial arts—or even with just getting our mind right when it comes to thinking (planning, preparing, and practicing) what we might do and could do in a self-defense situation.

Of course, we are not the first in history to face such a dilemma.

It is through studying the past examples of people much like ourselves, who have faced down their fears and overcome the bullies in their lives, that we will find both the inspiration and the techniques—requiring perspiration!—to help us face down our own internal and external bullies.

Where others have succeeded with firm gaze and sure step, we have only to narrow our own vision and concentrate on where we place our foot to succeed as well.

---

*For a more complete discussion of the philosophy and force of Cao Cao, see Haha Lung's *Mind Control* (2006) and *Total Mind Penetration* (2007).

Bodhidharma and the Bullies

> *"Things are not what they seem . . . nor are they otherwise."*
> —**Bodhidharma**, *The Lankavatara Sutra*

Much of the Asian lineage of martial arts can be traced back to an ancient form of fighting known as Kalarippayattu, the oldest practice of which is found in southern India. However, Indo-Aryan invaders from the north around 1900 B.C., who imposed their caste system on ancient India, also brought various styles of armed and unarmed fighting with them when they conquered the Indian subcontinent.

It is these Indian martial arts styles that Bodhidharma, the twenty-ninth Buddhist patriarch, took with him when he traveled from his native India to China.

We know little of Bodhidharma's early life before he became a monk except that he was born a noble and was said to have proven both his mettle and his metal in numerous battles.

As a well-to-do noble, Bodhidharma had access to the best martial arts instructors available at the time in India, as well as to foreign martial arts masters visiting India.

Whatever the particular revelation that convinced Bodhidharma to step off the leisurely royal road onto the winding, rock-strewn path of a humble Buddhist monk is not known. All we know is that we benefit from his decision.

By all accounts, Bodhidharma applied the same dogged determination and attention to detail to grasping Buddhism as he had previously done to learn the martial arts, graduating swiftly through the various levels of Buddha's teachings to become a recognized master and eventually earning the mantle of the twenty-ninth master in a direct line stretching back to Siddhartha Gautama, the historical Buddha a thousand years before.

But, in a tradition of breaking tradition that would soon become the hallmark of Bodhidharma's particular school of Buddhist thought, the master himself decided to go to China one day—some versions say he was answering a request from the Chinese emperor for qualified Buddhist teachers to come and teach Buddhism in China. Around A.D. 520, Bodhidharma made the journey to China (some say by dangerous sea voyage, others that he traveled across the treacherous bandit-infested mountains).

Arriving in China, Bodhidharma (called Tamo by the Chinese) was welcomed as royalty into the imperial court. The Chinese emperor immediately began reading off a list of all the Buddhist temples and shrines he had ordered built, all the scriptures he'd ordered copied, and all the good works he had done to promote Buddhism.

Bodhidharma listened patiently to this exhausting list of deeds the emperor had done in the name of Buddhism. But, finally, when the emperor got around to asking the visiting Buddhist master what merit all these deeds would garner him in his search for nirvana (enlightenment), Bodhidharma dismissed them all with a contemptuous wave of his hand, "Without daily meditation, no work has merit to carry you a single step closer to enlightenment."

Angered, the emperor at first thought to kill Bodhidharma but, realizing the monk's growing popularity, merely banished him from the imperial court.

At this point, so the legend goes, Bodhidharma considered returning to India but, realizing that if the emperor was any example, Buddhism was indeed in a deplorable state in China. So he decided instead to stay and teach proper Buddhist practice.

As a result, Tamo settled in a small Taoist monastery in Hunan province surrounded by a "small forest." Here, he taught the eager monks (and later nuns) a mixture of indigenous Taoism mixed with his own extreme method of meditation. From this fusion of Taoism and Buddhism came Shan Buddhism (called "Zen" in Japan).

The rest of the story is the stuff of martial arts legend:

Seeing that the Shaolin monks were too weak to stay awake during the marathon mediation session Tamo demanded of them, he taught then yoga-like exercises designed to strengthen the body and focus the mind (never telling them that these exercises could also be used for self-defense).

Later, after the monastery was threatened (some versions of the story say by local thugs and bandits, others say by an invading army of barbarians), Bodhidharma revealed the "hidden" fighting techniques inherent in his exercises.

Thus was born Shaolin kung-fu, the style from which nearly all Asian-based martial arts systems claim some lineage.

Many legends are told of Bodhidharma himself.

It is said he spent his first nine years at Shaolin in meditation in a nearby cave. To stay awake, he pulled out his eyelashes one by one. Where each lash fell, there sprang up a tea plant.

So intense was Bodhidharma's own meditation regime that, over the course of that nine years, his fierce stare (always present in portraits of him) actually bore a hole through the wall of the cave!

Even after his death, the legends continued.

It is said that many years after his death and burial a group of Shaolin monks returning from India saw a stranger who bore an uncanny resemblance to the late Bodhidharma walking across the mountains. The stranger wore but one sandal.

Alarmed by this, the Shaolin brothers finally opened up the cave where Bodhidharma had been laid to rest. To their amazement, all they found inside the burial chamber was one sandal!

Eighteen Hands and Five Animals

The fact of the matter is that even before Bodhidharma showed up on the doorsteps of the Shaolin monastery (and even more so after this twenty-ninth Buddhist master, first Zen master shuffled off this mortal coil), the Shaolin Order was constantly knee-deep in controversy.

As was the custom in many Asian countries at the time, anytime a respected military officer grew too old, was disgraced or disciplined harshly, or came under suspicion of being just a wee-bit too ambitious, often, rather than execute a knowledgeable officer who might be needed later, such military men were ordered by the emperor to become monks.

So it's not surprising that for every dedicated Shaolin brother seeking enlightenment we find, you could expect to discover another "involuntary monk" fuming over having been "exiled" to a monastery. Equally not surprising then is that the various Shaolin monasteries (there were many as the popularity of the order grew) became breeding grounds for dissent and sedition.

And it didn't help matters any when Bodhidharma introduced his new, devastatingly effective fighting art, originally known as the "Eighteen Hands of Lo-Han" (Lo-Han being another name for "monk").

Before long, some of the brothers (and sisters) of Shaolin were spending more time practicing their "Iron Broom" leg sweep and "Spear-hand" thrusts than they were meditating and memorizing Buddhist sutras. In short order, every would-be rebel, rogue, and ruffian—and, yes, bullies, within a hundred miles was beating a path to the monastery gate, trying to spy out the secrets of this new fighting art. Soon, the "secrets" of Shaolin Kung-fu began seeping out, giving birth to a dozen other styles of fighting and killing.

Early on, Bodhidharma had left instructions that this new style of Wu Shu kung-fu was only to be taught to Buddhist monks, because it was believed only a person who had taken a sacred pledge of nonviolence could be trusted with such a potentially deadly art.

With all this supposed scheming and "physical conditioning" going on behind the secretive monastery walls, it's hardly surprising that, over the years, several Shaolin monasteries, and eventually the entire order, came under suspicion by the imperial court and were banned and, in some instances, those suspect monasteries were burned to the ground. This happened on several different occasions, with the order falling out of favor with one reigning emperor, only to find renewed favor with a newly enthroned emperor.

Finally, in 1644 the original Shaolin Order (there have been many reconstituted claimants to the title since) was totally destroyed when the Shaolin brothers sided with a powerful resistance leader named Cuxinga who was fighting against the invading Manchu.

The last gasp of the order came when 128 Shaolin brothers held out against a besieging Manchu force at the monastery at Foochow.

Finally, betrayed by a traitor, only eighteen of the monks managed to escape with their lives. The number "eighteen" may simply be symbolic of the "Eighteen Hands of Lo-Han."

These surviving eighteen were then tracked across the length and breadth of China by Manchu assassins until only five remained. Known as the "Hung Brothers," these five monks founded a secret society dedicated to resistance against the Manchu from which the Triads, the Chinese "Mafia," claims descent.

The original "Eighteen hands of Lo-Han" consisted of martial arts techniques that would be considered "basic" and "fundamental" (i.e., boring) by many of today's martial artists used to more complex and flashy techniques—the kind you see in action-packed kick-flick martial arts movies. These included basic punches, open hand and clawing strikes, simple kicks, and basic leg-sweeping takedown techniques.*

The late Bruce Lee once commented that while defeating an opponent with a complicated martial arts technique is noteworthy, defeating that same

---

*As enjoyable and visually pleasing as such high-flying moves are for the silver screen, most real-life fights never involve such "fancy" moves.

opponent with a simple (basic) martial arts technique is the epitome of mastery.

Thus, when it comes to self-defense, simple is best. Simple is effective. What we will teach you is simple and effective martial arts self-defense techniques that work.

From these basic "Eighteen Hands," several specialized styles of fighting developed within Shaolin. This was a natural development, reflecting different individuals placing emphasis on specific techniques and on keen masters recognizing the natural gifts differing students possess.

For example, a long-legged individual might naturally favor kicks over punches because his longer legs give him a natural distance advantage over his opponent (i.e., he can kick his opponent before his short opponent has a chance to get close enough to effectively punch). Such long-legged kicks, accompanied by longer, sweeping arm blocks reminded people of the long thin legs of a crane as well as its flapping wings—thus was born crane-style Kung-fu.

A more squat, muscular fellow might favor judolike wrestling and grappling throws, giving birth to bear-style Kung-fu.

Today, there are hundreds of recognized kung-fu animal styles, ranging from the devastating to . . . well, the just dumb.

From Bodhidharma's original "Eighteen Hands" came the original Shaolin Five Animal styles: crane, leopard, dragon, snake, and tiger. Later would come other respected styles such as preying mantis and iron monkey. Other kung-fu styles would then emerge that combined elements of two or more of these original animal styles. For example, tai chi is believed to be a combination of the crane and snake styles (the legend being that a monk witnessed a crane and snake fighting one day, thus creating the style).

Don't panic. We're not going to ask you to sweat blood learning several styles of kung-fu . . . unless you'd like to.

A lifestyle that includes a daily regime of martial arts will benefit anyone—increased mental focus, increased confidence and self-worth, and increased physical health. We would encourage you to add such positive things to your life. But that is not the purpose of this book. We're all about dealing with the bullies in your life—and dealing with them today!

We are also not going to make you memorize the names of all the different kung-fu styles. All you need to remember about the various animal styles of kung-fu is that they developed in response to specific needs and in recognition of differing abilities. And this is the attitude we will take.

If you are tall, it's natural for your body to use those long legs to ward off something attacking you. If you are shorter, smaller in stature, Nature has given you an advantage for slipping in close to your attacker, thus avoiding his long-range kicks and punches.

Rather than teach you some difficult-to-perform, hard-to-remember "unnatural" martial arts techniques, we will concentrate on techniques that will emerge naturally from your individual body type and mind-set (i.e., temperament). Recall our example of "natural" body reactions in Figures 2 and 3.

Hu-Gui-Dao: Way of the Ghost-Tiger

Several styles of tiger-style kung-fu are taught today, all of which trace themselves back to the original tiger style taught at Shaolin.

The style that will most directly benefit us in our struggle against bullies is called hu-kuan, literally translated this means "tiger" (hu) "fist" (kuan) and refers not just to the physical aspects of fighting but also to the mental aspects (cunning) of the tiger as well.

The tiger is a much respected and feared animal in Asia. The dreaded Thuggee stranglers of India, the worshippers of the fearsome Goddess Kali, called themselves her "Faithful Tigers" and used the Bengal tiger as the inspiration for their stalking and killing techniques.*

The tiger is one of the twelve celestial animals that make up the Chinese zodiac. Someone born under the sign of the tiger (years 1938, 1950, 1962, 1974, 1986, 1998, 2010, etc., at twelve-year intervals) are said to "keep promises," and their natural weakness is that they are "suspicious by nature." (Lung and Prowant, 2002a)

Everyone knows the tiger is a fierce beast that patiently stalks its prey and approaches unseen, without disturbing or otherwise alerting its intended target. Once within striking distance, the tiger closes the remaining distance between him and his prey in an instant, striking surely and true the first time, knowing he might not get a second chance.

This is the same attitude we'll use as we learn to combat the bullies in our lives.

---

*For the complete history of the Thuggee cult, their terror and martial arts techniques, see Haha Lung's *The Ancient Art of Strangulation* (1995).

First, we will help you learn to recognize and then take advantage of your natural gifts—your body and mind temperament. We will then teach you how to recognize and, more important, release your flight-or-fight response. Finally, we will use this tiger mind-set to focus our energy toward our self-defense by confronting our bully with both the ferocity and unexpectedness—and effectiveness!—of the tiger. Thus, we will acquire both the claws and the cunning of the tiger.

All fear the claws of the tiger, and rightly so. But, all too often, while wary of the claws of the tiger, the prey falls to the cunning of the tiger.

How many great minds—master strategists all—do we need to tell us that our greatest battles are always fought in the mind—our own mind and that of our attacker, our bully. So, too, these masterminds tell us that defeating an enemy with our cunning will always be superior—and more satisfying—than having to defeat him with our claws.

But there is an even deeper understanding to be had when studying the tiger's use of cunning and claw. Cunning and claw are synonymous with stealth and striking.

Sometimes it is unavoidable to have to stand toe to toe with an enemy. But this Gary Cooper *High Noon* scenario—no matter how admirable—is not what we are realistically looking for when we study streetwise self-defense. If you recall from the movie, the sheriff (Gary Cooper) tried everything in his power to avoid direct confrontation and only resorted to gunplay as a last resort.

We need to adopt this same attitude: Fight only as a last resort.

While the samurai of medieval Japan were much admired for their fearlessness in battle, their standing toe to toe with their enemy, it was the ninja of medieval Japan that literally kept the fierce samurai tossing and turning in bed at night.

Ninjas don't fight fair. Stealth and sneakiness were their tools. Outnumbered and outgunned by the samurai, the ninja clans of medieval Japan were forced to think on their feet, to adopt and adapt new methods of fighting tactics that would give them the edge over the samurai. (Lung, 1997a) Far from being cowardly, this was sound strategy.

Would it surprise you to learn that the ninja also studied the way of the tiger, imitating many of his methods in order to develop their own methods of defeating their enemies. Claws for striking, cunning equates stealth.

Down through the ages, various cadre of fighters have successfully used stealth and the "surprise attack" (nowadays known as the "sucker punch"). A surprised enemy is a defeated enemy.

The ninja of Japan gleaned much of their own stealth from a ninja-esque group in China known as the Moshuh Nanren.

The Moshuh Nanren worked for the Chinese emperors as a combination Gestapo and Green Beret. As deadly as were their killing arts, the Moshuh Nanren's primary weapon was fear—a combination of secrecy, stealth, superstition, and ruthless willingness to wield same against the enemies of the emperor.

The Moshuh Nanren derived many of their techniques from "freelance" ninjalike rogues known as "vagabonds" or Lin Gui, a word that means "ghosts." Some of these Lin Gui were literally the "Ghosts of Shaolin," survivors from the Shaolin massacre, who went on to join (and found) a society against the Manchu, even criminal gangs. Other lineages of Lin Gui stretched back far before Shaolin, groups of mysterious rogues for whom stealth and secrecy were literally their bread and butter.

For a ninja to strike successfully, he had to get a samurai to literally drop his guard. This is no different from our goal of getting a bully to underestimate us, leaving us an opening that we can exploit.

Ninja called such techniques taisavaki ("shadowhand"), and this included any tactic or technique that allows you to get "close" to an enemy in order to make your counterattack more successful (see Lung, 2004b).

Let's simplify this idea: Say you are confronted by a violent bully who fully intends to do you grievous bodily harm.

If that bully would be nice enough to stand still and drop his hands long enough for you to hit him square in the throat with any of a number of open-handed martial arts strikes, there's a pretty good chance that fight would be over before it even began!

Unfortunately, your bully is probably one of those stubborn types who really doesn't like being hit in the throat and dropped to his knees gasping for breath.

You know if you could hit him in the throat, you could successfully extract yourself from danger. So all you really need to learn is a couple "tricks" for convincing that bully to allow you to hit him where it hurts, in other words, techniques designed to push aside his defenses and allow your strike to land quickly and effectively.

Remember: well-mastered tricks are called "techniques." Half-learned techniques are merely tricks. Tricks can get you killed.

Thus, before resorting to our claws, we will always try to use our cunning to surprise and mentally unbalance our bully. This element of surprise will give us the advantage we need to out-wit, and if need be out-fight, our bully. Whereas our confusing him does not succeed in stalling his assault, our cunning will also serve to put us into a strategic position from which to launch our physical counterattack—a simple, basic strike designed to stop our bully in his tracks.

This combination of tiger cunning and tiger claws works because our bully doesn't expect us to fight back (remember he "picks his shots," looking for the weakest and slowest) and because we have employed stealth (cunning)—he'll never see our counterattack coming! In Chinese kung-fu circles, this is known as Hu-Gui-Dao ("The Way of the Ghost-Tiger") because not only do we strike with the ferocity of the tiger but also we strike from such an unexpected angle as to appear almost ghostlike to our opponent.

4

Tiger Cunning:
Winning the Mental Game

"The best way to overcome an enemy is to make him your friend."
—Babbit (1936)

Your goal is to conquer two minds: your bully's and your own. How do we accomplish this? As counterintuitive as it may sound, we conquer our enemy by uniting with him.

The seventeenth-century Japanese swordmaster Miyamoto Musashi (1584–1645) put forth the concept of "melding" with your enemy in order to defeat him, calling his tactic "becoming your opponent":

> "Here is what I call 'becoming your opponent': This is as simple as thinking yourself in his place, standing in his stead. In life there exists a tendency to overestimate the power of an enemy. Consider a thief who, fleeing justice, is forced to barricade himself inside a house. PUT YOURSELF IN HIS PLACE: trapped, surrounded by his enemies, already doomed in his mind. He is now the pheasant, and those coming to kill him, the falcon! Study on this at length." *(A Book of Five Rings)*

The 1892 Japanese war book *Budo-Hiketsu Aiki No Jutsu* ("Secret Keys to Martial Arts Techniques") says that the ultimate goal of martial arts study is "aiki." "Ai" means "unification," while "ki" ("chi" in Chinese) means both "mind" and "spirit." Thus, aiki is "the union of mind and spirit." You may have heard of the Japanese martial art of aikido (that sneaky arm-locking, throwing stuff Stephen Segal does in his earlier movies). Aikido was founded by the Japanese master Morehei Ueshiba (1883–1969). Ueshiba added the syllable "do," meaning "the way of." (FYI: You'll be learning a couple of these sneaky moves in chapter 5!)

Aiki means not only the union (integration) of your own mind and body (which must take place first) but also intuiting your opponent's mind-set (a natural outgrowth of unifying your own mind first).

The *Budo-Hiketsu Aiki No Jutsu* goes on to explain how aiki can be accomplished by "taking a step ahead of the enemy," in other words, by you figuratively and literally being one step ahead of your bully.

Thus, there are two ways to look at this aiki concept: a (tactically) physical interpretation and a (strategically) mental one.

A physical interpretation of aiki teaches us to move before our attacker moves, before he initiates his physical attack, to be one step ahead of him in order to maneuver ourselves in perfect position from which to be safe (i.e., he can't hit you) and to launch an effective counterattack. (We will show you how to accomplish this more fully in chapter 5 when we give you your "tiger claws"!)

A mental interpretation of this aiki principle requires realizing what an enemy intends (sometimes before he actually realizes it himself) and then taking appropriate (preemptive) action, preferably nonviolent action. But, when violence is called for, we must not hesitate to display the aiki mind-set necessary to do what must be done to survive—up to and including violently defending yourself against harm.

Yes, this is similar to Zizhi-dao ("The Art of Control") we discussed in chapter 3, and it does incorporate our "Three Knows": know yourself, know your enemy, and know your environment.

SOLVING YOUR BULLY PROBLEM
THE PING-FA WAY

When we speak of Sun Tzu's *Ping-fa,* we are referring specifically to a treatise, an "art of war" book, a master's military/martial arts strategist's masterpiece. But ping-fa can also refer to the overall mind-set (craft and cunning) it takes to survive a threatening situation. This is all about problem solving.

The ancient Chinese Taoist masters developed and refined an eight-point system for teaching strategy that, first and foremost, emphasized practical problem solving (see Figure 5). Known as Pa-kua (pronounced "ba-kwa," meaning "Eight Trigrams"), this was first a philosophy that later became the strategic basis for a martial art of the same name developed by the Taoist alchemists at the Yu-hau Shan monastery. The martial art of Pa-kua specialized in confusing, circular movements designed to keep an opponent off balance.

The psychological (problem-solving) strategy of Pa-kua is built on this

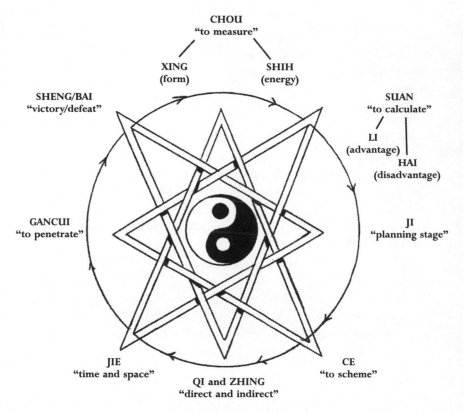

Figure 5. "Ping-fa Strategy."

same principle, only it's your enemy's mind you're keeping off balance. This strategy values the astute observation, realistic evaluation, succinct application, and, if need be, reassessment of any plan of action.

Ping-fa strategy isn't as complicated as it looks. In many ways, this problem-solving strategy is just a more expanded version of the five-step Western "problem-solving" model:

Step one: Clearly define the problem.

Step two: Brainstorm all possible solutions.

Step three: Prioritize possible solutions (gleaned from step two) in order of their best chance of success.

Step four: Implement prioritized solutions. Put your plan into action.

Step five: Follow-through and follow-up, adjusting as need be to compensate for shifting realities.

Let's see if we can spot the similarities between these five steps and the eight steps of Pa-kua Ping-fa strategy:

Chou (Measure)

Before embarking on any action (business venture, military campaign, or response to a bully confrontation), we must first consider (i.e., measure) two variables: Xing and Shih (pronounced "shing" and "she"), which are another way of saying "circumstance and flux." Xing is the outward appearance (shape) of a thing, a person, or a situation—the way it "appears" to be. For example, our bully appears to be unstoppable. In this case, Xing is the image we project to the world.

On the other hand, Shih deals with the true essence of a thing, the potential or stored energy within. In the case of a person, Shih is his real face, the one he keeps hidden from the world. If you expose his real face, you expose your bully for what he truly is.

When measuring people, Shih reminds us of Sun Tzu's "Know your enemy." Shih also reminds us of the second part of Sun Tzu's teaching, "Know yourself."

In any given situation, we must first measure the potential of ourselves. Do your resources and determination coincide with reality? What are you really capable of? Based on his past actions, what is your bully capable of? And what is the current situation? Is this the right time and place to attempt this?

All these observations must be realistically weighed (measured), before we decide on the appropriate action to take. In layman's terms, this simply means realistically sizing up your bully, trying to figure out what he's capable of.

Is he all bluster and bluff, or will he follow through with his threats? Does he have a history of violence? Of mental illness?

This is the stage where we clearly define the problem and realistically assess threat potential in order to move on to the next stage.

Suan (Calculate)

Having taken stock of the overall situation, the big picture, we must now calculate li versus hai.

Li means "advantage," what we have to gain by choosing one specific course of action over another. For example, if we give the mugger our wallet, will he be satisfied and i un away? If we quietly finish our drink and leave the bar, will the insults (and then assault) follow us out into the parking lot?

Hai involves what we have to lose. If we pay regular extortion to the bully on the playground, we may gain temporary respite. But what do we lose in the long run? Respect for self? And what might you inadvertently gain? Childhood trauma and anger that you then carry with you into your adult dealings. Hai is the cost we are willing to pay for safety and winning. Sometimes, that cost is too high.

Ji (Plan)

Having measured (chou) the worth of ourselves and the worthlessness of our enemy, then calculating suan (what we are willing to risk, gain vs. loss), we now come to the planning stage, which is part brainstorming, and part prioritizing. Having assessed our bully's threat level and calculating our own ability to respond, we now plan out our moves step by step, rearranging, and reprioritizing as new information becomes available.

This is a basic action-reaction scenario: Our bully presents a threat, we respond appropriately.

Of course, we need not wait for him to initiate the first move (especially in a potentially physical confrontation).

If you have reason to believe an enemy is about to move against you, you are fully justified in launching a preemptive strike, be it verbal or physical.

The operative word in that sentence being "reason," as in "reasoning, rational thought."

In any field of endeavor, whenever possible and time permits, we should first consult with the experts in the field of endeavor we intend to trod. This applies whether we're talking home fix-up or giving a bully his comeuppance. When confronted by the possibility of confronting a bully, it's always good to seek professional help.

In a school situation, that likely help should be school officials. In spousal bullying, police and social services should be your main line of official, professional defense, and shelter. And, in a workplace bullying situation, you should be able to go to your boss to lodge complaints about a bullying problem.

You should at least make an effort to seek outside help. If nothing else, it will weigh heavily in your favor when you need to justify your subsequent actions to a jury—how you diligently tried to get help from the police, school officials, and so on, before finally taking matters into your own hands!

Ce (Scheme)

Whereas planning (ji) focuses on the basics, the necessities and the logistics of the problem, ce concentrates on trying to figure out what countermoves (responses) your enemy might make to your countermoves to his initial moves.

Yes, it does sound a little like a chess game. But don't get stressed out thinking that, like in chess, you will have to "out-think" your bully ten or fifteen moves in advance. I think we've already established that your bully isn't the sharpest tool in the box—otherwise he'd have chosen another line of work!

One thing that remains constant across the board when talking about all bullies is that they are simplistic planners, their goals are simple, for example, thinking, "I'll grab this wimp's collar and he'll cough up his lunch money." The least little resistance (struggle, noise, avoidance) upsets the bully's plan and, more often than not, the frustrated bully is left scratching his head, before heading off in search of easier—less resistant, less confusing—targets.

Think of this scheming part of our Ping-fa strategy as your backup plan, contingency.

A famous strategist named Clausewitz once penned "No battle plan survives first contact with the enemy." That's why you should always have a plan b, "b" for "bully," that is.

Zhing and Qi (Direct and Indirect)

This is the stage of our Ping-fa problem solving where we decide whether we are going to confront our bullying problem head-on, or whether we are going to be able to use some sort of subterfuge to convince him into turning aside from his evil ways. Qi, indirect action, is always preferable—discouraging your bully, without having to resort to physical action. (Note the word "discourage", to take away, "dis," what little "courage" he has!)

Unfortunately, reality demands we always be ready (i.e., have a backup plan), for when negotiations go south and a physical response of some sort is called for, forewarned is forearmed.

Jie (Timing and Space)

Everything in its proper time. A time to talk, a time for action. Confuse the two and you run into a world of hurt.

Too often untrained individuals, facing a dire threat situation, hesitate just an instant too long . . . reacting an instant too late. This won't happen to you (at least not again) once we teach you how to release your inner tiger.

Jie also means "space," reminding us to take note of the distances between objects and people who might conceivably help or hinder our survival. This would be the "know your environment" part of the program.

To be proficient in martial arts, students must master a concept called "bridging the gap," closing the distance between you and your opponent as quickly (and as safely, without getting hit) as possible, in order to then disable your attacker as quickly and as efficiently as possible—preferably with one blow.

This same "bridging the gap, take the enemy out with one strike" attitude is one we should take with us into all of life's dealings.

Gancui (Penetrate)

This refers to getting inside your enemy's head in order to know what he's thinking and tell him what he should be thinking by using deceptive words and movement to sow daunting doubt into his mind.

Gancui also requires penetrating deeply and completely. In other words, when we strike, we give it all we've got. No half-assing. In karate, they call this Ikken Hisatsu, "To kill with one blow." This "killing with one blow" refers to both physical adroitness, but also to mentally "killing" our fear when we first feel it manifesting.

And while we may not be using an actual Tzuki-punch or Shuto-swordhand strike to bring down an opponent, when striking with our "Mind Fist" the same rules apply:

> "We first steel our own mind before we steal our enemy's mind." (Lung, 2007)

There is a story in the gospel of Thomas that tells of a wronged man who, having determined to kill his enemy, first practiced thrusting his sword into the wall of his home until he knew his arm (and, more important, his mind) was firm enough to do the deed. This should be our gancui mind-set in all undertakings.

Sheng and Bai (Victory and Defeat)

In the end, we win or we lose. But it's not always that simple. There's something called a Pyrrhic victory, a win that costs us too much to win. It's like a doctor saying, "The operation was a success, but the patient died," or like a battered woman staying in a toxic bullying relationship because she fears the loss of financial security.

While we all admire the feisty old lady who stands her ground against a would-be mugger, the victory of holding on to your purse isn't always worth the stomping that crack-head is willing to give you in order to take that purse from you.

Both Taoism and Buddhism, as well as the Western stoic school of philosophy, all teach that a person should remain "unmoved" by either success or failure. This doesn't mean we should all go around acting like Mr. Spock (although he was pretty cool, wasn't he). No, it simply means not losing our composure just because things seem to suddenly be going our way, just because we've stumbled onto a streak of good fortune. After all, this is exactly the kind of nonrational thinking state of frenzied excitement that professional conmen try to whip us into ("a limited time offer") in order to blind us with a brilliant (temporary) victory, so that we won't see our imminent defeat looming somewhere out there in the darkness they are about to lead us into.

Defeat is likewise distracting—not to mention often painful. If we can make another person depressed, even despondent by invoking their memory of a past, recent defeat, it's all the more easy to entice that person into doing something reckless (out of desperation) in order to reclaim their past feeling of victory.

There are two valuable lessons in this for us.

First, don't allow yourself to become depressed or despondent when facing down your bully problem. Your bully may look unbeatable, the situation may look hopeless, you may even have been defeated before, but tomorrow really is another day. The actions (or lack of action) you took up till today shows in the wherewithal and resources (or lack of both) you have on hand to deal with today's problems. Likewise, today we begin gathering the knowledge and the strength to deal with tomorrow, and the day after, and the day after that. Today's defeat means tomorrow I study harder. Today's victory means tomorrow I study harder . . . to make my next victory even more telling!

Second, never become blinded by victory to the point where you "drop your guard." Having instinctively counterattacked into your bully (whether verbally or physically), catching him by surprise, don't start dancing your victory jig just yet. Once you succeed in putting your bully down, follow through by escaping the area immediately, seeking shelter and help from others. Don't just stand there waiting for him to catch the breath you just knocked out of him (figuratively or literally). Barring escape, follow through by making sure he can't get back up. Do what you have to, to keep him on the ground and/or otherwise incapacitated, unable to resume his attack. (Hang on, we'll teach you how to do this in a minute.)

Yes, this does sound just a little bit like being just a little bit "ruthless." Be just a little bit ruthless. That bully you've just succeeded in knocking to the ground was planning on being a whole lot ruthless! The bully that successfully bullies you today will be back tomorrow for more lunch money. Worse still, the bully who successfully bullies you today might just decide to pick on one of your loved ones tomorrow. Tell yourself, "The buck stops here!" Innocent Bystander Effect be damned!

WHY FEAR IS THE TIGER'S FRIEND

"Anything can frighten.
One allows oneself to be frightened by what one does not expect."
—Musashi

The book of *Dune* warns us that "fear is the mind killer, the little death that brings total oblivion." And what was it FDR assured us? "We have nothing to fear, but fear itself."

Then there's the oft-invoked self-help class mantra designed to put fear into perspective by turning it into the acronym FEAR: False Evidence Appearing Real.

There is also the Japanese Shinobi-ninja philosophy that "fear never arrives" (Lung, 1997a). According to this way of looking at fear, what we are fearing right now is always in the future, whether years away, or minutes away, it's still not here yet. Since our fear has yet to arrive, we still have time to do something . . . hopefully the right something.

In a 1513 letter, the master strategist and acute observer of mankind Niccolò Machiavelli equates fear with lack of knowledge and advises us to overcome our fear by gradually replacing that fear with knowledge. We do so, according to Machiavelli, in the same way the wise fox overcame his fear of a lion:

The first time the fox sees a lion, the fox is ready to die from fear. The second time he encounters a lion, the fox slips behind a bush in order to better study the lion. By the third time the fox chances upon a lion, he has mastered his fear enough (through knowledge and understanding of this potential foe) that he is now able to talk to the lion. (Gilbert, 1961)

If Machiavelli is right, fear becomes the fox's friend. But fear is also the tiger's friend.

Not only is fear the tiger's friend because those wise enough and wary enough know already to fear the tiger—giving the proud beast a wide berth—but fear is also the tiger's friend—our friend—because the tiger knows how to overcome fear by turning (1) fear into focus and then turn focus into ferocity!

We will now learn how to do this ourselves, as the first steps in releasing our inner tiger.

We begin by mastering the "Four R's": Reality vs. really-like-it-to-be, recognize, release, and response.

Reality vs. Really-Like-It-to-Be

Brace yourself. It's time for some tough talk. You can lie to the world, but you have to be "real" with yourself. Or at least you should.

There's "reality," sometimes cold and dark or, worse yet, reality with brick in hand hiding in a cold, dark alley waiting for us to pass by. Would that it were not so. So many people spend so much of their time trying hard to ignore reality by wishing it away or by praying that the vulture of vulgarity and violence never shits on their mailbox.

These people don't live in reality. They live in really-like-it-to-be. Sorry, life isn't like that. No matter how we'd really-like-it-to-be otherwise, reality wins every time. It's best to prepare yourself and your loved ones. At the very least, prepare yourself for your loved ones.

Let's not be one of those people who can't tell the difference. To ensure this, we must strive to become more adept at making realistic assessments of our surroundings, the predators lurking therein, and, most vitally, ourselves.

Don't be one of the growing number of couch-potatoes who sit around playing video games on their fifty-two-inch screen, shoveling down handfuls of microwave popcorn, bemoaning their hard life, and ranting about the fact that the world isn't fair. What was it that the great (albeit a wee-bit cynical) American philosopher John Becker had to say about fair? "Fair is where hogs go to compete for ribbons!"

Recognize

There are two things you need to learn to recognize (and accept) if you are to turn fear into your friend.

Recognize What Your Bully's Body Is Telling You

First, learn to recognize the signs your bully is giving off that he doesn't know he's giving off, the "tells" of body and word that let you recognize a real threat when it comes knocking.

Opportunity never knocks twice, remember? Conmen always knock twice—and they keep knocking until you let them in. Bullies, they just kick the door in!

Those self-help gurus are right, many of our day-to-day fears are just "False Evidence Appearing Real," but there are also real threats out there that you should be afraid of—not so afraid that you freeze in your tracks, still threats that you need to practice recognizing before they get out of hand and get the upper hand.

This is why it's a good idea to get some knowledge of body language under your belt, those little subtleties of stance and gesture that can alert you that that person approaching you doesn't necessarily have your best interest at heart.

Recognize What Your Body Is Telling You

Learn to recognize the signals of readiness your body is giving off, not as evidence that you are some kind of coward, but as healthy signs of readiness.

Fear isn't always your enemy. Fear isn't necessarily a bad thing. You're probably alive today because sometime(s) in your life fear made you run like hell!

There are physical fears, mental fears, and spiritual fears, usually just called superstitions. There are likewise degrees of fear, from feelings of vague dis-ease, to chronic worry, to paralyzing dread. Our fears come from two places: from outside and from within.

Outside fears generally have more actual validity to them. There are some scary things in the world you should run away from. That's why Mother Nature hedged her bet by including the "flight" option in our "flight or fight" . . . or else die trifecta. That's why in some instances your survival-oriented brain perceives a threat (real or imagined) and sends an instant message to your muscles, "feet don't fail me now!" Or how about when, without taking time out to "think" about it, we instantly jump back from the snake laying at out feet. No, wait, it's only a piece of garden hose. But when it comes to danger, better safe than sorry.

FYI: Notice how fast your body jumped—without thinking about it—when it thought it was in danger? Think about that the next time you tell yourself, "I'm too slow to effectively defend myself against a bully." More on this in the next section.

Inside fears are another matter. Facing a perceived threat, a bully in your face, balling his ham-sized hands up, threatening to separate your head from your shoulders, what kind of "signals" are you receiving from your body?

- Has your mouth suddenly gone dry?
- Perhaps you're turning pale?

- You've broken out in a sweat (even though your skin feels cool to the touch).
- Your legs have begun to tremble (almost as if they can no longer hold your weight.
- You've got those damned butterflies in the stomach.
- And, inevitably, you begin to silently curse yourself for being "a coward."

Don't be so hard on yourself. You're not a coward. You're just misreading what your body is trying to tell you. All these signals are natural body reactions we all experience when faced with fear.

When faced with a physical threat, and knowing we're going to need our arms and legs for running and/or fighting, our brain reroutes energy (blood flow) to our extremities, temporarily shutting down unneeded body systems such as digestion—that explains those "butterflies." Your skin pales because blood flow is being rerouted to the muscles (needed for flight or fight) away from the skin As all-mighty adrenaline floods directly into our bloodstream in preparation for action, we sweat. This keeps us from overheating. Sweating also makes our skin "slipperier," harder for an enemy to grasp hold of. And we "tremble," which is a sign of the excess energy now coursing through us like a chained beast straining to be released into battle.

Do you finally understand? All these "cowardly" signs are really signs that we are seriously ready to open a can of whoop-ass . . . or else prudently exit stage left, post haste! Flight or fight. Not cowardice. Stop beating yourself up.

And now let's learn how to stop letting your bully beat you up! It's important to study the body to learn to recognize these signs of readiness for what they are. Any really good self-defense course or long-term course of martial arts training you take should be as "combat realistic" as possible, in an attempt to simulate an actual attack, in order to better trigger your body's response system.

That's also why it's important that you practice (not just read about) the self-defense techniques taught in this book, because merely understanding them intellectually (appreciation) is not the same as being able to use them when (heaven forbid) the time actually comes for the application of them.

Release

Even once you intellectually learn to recognize your body's signs of preparedness, it's no guarantee you'll be able to spring into action, using the stored energy in your body.

All too often, when faced with a dire threat situation, our body sends us these signs of readiness but even when we learn to recognize them as such, we still have not learned how to release our muscles to do what needs to be done. In other words, we "freeze" in place, making ourselves an easy target for even the slowest of bullies.

In Japanese Zen Buddhism, archery is often used as a metaphor to help the student understand—and obtain—enlightenment. Buddhism is the bow, the mind the arrow that, when properly aimed, sails true toward the target of enlightenment . . . or something like that.

We can use this same metaphor to understand what happens when our body reacts to a dire threat. When you're standing there facing down your bully, your body becomes tense, perhaps trembling just a little. This is the same as an arrow having been seated in a bow being drawn back. The longer the archer holds the arrow drawn back, ready for flight but not yet released, the more the archer's arm begins to tremble from the strain of holding back the arrow.

In the same way, your body perceives a threat, floods the body with adrenaline and tenses the muscle (draws the bow), ready to let fly (just like the arrow). However, when you hold yourself back (usually because you have not learned how to release your energy), your body may begin to tremble (not out of fear) but because it is straining for release—ready for flight or fight, as the situation dictates and survival demands.

If you've ever seen Japanese martial artists (karate, kendo swordsmanship, etc.) fighting, then you've also heard them fighting. Japanese martial artists give a sharp yell as they attack called a "kiai" ("spirit shout").

A kiai serves three purposes: First, an unexpected kiai startles your opponent, giving you a momentary advantage. The Japanese have a word "kotodam," which means "the spirits that live in words," and some believe that a forceful kiai carries with it this spirit, striking it into the enemy's mind like a dagger! Second, quickly expelling air from the lungs by forcefully contracting the diaphragm tightens the abdomen, making it less vulnerable to blows. Third, and perhaps most important, a kiai acts as a "release," freeing your mind from fear and doubt and forcing it to focus on the job at hand—victory!

Added bonus: On the practical side, in a street self-defense situation, yelling loudly when fighting off an attacker has the added benefit of attracting attention from other honest citizens who might also say "bystander effect be damned!" So, do not go quietly into that long goodnight. Make some noise!

When the mind is "shaken" out of its paralysis, suddenly all the fears holding you back are swept away, making your mind "a clean slate" on which to write your bully's obituary (figuratively speaking, of course).

This clear-minded, single-point focus is called "xi sui" by Chinese kung-fu masters. The term is sometimes translated into English as meaning "no thought," and there is a method of meditation that uses this very method to center and free up the mind from fear. (More on this in the following section on concentration and meditation.)

Many styles of traditional kung-fu believe it is better to keep the mouth shut during an attack (so as to better protect the teeth). Others believe the benefits derived from a forceful war cry is worth the risk. The late, great Bruce Lee was well-known for his elaborate (and entertaining) use of animal noises, all designed to unnerve his opponents.

For our purposes, we will use the Japanese spirit-shout syllable "kat," a war cry often used by Miyamoto Musashi as "katsu" (Tokitsu, 2004:410, n.150). Pronounced "cat," we find this syllable contributing to the Japanese word "masakatsu," which means "whatever it takes" or "by any means necessary" and carries with it the spirit of determination to succeed at all costs; to confront our enemy spirit to spirit with the inner assurance that our cause is just and our righteous spirit and focus will carry the day.

Also, because we are studying the way of the tiger, think of that great "cat" when you forcefully yell "kat!" when you practice your strikes against inanimate objects (such as a punching bag or thick mattress) and when the time comes to forcefully unleash your Inner Tiger against your bully.

Response

Once we have learned to release our Inner Tiger, we must make certain that, like water flowing through ditches, so, too, our energy flows effortlessly into a proper response, a response appropriate to a situation.

The Bible phrase "an eye for an eye" is often quoted as a general justification for striking back at someone who has offended against us. However, a more precise translation from Hebrew into English would render the phrase "no more than an eye for an eye," holding the meaning that the punishment should not be in excess, but should fit the crime. So, too, our response against aggression must be proportional and appropriate.

In a dire threat situation where you feel you or a loved one, or even a complete stranger you've decided to help, is in danger of either grievous bodily harm or possibly death, you must not hesitate, first in your decision to help a fellow human being and, more important, once you make the choice to meet the threat force for force, you must not hesitate to use appropriate force.

"Appropriate force" means not just using enough force to momentarily and temporarily stop an attacker from carrying through with his plan of attack, but also your using enough force to prevent that bully, madman, or terrorist from resuming his attack once you have foiled his initial effort.

If your attacker is fleeing the scene, let him go. At the most, follow him at a discreet distance so you can notify authorities as to his whereabouts. However, if there is any chance in hell your attacker will get back up once you've put him down, and/or regain consciousness and resume his attack, presuming you cannot reasonably escape the area of danger, then you are justified in doing whatever you have to, to keep him down.

Juries understand this. Let your conscience be your guide and the face of your loved ones he may attack tomorrow if you allow him to escape today. Let the punishment fit the crime. Let your response fit the situation.

TIGER FLEX AND FOCUS

Have you ever seen a little kitten stretching? It's no different from how a great Bengal tiger stretches. All cats stretch the same way: flex and focus.

First comes their "flexing" ritual, a release of lethargy and tension, stress reduction through first tensing and then relaxing the body; energy we can actually see rippling effortlessly along their powerful muscles and lithe sinews.

Then comes that great yawning of those fierce jaws, exposing their deadly fangs to the world, before—again effortlessly—there is an abrupt focusing their attention into a narrowed, knowing gaze, signaling they are ready to begin the hunt.

"Flex and focus." Write this out in big letters and hang it on your training area wall, or on your refrigerator, somewhere you can clearly see it everyday and several times a day. "Flex and focus" is your new Tiger-training mantra.

"Flex" means to stretch. First, this means we release tension by warming up our body and mind in preparation for a specific activity, and/or in preparation for taking on whatever today throws at us. Second, "flex" means seeking new challenges, "stretching" today's mind and body beyond yesterday's shortcomings in preparation for tomorrow's challenges.

Our initial mind-body "flex" breaks down the dams of stress and tension that bar the free flow of our stored energies, allowing these energies to rush headlong, forcefully, down the "ditches" of previous preparation and practice we've "dug" into our being. Like a rubber band suddenly snapping back, so, too, our mind and body "snaps" to attention—like the tiger's suddenly triggered hunting instinct—instantly focusing to pin-point attention, bringing our considerable energies to bear on any subject we choose to the exclusion of all superfluous distractions.

At last, our Inner Tiger has awakened! Flexed and focused, it is now ready to fight or flee to fight another day. In simplest terms, "focus" means to gather and direct the strength of body and mind.

There are five main techniques we can use to flex and focus ourselves, to awaken and then further free up our Inner Tiger. We call these the "flex and focus five": affirmation, relaxation, concentration, meditation, and visualization.

Affirmation

We begin awakening our Inner Tiger by boldly, loudly proclaiming, "Yes! I am right!" affirming to ourselves (and whatever part of the world that happens to be eavesdropping) that the action we have chosen—our path in life, if you will—is the correct one for us, appropriate to the situation.

You are in the right. It's your bully, and all the bullies of the world who are wrong, whose actions are evil, whose ways need correcting.

Knowing that your cause is righteous, that you are justified in taking a stand to defend yourself (and your loved ones, or even a complete stranger) makes all the difference in the world. Doubt leads to hesitation and hesitation—in a dire threat situation—all too often leads to vile injury and violent death. However, knowing you're right frees up your mind to do what is necessary and respond with appropriate action.

What was it Grandpa used to say? Nothing gets you right like being right. You need to get right before you give the bullies in your life some "get right"!

Relaxation

The more tense you are, the slower your mind and body respond. This is why "flexing" both body and mind are so important.

Learning techniques of relaxation are a vital survival skill that should be practiced daily, and not just before and after a stressful confrontation.

Relaxation Quick Fix #1

Keep a small, palm-sized rock in one pocket and a soft ball of fur or small plastic squeeze toy in your other pocket. When you need a burst of energy or quick infusion of mental clarity and strength, take a deep breath and squeeze the rock really hard, "willing" the hardness of the rock to "enter" you. Mentally repeat, "Strength." When you need a quick "relax fix," take a deep breath and squeeze the furry ball in your pocket, focusing your attention on the softness and pliability of the object.

This technique works, not because the "talisman" in your pocket has any special power, but because the deep breathing combined with your "visualizing" hard versus soft causes your mind to dwell on one or the other as you have directed. It's simple, but effective.

Another tried-and-true method for relaxing and helping focus your mind and body is hand yoga. In the East, hand yoga positions (mudras) are believed to help channel our inner energies—our chi (called ki, pronounced "key," in Japanese). Like the full-body postures of Hatha yoga most Westerners are already familiar with, hand yoga postures were designed to help us flex and focus and were developed for use when it was inconvenient to stretch out on a mat and do full-body exercises.

Each mudra is thought to channel the body's energies in different ways, alternately relaxing or otherwise invigorating the body, depending on the specific mudra used. There are hundreds of such mudras in existence, many of which can be seen on statues of Hindu deities and on depictions of the Buddha throughout Asia.

The nine mudras pictured in Figure 6 are from the Japanese Shinobi tradition:

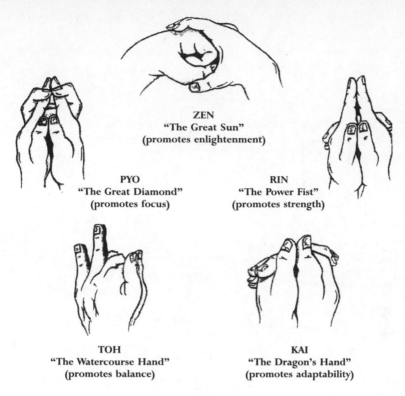

ZEN
"The Great Sun"
(promotes enlightenment)

PYO
"The Great Diamond"
(promotes focus)

RIN
"The Power Fist"
(promotes strength)

TOH
"The Watercourse Hand"
(promotes balance)

KAI
"The Dragon's Hand"
(promotes adaptability)

Figure 6a. Mudra Meditation, part 1.

To utilize these mudras, simply sit in a comfortable position and hold your hands together three inches in front of your solar plexus. Slap your hands together three times and/or rub them together until you feel a slight warmth, then entwine your hands into the positions shown. Close your eyes, take a couple deep, comfortable breaths, and mentally repeat the specific thought associated with the specific mudra you are using.

Even when done for only a few minutes, this hand yoga practice will help relax and center you by giving you renewed energy, insight, and direction to face today's bullies.

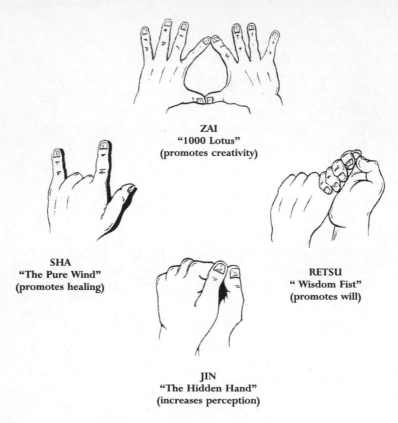

ZAI
"1000 Lotus"
(promotes creativity)

SHA
"The Pure Wind"
(promotes healing)

RETSU
" Wisdom Fist"
(promotes will)

JIN
"The Hidden Hand"
(increases perception)

Figure 6b. Mudra Meditation, part 2.

Relaxation Quick Fix #2

Engaging socially with others triggers neural circuits in the brain that then send relaxing signals out to the body, calming the heart, relaxing the gut, and switching off fear (Gold, 2007:57).

Concentration and Meditation

In China, meditative breathing exercises, which were designed to increase a student's powers of concentration, were part of Shaolin ying gong and jing gong body-mind training.

The following are some similar exercises that will help you further awaken your Inner Tiger.

Flower Breathing

In order to learn to relax and meditate properly, we must first learn to breath correctly. Many people go around acting like life literally stinks, breathing in gasps and chokes, rather than breathing in a full, sweet measure of life. As children, we breathed naturally. But as adults, so many of us breathe shallowly and irregularly. Many poison their lungs with tobacco or worse.

(Re)learning to breathe correctly is no mystery. Simply inhale as if you are smelling a flower, as if trying to get as much of a flower's wonderful fragrance into your lungs as possible. Having drawn in a full draught of air, hold this "flower breath" for a mental count of "one-two-three," then release a heavy sigh, allowing the air to flow out evenly at a natural rate. Having completely emptied your lungs, take another leisurely, full and pleasant sniff of "the flower." Meditators often use actual flowers or pleasant incense to encourage deep breathing.

Whenever possible during the day, take a few minutes to relax using this flower breathing. If time and circumstance permit, practice this exercise prior to your bully confrontation.

The "Furthest Away Sound" Meditation

Having used your flower breathing to relax, keep your eyes closed and listen for the furthest away sound that you can hear. At first, the furthest away sound might be close at hand: someone moving around in the next room, birds chirping outside your window, or cars passing out on the street. Now gently "push" your sense of hearing outward, beyond the furthest away sound you hear. Soon, you will begin to notice a thunderstorm approaching in the distance, an aircraft passing high overhead, and other far away sounds.

This exercise increases your powers of concentration and helps bring you more into tune with your surroundings. Extending your powers of physical hearing and mental concentration by seeking the furthest away sound will help you pay better attention to your immediate surroundings.

Practice "hearing," not just with your ears but with your whole body. Diligent practice of this exercise will lead you to realize that your ears are the last thing you need to "hear," your eyes, the last thing you need to "see."

"Breath Counting" Meditation

Close your eyes and observe the in-and-out flow of your breath. "Flower breathe" in while mentally counting "one." After comfortably holding your breath for a few seconds, slowly empty your lungs completely while mentally counting "two." Inhale again counting "three," hold, and exhale to the count of "four." If your mind wanders and you lose count, simply begin again with a "one" count.

Even five minutes of concentration on this meditation has a calming effect.

"No-Mind" Meditation

Close your eyes and practice your "flower breathing" a few times. Now clear your mind of all thoughts and distractions by mentally repeating the phrase "no-mind." Whenever other thoughts intrude, crossing your mind, gently draw your mind back by again repeating "no-mind." If necessary, repeat "no-mind" out loud until your mind becomes focused enough to permit reciting silently again.

If you continue to practice this "no-mind" meditation regularly, you will reach a point where merely reciting "no-mind" only once will allow you to instantly relax—any time, any place. Use this secret mantra to calm and center yourself when confronting your bully. Yes, this is similar to the clear-mind state kung-fu masters call xi sui we discussed earlier.

Regular meditation will help you relax, develop mental discipline, and give you greater self-mastery. If you'd rather rely on prayer, because "meditation" still makes you feel a little like you're holding some Satanic Asian hand, just tell yourself: prayer is when you do the talking, and meditation is when you do the listening.

Visualization

"By telling me WHAT you saw,
you tell me more about HOW you see."
—Only (2007)

In India and points East, they meditate on specially crafted geometric images to increase their powers of concentration and meditation. Called "yantra," these images range from the simplest (a dot or circle) to incredibly intricate designs known as "mandala." Students concentrate on these images of varying and increasing complexity in order to increase their powers of concentration.

For our practical use in fighting bullies, yantra "visualization" exercises will help us hone our powers of observation and visual retention so as to help you better "notice" when something is out of place:

- A suspicious car cruising your neighborhood
- A door or window in your home that you're certain was locked when you left
- The second time you notice that same man when you turned around suddenly

This exercise will also increase your powers of visual retention and recall:

- So you can remember every face in the park where your child went missing
- So you can more easily fix license plate numbers in your mind
- So you can more correctly help the police sketch artist draw an accurate picture of the suspect

Figure 7. Yantra.

Mind's Eye Exercise

Practice a few "flower breaths" while studying the "Buddha's Heart yantra" (Figure 7) for a full minute.

Now close your eyes and practice keeping the "after image" in your mind's eye for as long as possible. Don't be discouraged when the image eventually fades. That's normal. The goal is to keep the after image in your mind's eye for progressively longer periods of time, increasing your powers of retention and concentration.

It's not unusual for meditators using this "Buddha's Heart" yantra to see (i.e., imagine) various images within the yantra. Advanced meditators sometimes seek such images for the insights they bring. Indeed, you may notice that the Japanese kanji meaning "Buddha's Heart" lends itself to various interpretations. For example, many see in this kanji a dagger (of the discriminating mind) plunging down, straight into the heart of the matter (enlightenment).

Should you experience such an "insight" while meditating on this yantra, don't allow yourself to become overly excited. Merely note the "vision" for later introspection, before gently drawing your wandering mind back to the task at hand.

Kenji Tokitsu, in *Miyamoto Musashi: His Life and Writings* (2004), relates how traditional Japanese martial artists (in particular swordsmen) use "standing meditation" by standing completely still, while visualizing their movements, mentally rehearsing their various combat techniques in their mind, without moving. This is what some Western martial artists have taken to calling "mental katas."

Tokitsu goes on to relate a personal anecdote where he learned that visualization is part of an ancient Chinese training technique called De Cheng Quan. While on a sojourn to China in 1991, a certain Master Yu Yong instructed Tokitsu: "You imagine yourself as a powerful giant while imagining your opponent and everything that surrounds you as small. You are infinitely larger and stronger than they are and you dominate them." (2004:424, n.21)

The rationale behind such practice is clear to Tokitsu:

"The point is to create a psychological state that increases your combativeness."

By "combativeness," Tokitsu doesn't mean aggressiveness, rather he refers to preparedness to fight when the times demand it, to prepare ourselves mentally by experiencing our victory and our enemy's defeat beforehand. This kind of "prefight" visualization is well known to all professional athletes.

TING-JIN: SENSES TRAINING

As recently reported in *USA Today* ("Extra Eyes in Schools," August 9, 2007:A1), the percentage of public schools that used one or more security cameras on campus in 2003–2004 tallied up to: elementary schools 28 percent, middle schools 42 percent, and high schools 60 percent.

You can rest assured that the number of cameras in our schools has increased dramatically since 2004. Sadly, however, as we all witnessed at Columbine, all too often more cameras in schools—or in any public venue for that matter—simply means we end up with more grisly after-the-fact video feed for tabloid TV.

And while we all can appreciate more watchful eyes on our children in school, on our loved ones as they pass through the airport or subway, and even on ourselves when we (foolishly) visit the local ATM late at night, still, in the end, nothing's better for keeping us out of danger and getting us out of danger than our own two eyes. And that goes for the rest of your senses as well.

The "Buddha's Heart" yantra exercise will help you increase your powers of observation, visual retention, and recall, increasing the effectiveness of your eyes as tools and as weapons.

But don't neglect your other four senses. Train your sense of smell to notice out-of-place smells—perhaps alerting you to an intruder in your home? Or helping you remember the unique smell of an attacker—alcohol on his breath? Cheap and easily recognizable cologne?

Did you know you can also use your tongue to "smell" (actually taste) the air, plucking up sweet and acrid taste molecules out of the air?

When listening intently, especially at night, close your eyes and open your mouth to help you better catch sounds.

Use your "Furthest away Sound" meditation to increase your aural acuity. Become attuned to the normal sounds of your surroundings, your home, neighborhood, school, and workplace so as to more quickly pick up on out-of-place sounds.

Ask yourself: Would I rather look foolish diving for cover, having mistaken an automobile's exhaust "backfire" for a gunshot, or look dead for having dismissed a gunshot for a car's backfire?

In a variation on the old Native American tracker trick: Put your ear to the wooden or linoleum floor to tell if someone is moving in a nearby room. You're not really using your sense of hearing in this case as you are your sense of touch. You can also use your hands or bare feet to feel the vibrations of someone walking through your house.

Samurai would often spread rice and/or sand outside their sleeping quarters in order to better hear the approach of ninja assassins. Others would leave a deliberately creaky stair or floorboard in their house to alert them to intruders (see Lung, 1998).

Remember how, as a kid, in case of fire, you were taught to use your sense of touch to feel for fire on the other side of a door? You can use that same sense of touch on the hood of a car to tell if a car engine or appliance has been running recently. Did you feel that stranger's hand trembling when you shook his hand? Was his hand sweaty?*

HOW TO DEVELOP A SIXTH SENSE

Most people go around day to day with their heads glued to their iPods they miss out on so much of what's going on around them. Terrorists, muggers, and other bullies count on this.

Conversely, when you put some diligent study into increasing your awareness, simply through the full use of your five senses, folks are liable to start thinking you have ESP—a sixth sense.

Let them think that.

Having increased your awareness of your regular five senses, it will often seem to others, and sometimes even to yourself, that you have acquired access to a sixth sense, simply because you've become more attuned to life in general by actually paying attention to the people and places around you and by picking up on subtle and unconscious clues and cues given off by others—body language, hesitations, and fluctuations in speech.

Sometimes, when you get that "uneasy" ("hinky," "spooked," "rattled") feeling about someone, it's just a "bad feeling", right? Please, for safety's

*For a complete course in both Shaolin ying gong and jing gong "senses training," see Haha Lung's *Total Mind Penetration* (2007).

sake, better yet, for the sake of your loved ones, don't just shrug your shoulders and dismiss your "gut feeling" as silly. Remember that your "gut" evolved a few million years before that "higher reasoning" part of your brain . . . so listen to your gut. No, not the part where your gut tells you to reach for another Twinkie, the part where your "gut" stirs those short hairs at the nape of your neck.

What you think of as your "gut feeling" (maybe you call it your "intuition") is actually an older—yeah, less evolved—part of your brain called the amygdala.

Situated in the center of our skull, this area is where "flight or fight" lives. This part of the brain, sometimes referred to as our "lizard brain," controls many of our initial perceptions. (Remember the garden hose equals snake example?)

Perceiving a danger (real or imagined), this part of the brain gets the information first (before the "higher brain") and sends immediate signals to the spinal cord and muscles to react now!* In other words, it's your body trying to tell you something, dummy!

There's nothing mysterious about this. No real ESP involved. Your eye could have caught a discrepancy between a person's words and his body language that you're consciously not aware of. Or it could be a simple matter of you literally "smelling" fear (or the premugging excitement!) on the other person (from his sweating or else unconsciously giving off mood-affecting pheromones).

Learning to listen to your gut, to trust your gut-feelings, that is your real sixth sense, your real ESP: extra sensory protection!

Become attuned to body language—your bully's and your own. Become aware of unconscious "victim" signals you might be giving off, that your bully might mistake as an "invitation": walking with your hands in your pockets, head down; furtively glancing around, unable to hold eye contact, and so on.

Instead, practice giving off your "Tiger vibe." "Tiger vibe" is the air of control and confidence you'll begin to exude once you awaken and then tame your Inner Tiger!

---

*For a complete course in how this part of the brain works, often skewing how we perceive the world around us, see Haha Lung's *Total Mind Penetration* (2007).

DISCLAIMER

Chapter 5 that follows, the final chapter of this book, teaches dangerous and potentially deadly self-defense techniques. These techniques should never be taken and taught lightly, and never should they be applied lightly, nor with malice aforethought. Each and every lawful person has a right to defend himself and his loved ones to the fullest extent of his ability. This chapter will help you extend the ability you already possess.

Many of these techniques, while appropriate for teaching to children, should be done so only with special emphasis placed on teaching those young students when and where—only in a dire threat situation—such dangerous techniques are to be used. This is a decision that can only be made by responsible parents, hopefully under the watchful eye and sage advice of a qualified self-defense instructor.

5

Tiger Claws:
Winning the Physical Game

INTRODUCTION: "THE LAST RESORT?"

Whereas the first four chapters of this book concentrated mostly on nonviolent strategies and tactics for understanding and appropriately responding to the bullies in your life, this chapter takes a decidedly violent approach. This would be the "last resort" part of the program.

You've probably heard this all your life: "Violence is a last resort." Perhaps even, "Violence is the last refuge of the ignorant," that we should resort to violence only after we've tried everything else.

First off, we hope you never have to resort to any violence in any situation. Wouldn't that be nice. Living in Mr. Rogers' neighborhood.

That being said, those who cautioned you to only use violence as a "last resort" were wrong. Would that we had used violence first—when we had the chance—against that bully Osama bin Laden.

There are times when violence can be—and should be—an honest man's first reaction in response to a bully. At the risk of repeating ourselves, when confronted by a bully of any ilk or faced with a dire threat situation, where our Tiger Cunning would be wasted, we must nonetheless be cunning enough not to hesitate to bare our Tiger Claws!

Therefore, this chapter concentrates on giving you your Tiger Claws, both the power and the physical weapons you will need, to physically fend off a physical attack on your person, or on the person of a loved one, or when helping a complete stranger when your honor and humanity demand it.

Power means you have more choices in life. Once you awaken your Inner Tiger, you will then have more choices in life.

Choices. You may (prudently) choose to run from a dangerous situation. What was it Sun Tzu said, "There is some ground not to be fought over, some castles not worth attacking." But when you must fight—whether because you have physically been backed into a corner and left with no escape or because you have been backed into a moral corner and know using violence is the right thing to do, you will now have the courage—your Inner Tiger—as well as the weapons—your Tiger Claws—to make that decision from a position of strength, not weakness, not fear.

Choices.

THE THREE TYPES OF FORCE

There are three basic types of "force" in life:

- Force that barrels straight ahead
- Force that changes direction and sometimes reverses polarity
- Force that is a natural response (outgrowth) to one or both of the previous two forces

Think of it this way: "straight force" is the rock you throw into the pool. "Changing force" is the eruption of the water upward in response to the rock hitting the water. And "listening force" is the ripple that radiates outward, also as a result of both the straight force and the changing force.

As in life, so in kung-fu. Especially so in tiger-style kung-fu.

Zhi Jin ("Straight Force")

Zhi Jin is the force most of us are familiar with, straight ahead. See a problem, face it, deal with it directly by exchanging force for force. Tit for tat. An eye for an eye. Sun Tzu calls this cheng ("direct force"). What you would think of as basic head-to-head army operations.

Bian Jin ("Changing Force")

Bian Jin is called chi ("indirect force") by Sun Tzu. Military-wise, this is guerrilla warfare, hit and run, not suicidally facing a superior force head to head. Indirect force in the form of "sneaky" moves is designed to take advantage of an attacker's initial confusion, as well as any hesitation we sense in him.

These segue into the use of "listening force" because many of our moves will be in direct response to some fortuitous misstep taken by our bully. Fortuitous for us, bad for him!

Tin Jin ("Listening Force")

Tin Jin means responding to what the enemy does by instantly adapting to his maneuvers.

Tiger-Style kung-fu uses all three of these forces, as we will learn to do by choosing the most appropriate "line of force" to defeat our bully.

LADY TIGERS
(BE A MAN—START ACTING LIKE A GIRL!)

Throughout its history, China has given the world many examples of warrior women. From their classical heroines such as Mulan (yeah, that Disney cartoon was based on a real person), down to the twentieth century's Red Guard women warriors. There is even a somewhat anecdotal tale of how, in order to prove the validity of his methods, Sun Tzu was able to turn a giggling group of the emperor's concubines into a crackerjack bodyguard.*

And while we always hear about the "brothers" of Shaolin, the order had a nun's branch as well. In fact, it was a Shaolin Buddhist nun who taught the runaway bride Yim Wing Chun the secrets of Shaolin boxing for self-defense, allowing Yim Wing Chun to literally fight her way out of a forced marriage and a dismal future of spousal abuse.

---

*Sun Tzu's method involved the initial beheading of one of the gigglers but, after that, his instructions miraculously seamed to take root among the concubines!

Today, there is a popular martial art that still bears her name: Wing Chun

What's that? If you did decide to take the time to learn an Asian martial art, it certainly wouldn't be some "girl art" named after a woman? You male chauvinist pig! Wing Chun was Bruce Lee's original style, forming the basis for his own art: Jett Kun Do.

Wing Chun uses the concept of shun ("compliance," "going with the flow"). Realizing it would be nigh impossible to meet force with force, head on, not fighting a superior force, they adopted the philosophy of "Give way in order to get your way," Bian Jin and Tin Jin, what we know of today as the "Judo Principle." The Judo Principle: My opponent pushes, I pull. My opponent pulls, I push.

Evidently, Chinese women, Shaolin nuns at least, didn't need Sun Tzu to tell them, "When strong, appear weak," in order to draw an overconfident enemy into overextending his reach—figuratively and literally.

Some of the Shaolin nuns survived the 1644 Manchu massacre of the order. Some of these survivors went on to teach kung-fu, albeit in secret. Other Shaolin sisters are credited with founding a female secret society called the Black Lotus.*

In Japan, medieval Shinobi ninja clans also employed women spy-warriors known as kuniochi, which were said to be just as dangerous—if not more dangerous—than their male counterparts. One reason such women warriors were so dangerous is because men underestimated them.

This is an important lesson for us—male or female—when facing down bullies who we imagine are unbeatable. Bullies are always cocky, so sometimes pretending to be terrified can lull them into underestimating your willingness to fight back, thus they become even more overconfident, perhaps providing you with an opening you can take advantage of.

A second important lesson we need to learn from these female warriors is the way in which they were sure to use only techniques that worked for them. This meant taking into account their usual disadvantage in size and strength.

It's always impressive to see professional fighters (boxers, Ultimate

---

*For more on this deadly female "Triad" secret society (said to stretch the length and breadth of Asia . . . and beyond) see Sterling Seagrave's *The Soong Dynasty* (1985:261) and Haha Lung's *Total Mind Penetration* (2007).

Fighters, IFL) go at it toe to toe. It's also fun to learn powerful kicks and punches that can knock an opponent out with one strike. But, realistically, not every one can do that.

We're assuming here that you are not International Fight League material. It's doubtful such men have much problem with bullies. Professional fighters are taught to "take one to get one," in other words, to expect to get hit one or more times before being able to land a telling—finishing—blow of their own.

But not everyone has the option to "take one to get one."

Likewise, a well-muscled man can often overpower a less-muscled man, eventually wrestling him into submission. Again, many of us, for example a ninety-eight-pound woman lacking the size and strength of her attacker, doesn't have this option.

This is the third lesson we learn from these women warriors: Use brain over brawn, technique over testosterone. The Shaolin saying summed it up this way: "Use four ounces to beat one thousand pounds!"

Now some of you big bruisers are probably snickering, "But I am a well-muscled man, so I guess I can just bully my way through a fight!" by compensating for lack of proper technique with Zhi Jin, raw brute strength.

That's a plan. Want to know what's wrong with that plan? What if you get into a situation where you're tired, or drunk, or you've been cut and are losing blood fast—your strength literally dripping out of you? Where muscle fails you, technique will save you.

That's why, in this book, we'll stick to self-defense techniques that any ninety-eight-pound woman can use to dissuade, disarm, and disable a bully who has a size and/or strength advantage. In fact, most of the techniques we'll teach you can even be used by school-aged children. That's because these Tiger techniques rely, not on brute strength (though that's always nice to have!), rather these techniques rely on the element of surprise and body physics—Bian Jin and Tin Jin.

You can do this. And, yes, we're all scared. But you can first train your body and then trust your body to do what it needs to do to survive. "Train and trust," put that sign on your wall too, right below your "Flex and focus" sign.

Like the rest of us, you've got all the excuses in the world for not studying self-defense. Do any of the following sound familiar:

I'm too scared . . .

No, what you are is ready. Review the section on interpreting your body's flight-or-fight responses. And remember that those butterflies in your stomach are telling you they are ready to kick ass! Now shout your trigger word "Kat!" and unleash your Inner Tiger to do what must be done.

I'll "freeze up" when the time comes to fight back . . .

No, recognizing your body's signs of readiness plus using your trigger word will clear your mind (Xi Sui—no thought) and galvanize your body (instantaneous response).

I'm too old, too young, too little, too fat . . .

Doesn't matter. Not only is there something anyone can do to defend themselves no matter their age or size, but in addition all those things you think of as "liabilities" can actually be "assets," giving you advantages your bully doesn't have.

The elderly have been around the block a few times, enough times to learn how to outsmart a would-be mugger-bully. Many's the tale of how a senior citizen has faked a heart attack, chasing off would-be muggers more interested in a wallet than in catching a murder case. Also, that cane you're carrying makes a fine environmental weapon.

The young and the small often have an easier time escaping from an attacker—slipping from his grasp, perhaps escaping through an opening (e.g. through an attacker's legs, in a fence, etc.) a larger person can't fit into.

If you're overweight, practice suddenly pushing that weight against your bully, unbalancing him, knocking him to the ground.

I'm too slow . . .

Remember the garden hose you mistook for a snake? Moved pretty darn fast then, didn't you? Xi Sui—no thought allows the body to do what it does best: flight or fight at an instant's notice.

The same thing with burning your hand with hot water, the way you pulled your hand out from under the scalding water before you even registered the pain. That's how fast you are capable of moving.

Your bully thinks about grabbing you, thinks about hitting you. When your responses are Xi Sui—without thought—your "no thought" response is faster than his "thought" could ever be.

I'm too weak, I can't hit hard . . .

How strong do you have to be to stick your finger into a bully's eye, put a few pounds of pressure on his knee, or squeeze the next three generations out of his testicles?

I don't know how to do all that . . .
Well, we're about to show you how!

"400 FROM 4" BODY PHYSICS

"The journey of a thousand miles begins with a single step."
—Lao Tzu

It always looks daunting to a beginning student when he sees master's hard work on what looks like hundreds of different kicks. In fact, this seemingly insurmountable mountain of future study discourages many students from ever joining in martial arts study. However, once you explain to those students they only need to master four kicks—as opposed to four hundred—then learning the martial arts becomes more manageable.

From watching one of those Bruce Lee movies you might imagine there are hundreds (if not thousands) of different kinds of kicks in the martial arts. Actually, there are only four.

You heard right, only four. Though you'll never get traditional martial arts instructors to admit it, all the various kinds of kicks in the martial arts, from karate to kung-fu, Mui Thai kickboxing to Mo-Fo-Fu no-holds barred, can be classified into four basic types:

Front kicks: Kicks that shoot straight forward, either snapping up to strike with the toe (when wearing shoes) or with the ball of the foot (when barefoot), or else thrusting forward, striking with the heel.

Side kicks: Kicks that snap out from your hip horizontally, striking with either the side of the foot (sometimes called a "sword-foot") or else pushing/thrusting outward along the same plane to strike with the flat or heel of the foot.

Round kicks: Snap around and in or on an angled horizontal plane. These can be done with the leg whipping forward (called "Roundhouse Kicks") or with reverse-whipping motions (called "Hook Kicks").

Crescent kicks: At first glance, look like those kind of circling inward and then outward "Broadway Kicks," either inward or outward on a vertical plane to strike with either the inside or the outside edge of the foot.

From these four come the four hundred.

Likewise, from looking at all the fanciful stances you see martial artists posing in (many based on animal poses), you might become intimidated by how many stances you'd have to learn to advance in the martial arts.

But a careful look at body mechanics (physics) behind these stances will reveal that there are only three ways for a man to stand (see Figure 8):

- With his weight on his forward leg (a "Forward/Front Stance")
- With his weight on the back leg (a "Rear/Back Stance")
- With his weight evenly distributed (called an Even-"Horse Stance")

Even that fancy "Crane Stance" you remember from the first *Karate Kid* (1984) movie is simply an elaborate Back Stance. In fact, martial artists sometimes purposely use elaborate hand gestures to distract others away

Figure 8a. "Forward Stance"

Figure 8b. "Back Stance"

Figure 8c. "Even-Horse Stance"

from the fact that their fancy "Monkey Stance" or "Immovable Iron Warrior Stance" is still merely a variation on one of these three basic, easy-to-learn stances you'll find in all martial arts schools.

No, we're not going to make you learn a bunch of these fancy stances. So why bother to even learn these basic three, I mean if they just "come naturally" anyway? Because, by learning to recognize what stance your bully is in, you can narrow down what options he has and calculate what his punching, grabbing, and/or kicking attack will be.

How so? Because certain kicks can only be thrown from certain stances! Try it yourself:

Separating your feet about shoulder-width apart, lean your weight back (70 percent) onto one foot while facing the opposite direction. Congratulations, you are now in a "Back Stance," the most basic of martial arts defensive positions.

Now, say you wanted to kick forward at an attacker from this position. Notice that you can only kick with your forward leg, the leg that has only 30 percent of your weight on it. If you notice your bully standing in such a stance, without shifting his weight he can only kick you with his front foot. So that's the only foot you need to worry about being an immediate danger to you.

Are you beginning to get the idea? How about another example?

Say you are facing an attack by a bully crouched in what even an untrained eye would recognize as some kind of "wrestler's ready position": His weight evenly distributed, slightly squatting, his hands open (fingers splayed) obviously, ready to grab hold of you.

That's a "Horse Stance" he's in, weight evenly distributed. Quick quiz: Which of his legs can he kick you with?

Right, neither! Because both legs are supporting equal weight. In order to effectively kick, he's going to have to shift his weight 70 percent to one leg or the other. Here's why this is so important for you to know: So long as your bully's weight is evenly distributed ("Horse Stance") he can't kick you with either leg! So you can get close to him without worrying about him kicking (or kneeing) you.

Now on to you getting punched, or rather, learning how not to get punched while learning to strike into your bully with enough effectiveness to get him to break off his attack (before you have to break something off for him!).

Did you notice how that bully's fingers were splayed open?

In the same way that there are only three basic (natural) stances from which all other fancy martial arts stances derive, and four basic kicks from which evolved four hundred kicks, so, too, with the hand positions you will use to strike back against your bully.

While at first glance it might appear there are dozens of different ways a martial artist can hold his hands from the simple fist to those karate chops, to strange-looking "Preying Mantis Hand" and "Eagle's Claw," in actuality there are only three hand positions (see Figure 9):

The Closed Hand is the fist, made by the hand gripping itself tightly,

Figure 9a. "Closed Hand."

a. Closed-hand fist punching forward with two-knuckle "boxers" striking or one-knuckle "Chinese-fist" striking.
b. Striking backward ("Backfist"), striking with the two top knuckles (of the index and middle fingers).
c. "Hammer-fist," pounding downward.

thumb wrapped around the outside. The fist is the number one most likely attack you will need to learn to defend against, because it is the most common weapon in your bully's arsenal.

Western fighters and Karate-ka usually opt for the horizontal fist (thumb on the bottom), usually striking with the prominent knuckles of the index and middle fingers. Some kung-fu styles prefer Vertical-fist strikes (thumb on the side, pointed down, index-finger knuckle extended).

In Asian martial arts, in addition to using the closed hand for straight forward knuckle "punches," you can also pound downward with the bottom of the fist using a "Hammer-fist." You can also strike outward with the closed vertical fist, striking with the knuckles in what's known as a "Back-fist."

The Open Hand, correctly called a "Sword-hand" (Jp. Shuto), what the untrained call a "karate chop," is used for striking down—vertically—onto an attacker's collarbone, or else used on a horizontal plane to strike into the side of his neck or temple. This kind of "hand" can also be used on the reverse (thumb side) to strike (e.g., up into the groin) in what is known in karate as "gyaku shuto" (Reverse Sword-hand).

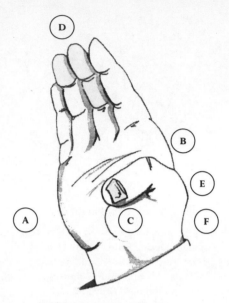

Figure 9b. "Open Hand."

a. "Karate chop" aka "Shuto."
b. "Ridge-hand" aka "Reverse Ridge-hand" aka (Gyaku-shuto).
c. Palm-hand strike (fingers bent back).
d. "Spear-hand" (stabbing with fingers), aka Nukite strike.
e. Thumb-strike (e.g., jabbing into eye, throat, etc.).
f. Full-hand "slap" (target arteries and veins just below the ear (side of neck) to affect bloodflow to brain, causing dizziness, disorientation, unconsciousness).

This configuration of the hand can also be used for stabbing straight forward, spearlike. This is called "Nukite" strike in karate. This rigid-fingered "Spear" can be used to stab into an attacker's eyes or throat, even by untrained individuals.

With the fingers bent back, you can also strike into an attacker with the palm-ball of your hand, as with the Claw-hand.

The Claw Hand looks just like its name—fingers splayed, as if to imitate an animal's claws.

Some schools of martial arts use variations of this basic claw hand,

Figure 9c.
a. "Tiger-claw" finger-rakes. See also Figures 20 and 22.
b. Thumb-gouge.
c. Palm-strike (preceding Tiger-Claw rake). See also Figure 20.

emphasizing specific striking methods. For example, "Eagle Claw" kung-fu overlaps the ring finger onto the little finger, allowing the former to reinforce the latter (thus giving the impression of a four-taloned eagle's claw). Likewise, "Preying Mantis" style kung-fu uses the thumb to reinforce the striking-then-pinching index and middle fingers. With your fingers splayed, you can also strike into an attacker using the palm-ball of your hand (e.g., striking upward, targeting under his chin and/or under his nose). Many of your Tiger-style defensive counters will use this easy-to-use Claw-hand variation.

While there are many variations for the use of these three hands, odds are you will run into only two of them in an actual street confrontation: the punching fist and the grabbing open hand.

However, whereas it is highly unlikely your bully will use many variations of these hands, keep in mind that all of these techniques are available for you to use defensively. Even when the best "defense" is a good "offense!"

THE BIG FIVE NEMESIS (OR "NARROWING DOWN THE FIELD")

In Sun Tzu's *Ping-fa,* the master strategist tells us: "Not knowing where I will attack, my enemy must prepare everywhere. Forced to prepare everywhere . . . he is strong nowhere!"

When the untrained eye looks at a bully, a person thinks, "Oh my God! There are so many ways he can attack me. I can't possibly defend against them all!"

There are two untruths in this way of thinking.

First, there is something you can do about your bully, and you can beat him—given enough focus and ferocity—and your Inner Tiger has plenty of both! Second, your bully doesn't have an unlimited number of attack strategies to use. Just the opposite in fact. The average street punk has a very limited number of attack options (we call them "attack vectors"). He's generally limited by his lack of formal martial arts training and his stupidity.

For example, 90 percent of the hand blows you will encounter in any fight with a bully will be the straight fist punch. It is unlikely your bully will use a "Hammer-fist" variation, and even more unlikely he would resort to an "Inverted-fist" strike—which you will learn to use. An "Inverted-fist" as seen in traditional karate (and to a lesser extent in kung-fu) whips the fist into the target with the thumb pointed downward (see Figure 15).

The same goes for fancy kicks. Of the four kicks (and their variations), 90 percent of the time the only kick you have to worry about from your bully is the straight "Front Kick."

Granted, it's quite possible for your bully to be "combat trained" or to have taken time to learn traditional martial arts, but remember that the odds are in your favor.

Thus, the most common kicking attack will be a "Front Snap-Kick" targeting your groin, or a front kick "stomping" you once you have been knocked to the ground.

That's why we say there are only five basic physical attacks you can expect from your bully. Once you take the time to familiarize yourself with these five attack vectors, and add that knowledge to the fact you've have already learned that how a bully stands (his "stance") and how he holds his hands (closed or open), then you will have all the clues you need to instantly decipher how he intends to attack. In other words, factoring in his stance plus his hand positions, you will be able to instantly narrow down—to a manageable few—the limited number of attack moves he can come at you with.

Now, instead of having to worry about dozens of possible attacks, by reading his body language (his attack vectors) you will know what he is planning to do—often before the knucklehead knows what he's going to do himself!

The average bully has two attack vectors: strike you, and/or else grab you—after which he will either put you in a choke hold or else slam you to the ground and possibly try to stomp you.

Here are the five most common attacks you will have to defend against:

1. A punch
2. A grab followed by a slam
3. A grab followed by a choke
4. A kick
5. An attack by a weapon

We'll teach you viable defenses for each of these. First, let's give you your claws.

THE THREE PERIMETERS

When facing a ruthless attacker, a confrontation from which you cannot immediately escape, one likely to end in bloodshed and possibly death, you have "three perimeters" of defense—keeping in mind that the best defense is often an immediate offense.

Think of this as the same as the defenses of a castle or a military base— an outermost perimeter, bolstered by a middle line of defense, and backed-up by an innermost perimeter of even more defensive measures. Even if an enemy succeeds in breaching the first perimeter defenses, he is sure to be stopped by your second and third lines of defense.

Translated into no-nonsense self-defense use, our three lines of defense—in order of preference—are: using a weapon (Kobudo-jitsu); fending off an attack with kicks, punches, and other strikes (Dakentai-jitsu); and finally closing in and grappling (Jutai-jitsu) an attacker to the ground.

Kobudo-jitsu

As a general rule, the further you are away from an (unarmed) attacker, the safer you will be. Likewise, anytime you can keep an object (e.g., a chair, garbage can lid, etc.) between you and your attacker, your chances of sustaining an injury are decreased.

Talk of having to use a weapon may make you feel uneasy but, remember, when we talk of weapons we're only being realistic.

Asian martial arts developed in many cases, not because the practitioners morally shunned weapons altogether, but more often than not because they were forbidden weapons by tyrannical rulers and ruthless conquerors.

Karate was born on Okinawa in response to invading samurai forbidding the indigenous population from possessing weapons. As a result, unarmed combat styles flourished on Okinawa: shorei-te, naha-te, to-te, all of which contributed to the eventual development of kara-te.*

Besides honing their unarmed skills, Okinawans also gleaned environmental weapons from their surroundings, in the process creating many of today's well-known martial arts weapons: the three-pronged sai (originally used for spearing fish), the bo-staff (used for poling boats), the tonfa (now carried by police worldwide who call it a PR-24, originated as a handle on a rice grindstone), and the dreaded nunchaku ("numb-chucks") fighting stick joined by a cord (originally a rice-flail).

While the concept of gleaning weapons from your environment is ancient and universal, the term "environmental weapons" was coined by Ralf Dean Omar in *Death on Your Doorstep: 101 Weapons in the Home* (1994), which is required reading for anyone interested in a complete course in the use of everyday objects as environmental weapons. See also Omar's *Prison Killing Techniques: Blade, Bludgeon and Bomb* (2001), an in-depth study of how, despite stringent security, prisoners worldwide continue to manufacture ingenious weapons.

Weapons recognition and use was a regular course of practice at all Shaolin monasteries, if for nothing else than for the fact that, in order to defend against a weapon, you first need to familiarize yourself with what that weapon is actually capable of. Untrained individuals often have an inflated idea of how dangerous a weapon is.

Well-trained soldiers tell you "hand-to-hand combat is something you do in between weapons." In civilian terms, this means a soldier only resorts to hand-to-hand combat with an enemy as a last resort (e.g., when that soldier's firearm has jammed or when he is caught without a weapon).

---

*"Kara" means "empty," and "te" means "hand," thus "empty hand."

The Japanese term "Kobudo-jitsu" translates to "the art of all weapons," meaning that we can use anything and everything we can get our hands on to defend ourselves. This goes beyond our learning to use a firearm, or even carrying chemical mace and/or a stun gun, which are all viable options and permitted in most places.* Beyond weapons you need permission to buy, carry, and use, there are thousands of environmental weapons laying around you at any given time—anything and everything you can snatch up to aid you in your fight for survival.

Recall that we already decided that when you feel that you, a loved one, or a fellow honest citizen is in danger of severe harm and/or possible death, you are justified—some would say obligated—to do whatever it takes to save your life and/or the life of those in your care.

Brandishing a weapon, whether one you "brought to the party" or one you've gleaned from your environment, is often enough to chase off less-committed bullies, just as steadfastly standing your ground unarmed is enough to dissuade those bullies looking for "an easy score." However, when facing down more committed (i.e., more desperate or psychopathic) bullies, it may become necessary to actually use a makeshift weapon.

Weapons rule #1: Never pick up a weapon unless you are fully committed to using that weapon. Pray you don't have to use it, but be prepared to use it if need be.

Weapons rule #2: If someone shows you a weapon, odds are he is trying to scare you.

While it's true brandishing a weapon will sometimes scare off an attacker, in a dire threat situation it is most often the weapon your attacker doesn't see that saves your life. Example: Whereas a committed (psychopathic) attacker might only snicker at seeing that No. 2 pencil you're brandishing to try to ward him off, that same assailant will be screaming when the No. 2 pencil you keep concealed until the very last minute suddenly appears eraser-deep in his eye!†

---

*Always be sure to obtain proper permits and to obey all local, state, and federal laws governing the purchase, carry-concealment, and use of any such personal safety devices. (Our liability lawyers made us put this disclaimer here!)

†Legal argument (excuse?) side: A weapon you instinctively snatch up from your surroundings during a life-and-death struggle is a whole lot easier to justify (in a court of law) than a weapon you premeditatively "brought to the party."

Environmental weapons are generally classified into four categories: blockers, blinders, bludgeons, and blades.

Blockers are any object you can put between you and your attacker. This can be something as small as a book you hold up to ward off a knife attack. You can use a chair, a table, a trashcan, or anything else to place between you and an attacker to keep him from reaching you.

The heroes who succeeded in barricading the doors in the classrooms at Virginia Tech, thereby preventing Cho from exacting an even higher toll on his fellow students, is an excellent example of using an environmental weapons blocker.

Long sticks, a golf club, or umbrella, all these can be used to keep a bully far enough away that he can't touch you. Chemical mace and a Tazer or stun gun would also qualify as blockers because they are designed not only to disable an attacker but also to keep him off you.

Blinders are anything you can throw at or spray on your bully to temporarily blind him, giving you time to either escape or use countermoves designed to completely disable him from pursuing his attack. Sometimes blinders are used simply to elicit a "flinch reaction" from your attacker, giving you precious seconds to either flee or counterattack with a more permanent solution.

Of course, any stiff jab to the eyes (fingers, stick, etc.) can disable or destroy the eye, and/or cause both eyes to tear up, temporarily blinding your attacker. Spitting water, coffee, hot sauce, tobacco juice (a disgusting habit by the way) into a bully's eye can also blind him long enough for you to make a move.

Bludgeons are objects that can be thrown at an attacker to elicit a flinch reaction and/or strike and stun the attacker. Bludgeons include everything from the rock or brick you pick up off the ground, to—literally!—the kitchen sink. (Remember the rule that "anytime your hand touches the ground, fill it" with dirt, a rock, something.)

The preferred target for any bludgeon is the skull, hitting hard enough to knock out your attacker. Barring this, a strike to the face can blind him with blood. A strike to his extremities (hands, arms, legs) can disable him.

Blades are objects that are sharp or pointed and that can be used to stab or cut your assailant. These range from a ring of car keys, to pens and pencils, to sharp-edged trophies and trinkets, to actual kitchen knives and other utensils. Stabbing a pencil into a punching fist can dissuade a second punch. However, as with bludgeons, the face, throat, and side of the neck have the most dramatic effect.

As already mentioned, your best advantage is not to let your aggressor see your blade (especially if it is a makeshift blade such as a pencil) until you make your move.

Keep in mind that these three categories are not exclusive and that there is much overlap within the three. For example, whereas a heavy-handled knife would by definition be a blade, you can also use the butt-end of the knife as a bludgeon to strike into and stun an attacker. Likewise, while a large book or metal tray can easily be used as a natural blocker, the edges of such objects can be used like a blade to stab into an attacker's soft tissue (e.g., eyes, throat, and groin).

Take some time out right now, wherever you are (at home, at work, in the park) to see how many environmental weapons you can spot in your immediate surroundings.

Dakentai-jitsu

If we are unable to flee and do not possess a weapon or are unable to quickly find an environment weapon, then we must either comply with our bully's demands, or else physically fight our bully off. Fighting a bully off means hitting him: us hitting him before he hits us. It's not rocket science. It's survival.

We didn't ask for this fight. But now that we are in the fight, life suddenly becomes simple: We keep him from hitting us while we hit him and keep hitting him until he is no longer capable of hitting us again.

Dakentai-jitsu literally means "the art of striking."

When the untrained face a bully, they falsely think themselves unarmed when, in actuality, they possess dozens of natural body weapons that—with no or little training—they can effectively use to defend themselves, their loved ones, and their fellow honest citizens.

What are these natural body weapons?

Your hands (for striking, grabbing, and clawing); wrists, forearms, elbows, and shoulders (for striking); head (for butting); teeth (for biting); hips (for unbalancing and then Judo throwing an attacker); knees and shins (for striking); and feet (for kicking and stomping and for sweeping a bully's own feet out from under him).

But your natural body weapons arsenal doesn't stop there, because there are dozens of ways to use each of these natural body weapons. That means—right here, right now—you're packing hundreds of weapons you can use to defend yourself against your bully!

We'll go into details into how to effectively use each of these natural body weapons in the section that follows on countering.

Jutai-jitsu

If you are forced to fight off an attacker, kicking and punching him from a distance is preferable to having to wrestle him to the ground. Remember that, in general, the closer you are to an opponent, the more danger you will be in. Wrestling (grappling) with an attacker can allow that attacker to use his superior height, weight, and muscle to his advantage.

That being said, there will come times when you'll find yourself grappling in close with an attacker.

Perhaps the worse-case scenario that comes to mind when having to grapple with a crazed attacker would be fighting for your life while trying to wrestle a gun away from a crazed campus killer and then restraining that madman until authorities arrive. But what about your little son or daughter trying to break free from an attempted abductor—trying to fight off a pervert who outweighs them by one hundred pounds?

Both of these are horrifying scenarios we pray none of us ever have to face. While doing a little praying, it's also smart to be doing a lot of preparing!

At such times when we must close with an attacker, it is important that whatever self-defense move(s) we do, that we do them unexpectedly, instantaneously, and devastatingly. "Devastatingly" means with full force and ferocity, our Inner Tiger unleashed!

This requires we, first, learn to instantly move ourselves into an advantageous position, one from which we can correctly block, defending ourselves, while simultaneously countering with enough power to get the job done. Positioning, blocking, countering, and bringing enough power to bear . . . you've just read the outline for the rest of this book!

150

POSITIONING

"Avoid rather than block."

—Shaolin precept

"Positioning" is 90 percent of the self-defense game. This simply means responding to a threat by moving yourself out of the line of fire, by simultaneously placing yourself in a safer position from which to counterattack your bully.

This is the kind of movement you see boxers and wrestlers doing—circling one another, sizing one another up—each one jockeying for the best position from which to launch his attack and counterattack.

Don't worry, what you need to learn is much simpler.

Remember the example that, if your bully would be so kind as to allow you to slip behind him without trying to hit you, from that safe position, there's a pretty good chance we could clean his clock for him. Unfortunately, there's a better chance your bully is going to do everything in his power to keep you in a disadvantageous position, a position that works to his advantage. For most bullies, this means he wants you "boxed up," that is, facing him, your shoulders aligned with his, with your centerline exposed (see Figure 10).*

So instead of standing in this boxed position, you want to move into a better position. A position where your bully can't hit you and you can hit him.

Relax, don't panic. We don't expect you to learn some kind of fancy *Matrix* (1999) flip or flying anything. You're going to learn two very simple positioning moves that will keep you from getting hit, while placing you in the perfect position to counterattack.

Spearpoint Stepping

"Spearpoint stepping" teaches you to move forward, closer in to your attacker without getting hit.

---

*Your centerline is an imaginary line running down the front of your body, from between your eyes to your groin.

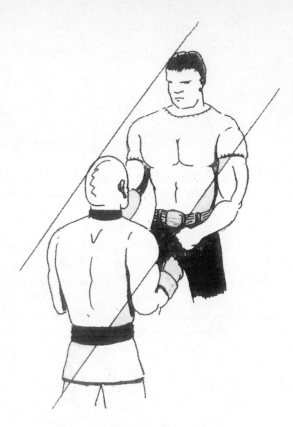

Figure 10. "Boxed-up" prefight position.

I know, this sounds scary, even counterintuitive: stepping closer to your attacker? Seems like you should be going in the other direction, huh?

It's true putting (and keeping) as much distance as possible between you and an aggressor is always smart—when retreat is possible. We're talking about when you know you're going to have to fight. When the option of flight has . . . well, flown.

When your enemy's eyeing you like tonight's rump roast, at least make him fight for his supper!

Having boxed you up, as your bully steps straight forward to punch you, you want to step diagonally forward, on the same side he's punching from.

Think of this as resembling a spear point. Your attacker is the spear

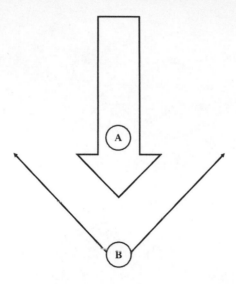

Figure 11.

a. From a boxed-up position, shoulders aligned, your attacker moves directly forward toward you, like a spear thrusting forward.
b. Counterposition yourself by taking a step forward and diagonally, which places you outside his striking arm (or kick).
c. Having avoided the thrust of his spear, counter with strikes of your own. See Figures 12–15, 18–29, 37, 38, and 43.

point coming straight at you. What you want to do is step diagonally forward, allowing the point of the spear to miss you (see Figure 11).

In practical application, you've stepped forward diagonally, slipping outside his punching arm, while putting yourself in a perfect (safer) position for counterattacking.

Notice the use of the "Cross-Block" in Figure 12.

Practice this "Spearpoint Stepping" and "Cross-Block" with a partner. Take turns punching/defending, with one partner stepping forward to punch while the second counters with the "Spearpoint Step" and "Cross-Block" to establish a back-and-forth rhythm. Think of your legs as springs.

Once you can perform the "Spearpoint/Cross-Block" smoothly, add a counterpunch (as in Illustration 12). Then experiment with other counterstrikes from this position as your knowledge of your natural body weapons increases.

Figure 12a.

a. Spearpoint stepping forward and diagonally to avoid attacker's punch (or kick).
b. Strike into his punching arm with a forceful "Cross-block" strike.
c. Having positioned yourself through "Spearpoint Stepping," now counterstrike into his centerline.

Did you note how when your bully throws his "leading hand punch" that he places his weight on his leading leg? Thus, when you "Spearpoint Step" into his leading side, you automatically move yourself out of the box, out of reach of both his rear hand and foot, preventing him from striking you with either.*

---

*"Spearpoint Stepping" is part of what Chinese kung-fu practitioners call kai men ("open the gate," meaning to penetrate, to slip past an enemy's defense. Kai men can also mean simply "skills," in this case, fighting skill, and is similar to the Japanese concept of taijitsu ("skill with the body").

Figure 12b.

a. Having positioned yourself outside your enemy's attack . . .
b. Counter up inside his defenses, along the line of his centerline, unbalancing him.
c. Use the force of your counter (e.g., an upper-cut) to drive him backward, allowing you to seize a hold on him. (See Figure 28.)
d. Close in, further unbalance your attacker by kicking forward and/or back (i.e., "Kickback Throw") into his legs.

Pivoting

The second move you'll add to your resistance repertoire will not only help you move out of danger more safely but will also increase the effectiveness—and power—of many of your countering moves, specifically adding power to takedown techniques such as the "Wrist-lock," "Arm-bar" (see

Figure 13. "Arm-Bar."

a. Having spear-stepped outside your attacker's punching arm, you seize a firm hold on his wrist . . .

b. . . . simultaneously strike into (applying pressure to) his elbow, which should be pointing toward your centerline.

c. Having secured your Arm-bar, you can also pick up your rear foot and pivot around (180°) behind your attacker, throwing him to the ground.

d. Augment this pivoting throw by extending your leg, tripping him.

Figure 13), and "Hair-twist," all of which you'll learn to do in the following section on "Your Takedown Techniques."

Pivoting consists simply of picking up one foot, turning, and placing that foot down 180 degrees in the opposite direction.

This unexpected reversal on your part throws your bully's attack vectors out of whack, at the very least making him stall, often allowing him to be pulled off balance and thrown to the ground.

BLOCKING

"Block rather than strike."

—Shaolin precept

In kung-fu, blocking is referred to as peng jin, meaning "warding force," as in deflecting an attack rather than meeting force-for-force.

The good news is you don't have to learn to block because your body already knows how to instinctively block (as shown in Figure 2). What you need to learn to do is block correctly (as shown in Figure 3). Blocking correctly means always blocking at an angle so as to better deflect the force of a blow.

When it comes to blocking, we instinctively throw up our hands (and, when on the ground, our feet) to protect ourselves. With a minimum of practice, you can also learn to use your elbows, and even your knees, to ward off an attacker.

The Chinese general Cao Cao is (in)famous for creating iron-wall kung-fu. Based on his many successful military encounters, you can use the elbow as a primary blocking-striking tool when close in.

"No-Block": The Secret to Blocking

The secret to good blocking is that there are no blocks, only strikes.

Each time you block, deliver that block as if it were a strike. This applies whether you are blocking with your body or with an environmental weapon. So it's not really a block, it's a "no-block" (see Figure 14).

For example, you are blocking a punch to your head with what karate-ka call a "Sword-hand block," like a karate "chop." Well that's just what it is. Don't think of it as blocking your attacker's arm with a open-hand karate-

Figure 14. "No-Block Striking."

a. Rather than passively blocking into your attacker's punching arm, strike into the attacking arm with a sword hand Uke-Shuto, damaging the arm and upsetting your attacker's punching rhythm.

b. Follow through and augment your initial Uke-Shuto block-strike by further deflecting (i.e., slamming into) your attacker's extended arm at the elbow with your other hand.

chop, think of it as trying to destroy his attacking arm with your karate-chop!

Anytime you throw your arm up to block (e.g., Figure 3), don't just raise your arm—slam your blocking arm into the attacking arm, doing as much damage as possible to the attacking arm, making your bully think twice about throwing another punch.

This "no-block" tactic is part of the hu-gui strategy, the "Ghost-Tiger" way of deliberately confusing and surprising an enemy by doing unexpected moves and/or by hiding your intention (your real move) behind a simpler initial move.

Chinese hu-gui is very similar to, and may have helped inspire, the ninjalike techniques of other lands, for example, the Hwang-do shadow-warrior techniques of Korea and the Taisavaki "shadowhand" techniques of the Shinobi ninja of medieval Japan.*

The Chinese term gui (pronounced "kway," also spelled kuei) means both "ghost" (meaning our attacker should never see your counterattack coming) and "demon" (meaning, when you strike, you attack like a ferocious demon, striking terror into your bully's heart!).

Keeping your fighting strategy, tactics, and techniques hidden from your enemy till the last possible instant is just common sense, thus, standard operating procedure for Asian martial arts strategists and their schools. Traditional Japanese martial arts schools call this ura ("inner, hidden") traditions and technique:

> "Keeping secret the existence of a particularly effective technique was a customary approach in all the ancient schools of the martial arts. The secret technique was usually concealed behind the cover of another technique that was close to it." (Tokitsu, 2004:34)

Now back to our sword-hand "no-Block" meets hu-gui Ghost-Tiger scenario:

Having Spearpoint-stepped into position . . . block-strike hard into his attacking arm. But then, as he instinctively retracts his damaged arm, instead of pulling back ("rechambering") your still extended blocking arm, whip your blocking hand around into an "Inverted Punch" targeting his exposed temple (see Figure 15). Sliding your leading foot a half step forward adds more impact to this strike. (We go in-depth explaining the "Collapsing Principle" in the subsequent section on "Countering.")

The hu-gui hidden move in this block-counter is that instead of blocking, you have attacked into his attacking arm and then used the momentum from your "no-block" to launch a totally unexpected second strike into his temple!

Keep in mind that anything and everything you can fill your hand with can be used to block an attack. That being said, the same rule still applies: There are no blocks, only strikes:

---

*For a complete course on such techniques, see Haha Lung's *Knights of Darkness* (2004), and Haha Lung and Christopher B. Prowant's *Ninja Shadowhand: Art of Invisibility* (2004). and *Shadowhand: History and Secrets of Ninja Taisavaki* (2002).

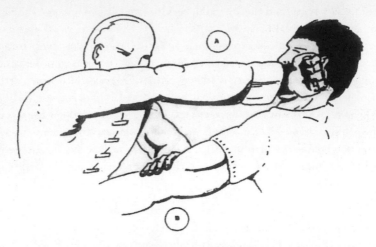

Figure 15. "Inverted-Fist Strike."

a. Having successfully block-striked your attacker's punching arm using the technique in Figure 14, as soon as your hand strikes the outside of his punching arm, immediately whip your arm around (i.e., invert it) to strike into the side of his head (targeting his temple).
b. Use your other hand to maintain control of his extended hand.

- As your bully punches you, block-stab into his punching hand with the pen or pencil you've kept concealed behind your back.
- As your attacker thrusts at you with his knife, don't just hold up that thick book as a shield. Slam it into his knife hand, possibly knocking the knife from his hand.
- Trapped in a classroom with a gunman blocking the only exit, don't passively hide behind a folding table or chair. Holding that chair in front of you, rush forward, slamming that chair into him and/or stabbing him with the legs of the chair. If another person is hiding behind the table with you, lift that table together and slam it into the gunman—pin him to the wall with the table to overpower and disarm him and/or to escape to alert the authorities.
- You've barricaded the door with a table, chairs, or your own body to keep a gunman out, but he's still trying to force his way in. Counter-

attack by spraying a fire extinguisher or fire hose through the crack still in the door, or through the bullet holes he's already made. If necessary, use the empty fire extinguisher or heavy fire hose nozzle to further beat back the invader. You can also unnerve (choke/blind) him by spraying water from a garden or maintenance hose, or by using aerosol paint, bug, or hair spray. Likewise, slippery liquids (oils, and other household chemicals) can be squirted under a door to unbalance him. NOTE: When barricading a doorway with your body, don't stand directly in front of the closed door (as your attacker may fire blindly through a thick door). As is practical, either crouch low or else stand to the side of the doorway.

More on fighting a bully armed with a weapon in a minute.

Getting Your Ground-Game Together

When shopping around for competent self-defense-oriented martial arts training, always ask the instructor to demonstrate his style's "ground technique," in other words, how his students continue to defend themselves once they've been knocked or thrown to the ground. If that sifu or sensei brags, "My students never get knocked down," walk away. Look for another—more realistic!—school.

Japanese traditionalists have a saying, "Even monkeys fall out of trees." Sooner or later, every fighter ends up on the ground. So it's important to know how to defend yourself, how to block and counterattack, even when you find yourself on the ground.

Blocking from the ground can actually be easier than blocking when standing. That's because when you're on your back on the ground, and your attacker is still standing, he has to reach down to punch you—making him especially vulnerable to being pulled off balance and you kicking up at him. Conversely, without leaning down—and risking bringing himself into your hitting range—all he can do is try to stomp you.

In keeping with our "no-block" rule, even when you're knocked to the ground, you do not merely cover-up and defend passively—like a turtle. Have you ever heard of the term "Crouching Tiger" before?

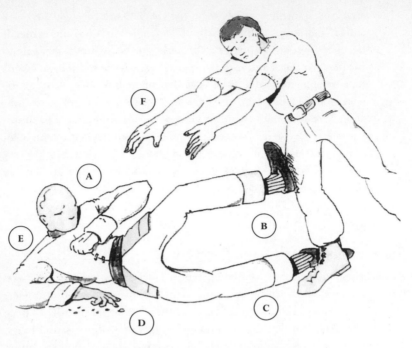

Figure 16. "Defending from the Ground."

a. Having been knocked or having fallen to the ground, immediately bring one of your arms up across your chest as a guard. Keep your elbow pointed toward your attacker.

b. Bring one leg up ("cocked," "chambered") to both guard (against his stomping down feet) and in order to kick into your attacker, kicking in and up targeting his knees and groin. Target his upper body when he leans down in to strike with his hands.

c. You can also use your extended legs to "hook" his ankles, pulling him off balance. This technique works especially well when you push at his knee with one foot, while pulling at his ankle with your other foot.

d. Any time your hand touches the ground, fill it with a weapon (dirt, rocks, etc.), even grass can be used to temporarily blind an attacker).

e. Keep moving while on the ground. Constantly shift side to side, alternating which hip your weight is centered on, which leg you can kick your attacker with.

f. Grab his extended arms, pulling him off balance. See Figure 33.

INCREASING YOUR SPEED AND POWER

When asked what the secret was to winning battles, the successful—albeit impatient—Civil War general Nathan Bedford Forrest snapped, "It's whoever arrives first, with the most!" "First" equals speed. "The most" equals power.

We are intimidated by our bully because we believe our bully possesses more speed (to hit us before we can do anything about it!) and that he possesses more power (to make that hit hurt really bad!).

But you're pretty fast yourself, remember?

Remember how fast (and far) you jumped when you mistook that garden hose for a snake? Remember how fast your hand moved when it got caught under that scalding water?

The late, great Bruce Lee, renowned for both his speed and his power, was once asked by an interviewer what the secret of his art was. In response, Bruce casually tossed an apple at the reporter's face. Instinctively, as fast as a cobra, the interviewer's hand shot out and effortlessly snatched the apple from the air.

"That," smiled Bruce, "is the secret."

In other words, there is no secret, it's instinct. It's the xi sui principle of "no thought" you've already mastered through your (daily?) relaxation, concentration, and visualization exercises. And it's your having practiced your "Kat!" kiai trigger-release.

Speed

"120 milliseconds. That's how fast your brain distinguishes cues that have caused you to make mistakes before. This early warning signal prevents falling for the same trick twice."
—*Psychology Today* (September–October 2007)

How about some martial arts math? (Groans all around!)

I + F = S. In turn, F + S = P.

I = instinctual reaction (which you might have to spend some time remembering. That's what your relaxation, concentration, meditation, and visualization exercises are for).

F = form. Form refers to pattern movements performed smoothly and effortlessly, preferably without superfluous, distracting thought (xi sui).

Martial artists, as well as professional athletes, call this "muscle memory," performing repetitious training designed to establish a "habit" of moving a certain way into the muscles themselves. This is no more complicated than your being able to write your name without having to look at the paper. That's muscle memory.

We fall back on our already established analogy, that of patiently digging ditches; digging those ditches with an eye toward both direction and depth, in anticipation of our future needs.

S = speed. Speed is the velocity at which the previously dammed water rushes once released into those ditches. In the same way, once released, our body energies react instinctively and appropriately to a threat, often before our conscious mind has even analyzed the threat.

P = power. As already mentioned, in this equation, power is simply the ability to get the job done.

Ergo, our first formula reads: I (instant xi sui reaction, sans resistance, hesitation) plus F (practiced and perfected form) gives you S (speed).

Our second formula is even more promising: F (form) + S (speed) = P (power)!

Here's a good example of how the second formula finds practical use:

Take a simple bath towel. If you swing it in a wide arc, it only lightly slaps against a person. Now, take that same towel, rattail it by spinning it up tight, stretch it between your arms with tension, and then let go, snapping it forward like a bullwhip. What happens? Anyone whose ever been snapped by a wet towel in the shower knows the answer to that one—it hurts like hell!

But what changed in this equation? It's still just a towel? Same towel, same target—your butt! The two new factors are form (rattailing the fabric) and speed (the intentional creation of tension followed by a sudden dynamic release of that potential tension-energy). By perfecting the form (i.e., rattailing the cloth), then adding speed (through tension and sudden release), we create power (the impact of the speeding towel connecting with your butt!), turning a harmless towel into an environmental weapon capable of putting out an eye as efficiently as any bullwhip. In fact, the same physics principles apply to a bullwhip.

This same principle can also work for us, increasing the impact (power) of our striking. Once we learn the correct form of a martial arts move, we

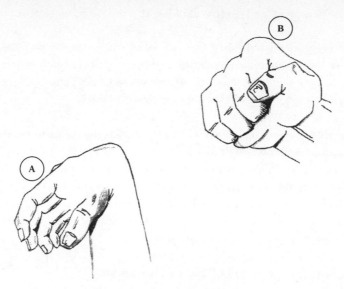

Figure 17. "Snapping Back-Fist."

a. Practice shaking your hand at the wrist (fingers relaxed), as if trying to shake off some water . . .
b. Flexing your arm forward toward your target, suddenly tighten your fingers into a fist an instant before striking your target.

then practice to create mind and muscle memory patterns. Then, when threatened, before our conscious thought can hesitate, our practice pays off as our (re)awakened Inner Tiger jumps to defend us.

You can see in Figure 17 how easy it is to apply this principle to improve your striking power, in this case, your ability to instantly "snap" a lighting-fast "back-fist" strike into an attacking bully.

Begin by relaxing your wrist, waving your limp hand loose back and forth (thumb pointed up). Now, the next time your wrist bends forward (leading your hand), suddenly tighten your hand into a fist. Did you feel that? Did you feel the "snapping" power? In the same way the rattailed towel gathered and then released energy (power), your hand just did too.

Now practice hitting with your top two knuckles—in a real fight, you would target your attacker's jaw line and temple.

"Form plus speed equals power!"—this is one more for your inspiration collection.

Power: How to Get It, How to Use It

*"I suggest joining a school that has real-life situation training and
kickboxing training. Developing striking power is essential to be
able to execute self-defense tactics."*
—Sensei Don Niam in *Cruise* (2007:4)

Power doesn't mean brute force. Power means the ability to get the job
done, and to get it done right the first time.

For example, in martial arts, subtle jujitsu and aikido moves get the job
done—putting the bully flat on his back—but they do so for the most part
without the use of overt force and without using more force than is necessary to contain the situation. In kung-fu they call this jin or jing ("trained
force"), force (power) developed through practice.

Your Body Weapons and How to Use Them

"Warned is wary. Warned is wily. Warned is winning."
—Joshua Only (2007)

First let's take a quick inventory of the personal body weapons you can
use at any time, any place, to defend yourself against a bully. Then let's learn
the "Collapsing Principle," which allows us to combine these weapons into
effective defenses and devastating counterattacks . . . which, by now, you realize are one and the same.

Your Personal Arsenal

Hands. Study "The Three Hands" (Figure 9). Not only can your hands
block (no-block) a bully's kicks and punches but also your hands can wield
weapons, conventional and environmental.

Wrists. The top of the wrist bone (called in some Asian martial arts
schools "Crane," in others "Turtle's Head") can deliver stunning vertical
blows (up into a bully's chin, into his groin) as well as horizontal strikes into
an attacker's solar plexus and into his temple (similar to the "Inverted Fist"
strike in Figure 15).

Forearms. Forearms can not only be used to block but, in keeping with
our no-block strategy, the forearm can also be used to counterstrike an at-

tacker (by wedging it under his chin and into his throat). The forearm can also be used as a fulcrum when levering the bully's arm into an "Arm-Bar" lock (read: break!). See the "Finding Your Takedown Technique" section that follows.

Elbows. The elbows (aka "short-wings") can be used to both block and strike into an attacker, for example, by striking upward like a boxer's "Uppercut" (targeting the chin when standing, the groin when kneeling). The short-wing can also swing inward horizontally to strike targets along the centerline (e.g., solar plexus, throat, jaw line, and temple). When grabbed from behind by an attacker, strike backward with the elbow vertically and/or horizontally targeting his ribs and along his centerline. From the front, you can also strike downward, targeting the bridge of your bully's nose and his collarbones.

Armpits. The armpits (aka the "Eagle's Nest") can be used to pin (trap) an attacker's hand, preventing him from striking you, making him more susceptible to your arm-locks and takedowns.

Shoulders. The shoulders can be used to unbalance an attacker. Think NFL! Even a small, lightweight child can topple an attacker three times his size and weight by forcefully slamming his shoulder into the attacker's knees (see "Finding Your Takedown Technique").

Head. Use the slight ridges on either side of your forehead to head butt your attacker (targeting his nose). When a bully encircles you from behind and pins your arms, head butt backward, targeting the bridge of his nose. You can also head butt him in the solar plexus and stomach (like a mountain goat), knocking the breath from him, as shown in Figure 18. Having stunned your attacker, you can now head butt upward into his chin and/or use your arms to pull his legs out from under him.

Voice. Never underestimate the power of a good scream! And not just your Tiger-roar kiai "Kat!" used for releasing your power. Screaming at the top of your lungs can not only unnerve your attacker but can also draw the attention of others.

Teeth. Bite anywhere you can. All is fair when you're fighting for your life. Plus, bite marks make great evidence in court. You can also spit into an attacker's eyes, temporarily blinding him. Saliva can elicit a flinch reaction from an attacker that can be used to your advantage. Other substances are also effective, such as tobacco juice or dip (need I mention that these are really nasty habits?); any kind of drink (coffee, soda, etc.); or hot sauce or

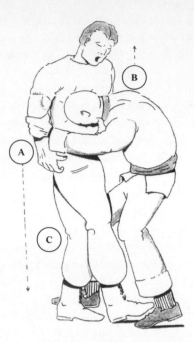

Figure 18. "Head-Butt Combination."

a. Having gained control of your attacker's arms by pinning them to
his side, drive the top of your head into his solar plexus as
forcefully as possible. This will knock the air from your attacker,
unbalance him, and make him pitch forward.

b. As the force of your head butt causes your attacker to lean
forward, immediately thrust your head upward, slamming into his
chin. The force of this collision will cause your attacker pain,
disoriente him, and possibly knock him out.

c. Variation: Having unbalanced your attacker with your initial head
butt, release your grip on his arms as you squat and slide your
hands down his body to scoop his legs forward, toppling him to
the ground. See Figure 27.

d. Variation: When attacked by a "sagger" (i.e., someone who wears
extremely baggy pants, often already hanging low on his hips),
and after head-butting into his solar plexus, slide down his body,
seize a hold on his already drooping pants, and strip those pants
down to his ankles before then forcefully jerking your grip
forward suddenly to topple him to the ground.

Note: In both c and d, do not lose contact with your attacker's body as you slide
your hands down his body.

pepper water. Depending on your level of determination (read: desperation!) you can even temporarily hold a more toxic chemical such as bleach in your mouth for a few seconds in order to sprew it into an attacker's eyes. You can also blind an attacker by spitting his own blood back in his face—from that plug you just bit out of him!

Weight. Heavy-set people can always slam their superior weight into a leaner bully, unbalancing him. Teach children to go "deadweight," dropping to the ground when someone tries to abduct them. It's harder to drag ninety pounds of dead weight into a nondescript van with muddied-over license plates than it is walking a compliant victim. Likewise, teach your children to hold on tight to their bicycle (or to any nearby post, fence, etc.), adding the weight of this object to their own.

Kid tip: Get a dog. A dog's the best antiburglar device you'll ever invest in. Even a tiny—noisy!—dog will help discourage burglars. Likewise, encourage your child to take the dog with him when possible. A child walking with a dog—even a tiny noisy dog—can discourage a predator from approaching.

FYI: Adults walking, jogging, or even riding in a car with a dog are also less likely to be approached by street thugs.

Hips. The hips can likewise be slammed into an attacker's side, unbalancing him. Bony hips make especially good jamming weapons. Many martial arts judolike throws are predicated on jamming your hips in under an opponent's hips and lifting them off the ground. Carefully practice this with a friend.

Knees. The knees are well-respected—and feared!—weapons in nearly all martial arts. A fast-rising knee to the groin can end a fight, as can pulling an attacker's head down into your rising knee.

Shins. The shins can strike into an attacker's legs, unbalancing him. It's not necessary to "toughen" your shins (especially the psychotic way they do in all those kickboxer movies!) because you aim your shins against the meatier sides and calf of an attacker's lower legs when sweeping him to the ground.

Feet. As already discussed, there are hundreds, perhaps thousands of kick variations in the martial arts, but there are still only four types of kicks. The two main kicks you can easily learn to use are the straight Front-Kick (targeting the groin or knee) and/or the Round-Kick (attacking and sweeping his leading support leg with your instep or shin).

While it might not sound "sporting," you can also kick an attacker once

MIND FIST

you've knocked him to the ground (targeting head and body, kicking up into the groin from behind) and stomp him (targeting his hands, sweeping his supporting arms out from under him) (see Figure 16).

The Collapsing Principle

Asian martial arts, unlike Western boxing, takes advantage of all the previously mentioned body weapons, not just the fists. This is a major difference between a sport such as boxing, and a martial (war) art whose philosophy is "Masakatsu!"

Western fighters typically punch one hand and withdraw it while punching with the other hand. This is known as the "Old One-Two" or, in modern parlance, hitting someone with "a two-piece."

Asian fighters in general, and kung-fu practitioners in particular, strike differently. Instead of striking with one hand, retracting it, and then striking with the opposite hand, kung-fu fighters strike multiple times with the same hand and foot before retracting it. This is known as the "Collapsing Principle" (see Figure 19).

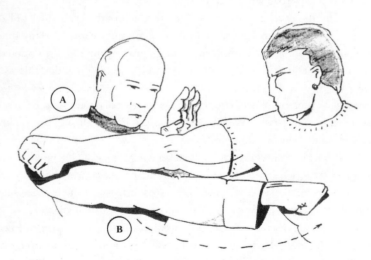

Figure 19a. "Collapsing Principle."
a. Having Spearpoint-stepped past your attacker's initial lunge . . .
b. Counterstrike into his centerline with a punch, Palm-strike, etc. of your own . . .

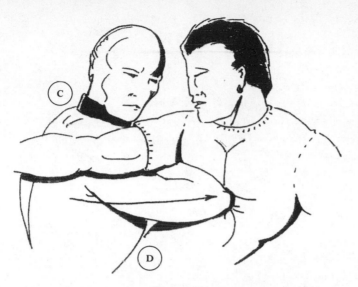

Figure 19b.

c. Immediately upon connecting with your strike, "collapse" further into your attacker with a follow-up "Short-wing" elbow strike before he has time to fully absorb the shock of your initial strike.

d. Variation: Follow through with the "Wolverine" takedown from Figure 27.

For example, a connecting punch to the body by a boxer might be followed by a corresponding punch from his opposite hand. One-two, left-right. However, when a kung-fu fighter connects with a punch, rather than withdrawing the striking hand, he takes advantage of his forward momentum to "collapse" into an elbow strike.

Many tiger-style kung-fu strikes are based on this principle: striking with one body weapon and immediately "collapsing" inward to strike with another body weapon.

Another example: You strike upward into your bully's chin using a Palm-strike. Having stunned him with this strike, you immediately follow up (complete) the counterattack by striking inward and then raking down his face with your Tiger-claw (see Figure 20).

As you can see, this initial Palm-strike "hides" the follow-up Shadow-hand Tiger-claw rake. This is indicative of all Tiger-claw strikes, where an ini-

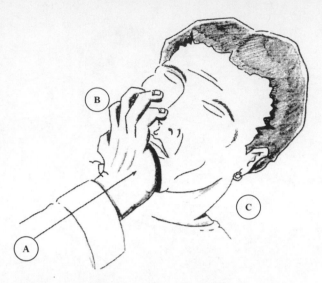

Figure 20. "Tiger-Claw" Strike.

a. Having evaded your attacker's initial lunge by Spearpoint-stepping, strike up into his chin (or under his nose) with a Claw-hand Palm-strike.

b. Immediately upon solidly connecting with your Palm-strike, curl your fingers down into a Tiger-claw, first digging into the soft tissues of the face, before then raking downward.

c. For a variation, see Figure 22.

d. *Follow-up technique:* Your initial Palm-strike to the chin will force your attacker's head back, exposing his throat for possible counterstrikes (e.g., Spear-hand thrust, "Tiger's Mouth Strike" aka "Reverse Ridgehand," horizontal elbow, etc. (see Figure 9b).

tial Palm-strike "softens" up flesh and muscle, making it more susceptible to the subsequent Tiger-claw rake.

This Collapsing Principle works for leg strikes as well.

Having "checked" your attacker's advance by using a "Chinese-Cross" Kick" (pressing/stomping your insole instep into his leading knee—see Figure 21a) without placing your kicking foot down, twist your foot around to strike his rear leg with a low-level "Side-Kick" (striking with the sole of your foot, as in Figure 21b).

Figure 21a. "Chinese-Cross Jamming Kick."

a. Shifting your weight slightly forward into a front stance, raise
   your rear foot up to knee level, before twisting your leg forward
   and forcefully striking downward with the inside edge of your
   foot (as if targeting an attacker's knee and/or shin).

Note: Simply pushing against an attacker's knee is enough to stifle his
   forward momentum and/or topple him (see Figure 27).

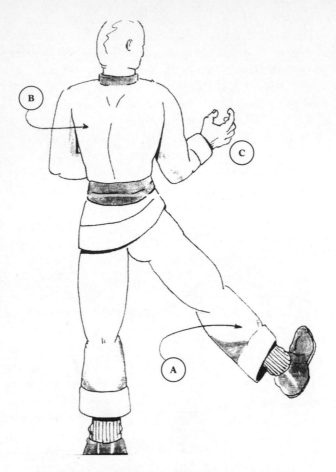

Figure 21b. "Chinese-Cross Kick Follow Through."

a. Having successfully struck your attacker with your initial Chinese-Cross Kick, as your striking foot "rebounds" (automatically rechambering itself) rather than setting your foot down, twist your hip forward to launch a low-level Side-Kick targeting the knee of your attacker's other leg.

b. Add force to this Side-Kick by twisting your entire body forward, putting your full weight behind it.

c. "Always land with a hand." Remember, the most important part of kicking is the "landing." Always "land" with your hands in guard position and/or be ready with a follow-through hand block-striking technique.

Some More Kung-fu Secrets

Now, because you've been studying so hard, practicing your bully fighting skills diligently (and daily?), we're going to reward you by letting you in on the secret of both the kung-fu "1-to-3 Inch Punch" and the dreaded "Poison-hand." Both of these strikes, the stuff of kung-fu legend and a thousand fanciful Hong Kong kick-flicks, are based on the reality of the Collapsing Principle.

The secret is that every time the body gets struck, it tenses . . . then it immediately relaxes. The Western method of "one-two" hitting allows a struck part of the body to tense-relax-tense in synch with the "one-two" punching rhythm. The Collapsing Principle, as used in the "1-to-3 Inch Punch" doesn't allow for this kind of tension-relax-tension by the body.

For example: Having stabbed into the opponent's body with a vertical "Pear-hand strike" (thumb on top), rather than retracing the striking hand (giving the enemy fighter's body time to "relax" in that spot), the kung-fu fighter immediately "collapses" his hand from Spear-hand into Vertical Fist. The kung-fu fighter then has the option of continuing his Collapsing Principle charge by collapsing from his Vertical Punch into an elbow strike, and so on.

Demonstrations are often given where a kung-fu striker places his extended fingers against a volunteer's body and then "punches" from only three-inches away (the length of his fingers), sending the volunteer flying, thus "proving" the power of the "1-to-3 Inch Punch."

Oh, the "1-to-3 Inch Punch" really works, just not the way it's often portrayed.

What's actually happened is that the kung-fu demonstrator first pokes his fingers against the volunteer's skin, triggering that person's natural "tense reflex." The kung-fu man then pulls his hand back slightly until he feels the volunteer instinctively relax, at which point the kung-fu man suddenly tightens his Spear-hand into a Vertical Punch, which he often augments by shifting his weight forward, from an even stance to a forward stance.

This simple technique of multiple strikes using the Collapsing Principle was often mistaken in ancient times as being somehow "magical," because to untrained on-lookers, it appeared that the kung-fu fighter had only hit his opponent with one strike when, in actuality, he had hit his opponent rapid-fire with several strikes, all proceeding out of one forward attack movement. Other on-lookers believed such fighters possessed the secret of the "Dim mak," the dreaded "Death's Touch." Of course, the kung-fu fighters did little to discourage such beliefs on the part of their enemies.

Now you know the secret to both the magical "1-to-3 Inch Punch" and to the dreaded "Poison-hand." It's a good thing you are not a bully!

FYI: "Collapsing" into an opponent was also the basis for the renowned Chinese poet Li Po's creation of "drunken style" kung-fu, in which a fighter mimics the weaving in and out of a drunk man, before "collapsing" into his opponent with multiple unexpected strikes—punch becomes elbow strike which becomes shoulder blow which becomes head butt, and so on.

COUNTERING

Now that you've learned to identify your tactical personal body weapons, and learned a little of how these weapons can be used to both battle back your neighborhood bully, as well as potentially save your life in an emergency dire threat situation, now let's look at specific ways we can easily apply those personal body weapons.

Finding Your Three Hands

Western fighters are in love with the straight punch, "the Haymaker," the knock-out punch. But don't forget there are several ways to use the Closed Hand and, right behind that, you have two other tools: the Open Hand and the Claw.

Using Your Closed Hand

For practical purposes, when needing to perform a good, solid straight punch, fill your hand with a D-sized battery, a thick pen, even a rock, anything that will reinforce your hand and add weight and firmness to it.

When you can't deliver a solid knuckle punch, use your Hammer-fist instead. In order to strike solidly with a Hammer-fist, we "Open-to-Close," meaning, as we strike toward our target (the bridge of his nose, his collar bone), we leave our hand open till the last instant before impact when we suddenly close our open hand into a tight fist. This is similar to the snapping motion of the towel we discussed earlier.

Practice doing this on a firm pillow, before moving on to firmer surfaces. Straight out of a *Rocky* (1976), once you've practiced this technique on a firm pillow, try doing the same Hammer-fist blows on a large ham, something that closely resembles the feel of actually hitting human flesh and muscle. (Don't worry, you can do this in the privacy of your own kitchen, so no one will be laughing at you.)

Of course, you can also reinforce your hand with the battery, gripping it tight while performing your Hammer-fist and/or Back-fist strikes.

Using Your Open Hand

When "Karate chopping" down on an attacker's collar bones or bridge of the nose (from a side position), use the "Close-to-Open," striking at your target with a Closed Hand, snapping it open into a "Sword-hand" an instant

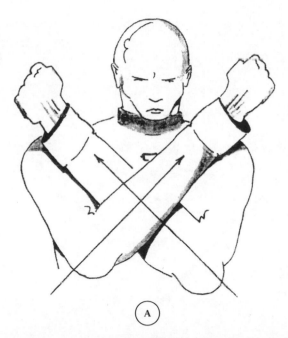

Figure 22a. "Tiger-Claw Defense Against a Grab-Choke."

a. As your attacker attempts to grab you with both hands (or after he has already seized a grip on your throat or lapels), press your body weight into your attacker, suddenly and forcefully thrusting your crossed arms up between his two arms (as close to his elbows as possible).

before impact. Remember also that you can use the reverse (thumb) side of your Sword-hand to strike (e.g. up into the groin). This Gyaku-Shuto is sometimes called "Monkey's Paw" by Chinese kung-fu men. Your Open Hand also doubles as your "Spear-hand," with fingers and thumb being used to stab into a bully's "soft" targets (eyes, throat, armpits, groin). You can also bend your wrist and fingers back to strike with the palm of the Open Hand.

Using Your Claw Hand

We've already discussed how an initial "Palm-blow" is used before a "Tiger-claw" rake is employed (see Figure 20). Tiger-claw rakes can also be used in conjunction with one another, for example, in a Double Tiger-claw escape from a front choking situation, as shown in Figure 22.

Rather than simply "scratching" your fingers against your enemy, a

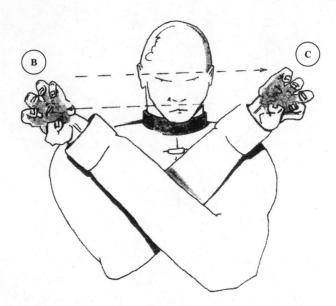

Figure 22b.

b. **Having successfully loosened your attacker's hold, open your closed fists into Tiger-claws, simultaneously ripping in one direction across his eyes . . .**
c. **And in the other direction across his throat.**

proper Tiger-claw starts with fingers splayed somewhat before the fingers suddenly tighten inward, seizing a hold on the flesh, digging in, then literally ripping along the flesh and muscle. Chinese kung-fu masters call this kind of devastating Tiger-claw attack/counterattack bo-pi ("flesh peeling").* Yes, it sounds brutal and it is—brutally effective.

For example: Having blocked an attacker's arm with a Palm-block, your Palm-block immediately transforms into a Tiger-claw which "bites" into his arm. This Tiger-claw then "rakes" down the length of his retracting forearm (damaging the arm as it descends), to then seize a grip on the wrist, from which you can then apply an effective Wrist-lock (see "Finding Your Take-down Technique").

Strengthen your fingers for performing the Tiger-claw by practicing tightly gripping balls (racquetballs, not his balls . . . that will come later!) and by massaging thick clay, wax, and so on. It's not necessary to have "fingers of steel" because these Tiger-claw techniques target a bully's "soft" tissue.

Experiment with performing these types of hand strikes quickly and solidly. Form + Speed = Power. Practice against firm surfaces until your hands and arms can absorb the referral shock of such impact without undue pain.

FYI: There's no reason to "deform" your knuckles or striking palms of hands like professional fighters and sundry masochists seem to enjoy doing.

Finding Your Two Kicks

Good kicks come from your knee and are guaranteed to drop your bully to his knees! Practice raising your knee up quickly and, once your knee reaches its apex, snap (or thrust) the foot outward. A good, solid basic "Front Snap-Kick" (see Figure 23).

The other basic kick you need is the "Forward Round-Kick," where you sweep your leg (shin or instep) in to strike-sweep the side and back of your bully's leg (see Figure 24).

Additional kicks, such as the Side-Kick (see Figure 16), the Crescent Kick, and all the possible variations of the Four Kicks, you can learn at your leisure, as befits your particular pasttime and paranoia. Likewise, when

---

*Not to be confused with the ancient Chinese torture method of the same name!

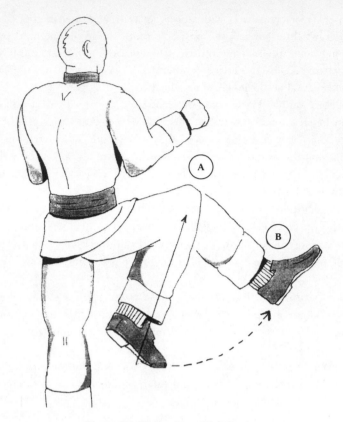

Figure 23. "Front-Snap Kick."

a. Having assumed a back-stance, quickly and forcefully raise your knee up to belt level...

b. As soon as your knee reaches belt level, forcefully thrust your foot forward using the "hinge" of your knee. As soon as your foot impacts with your target, withdraw (rechamber) it immediately.

Strike with your toe (when wearing hard-toed shoes), with your toes curled back or down (when bare-footed) and/or with your heel in either instance.

Remember to pull your kicking foot back twice as fast as you thrust it out in order to prevent your attacker grabbing hold of it.

Land with a hand.

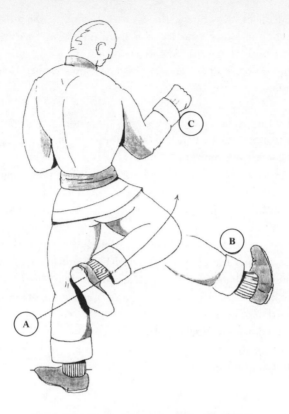

Figure 24. "Roundhouse/Sweeping-in Kick."

a. Assuming a front stance, fold your rear knee in as you swing it forward in a horizontal rising motion (as if you intend to strike with your knee) . . .

b. At the apex of your swing, suddenly release your knee fold, allowing your foot to fly forward, striking the target.

Depending on your mastery of this kick, targets start at your attacker's ankles, knees, and thighs, and work their way up to his trunk and even his head.

c. The higher up the target on his body, the more you will need to "torque" your body forward. To maintain balance, your supporting leg foot will naturally rotate away the higher up you kick.

Immediately upon striking your target, either retract your foot along the same route it took toward your target, or else drop your leg forward, into a forward stance. Always land with a hand.

plotting your defensive strategy, the Front-Kick and a sweeping-in Round-Kick (intending to knock your legs out from under you) are the two kicks you are most likely to have to defend against on the street.

Awareness, preparedness, and a solid stance are your best defense against a kicking attack.

The most important part of kicking is the landing.

Learn to throw kicks that are fast enough to prevent an enemy from "catching" them. But, more important, kicks that don't knock you off balance—in effect, doing your bully's job for him! When practicing your kicks, practice landing (recovering) in a back stance, both hands up ready for blocking, in a defensive posture that will allow you to either continue the fight, or else flee to safety.

The rule for holding your hands up defensively is: "One in, one out, one up, one down," meaning you should have one hand further out, while keeping your other hand closer in (as a secondary line of defense). Likewise one of your hands should be up ("high guard"), while the other is held lower ("lower guard"). It doesn't matter which hand is held where, only that this "One up, one down, one in, one out" discipline be adhered to.

Take note of the surface you are standing on as some surfaces allow you more traction for kicking, while others are too slippery (ice, linoleum, etc.).

Finding Your Takedown Technique

In the movie *Harry in Your Pocket* (1993), the late, great James Coburn (a student of Bruce Lee by the way) plays Harry, a master pickpocket who has one rule, "Harry never holds," meaning that, once Harry lifts your wallet, he immediately passes it off to a confederate.

"Harry never holds" is the same rule you will use when applying arm or wrist locks: You never "hold," as in trying to restrain your bully until he cries "uncle." (Oh, he'll cry "uncle" and promise never to do it again. And then, when you let him up, he'll kick your ass and break both your arms!)

So you break his arm first. I know, tough talk. It's a tough world. And you need to decide, here and now if you haven't already, to be tough. If not for yourself, then for your wee ones, and your elderly. And for the other passengers on the plane who'd like to get home to see their loved ones again too.

Life is tough, and so as long as there's some of that life still flowing through your veins, you should be tough too. Tough enough to break an attacker's arm if need be.

The two most oft-used arm trapping techniques used in the martial arts are the "Wrist-lock" and "Arm-bar" (see Figures 25 and 26). American martial artists often refer to these as "AK-1" and "AK-2," respectively. "AK" being short for aiki-jitsu, the more combat-oriented style of grappling from whence derived the modern aikido. AK-1 can be applied in a defensive situation anytime a bully seizes a hold on you, for example, a lapel grab or a choke. AK-2 can be used to augment AK-1, or used by itself anytime you succeed in trapping a bully's extended arm.

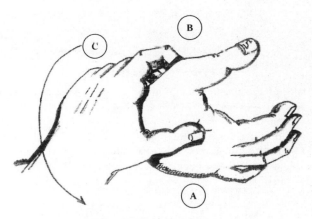

Figure 25. "Wrist-Lock."

a. To successfully apply a Wrist-lock (aka "AK-1"), first forcefully jam your thumb into the back of your attacker's hand.
b. Simultaneously, dig your remaining four fingers into the palm-base of his thumb.
c. Having obtained a grip on your attacker's hand, now twist his wrist around by pulling with your four fingers from the thumb-side of his hand while simultaneously pushing your thumb harder into the back of his hand.

   The combination of this push-pull action will automatically twist his wrist painfully back toward his inner-forearm.
d. Augment this technique by stepping back and/or pivoting away from your attacker while maintaining your Wrist-lock on him. (See Figures 13, 31, 35, and 36.)

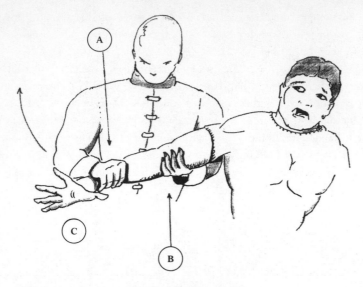

Figure 26a. "Arm-Bar."

a. Having secured a firm hold on your attacker's wrist or forearm, press down on his wrist or forearm . . .
b. . . . while simultaneously using your other hand as a fulcrum to apply pressure to his elbow.
c. This Arm-Bar can also be applied simultaneously with a full AK-1 Wrist-lock to create a double lock.
d. For variations, see Figures 34 and 36.

The application of both AK-1 and AK-2 are simple to perform and take no strength to apply. However, they do require maneuvering into the right position. (Remember that part a while back about martial arts being 90 percent positioning?)

Any time you succeed in turning an attacker's arm, the rule is "look for the elbow," that is, turning his arm so as to expose the elbow. Because, if you can "see" the elbow when you turn the arm, then you can lock-out the arm by applying pressure to that elbow. And then you can break the bully's arm.

Tough talk time again: Remember that desert hiker whose arm got trapped under a boulder, who would have died had he not had the courage to use a small penknife to cut off his arm? In a desperate situation, one de-

Figure 26b. "Arm-Bar Variation."

a. Having successfuly Spearpoint-stepped out of the line of fire, apply the AK-2 Arm-bar by trapping your attacker's arm in the crook of your elbow, using your chest as the counter fulcrum.

You can also pin your attacker's arm under your armpit, known in martial arts circles as trapping him in "the eagle's nest."

b. Using your chest as a fulcrum frees up your hand from counterattacking.

c. Augment this trap-counterattack by sweeping uyour attacker's leg out from under him (e.g., by using a "Kickback" throw).

manding you make tough choices if you want to survive to see your loved ones again—you do what you have to.

But, by the same token, you don't know how desperate your attacker is. If he is truly desperate, even the best of arm locks and wrist-holds won't restrain him for long. Sooner or later he'll get loose and then you'll have to start the fight all over again, except this time he's "hip" to that one "trick" that might have just saved your life had you followed through with it by breaking his arm.

Figure 27. "Wolverine Leg-Lock Takedown."

a. Having closed with your attacker, while he is in a forward stance (i.e., his weight on his forward leg, preventing him from kneeing you), immediately drop down and forward, crossing your hands behind his leg as you forcefully lean your shoulder into his forward knee.

b. Pull with your crossed arm as you lever your weight into his knee, dumping him to the ground.

c. Variation: See Figure 18 and/or when fighting from the ground, see Figure 16.

Note: This technique requires no strength to perform correctly, even a child, properly instructed, can knock down a grown attacker.

And that's why "Harry never holds." Break the arm. Put your bully out of the fight permanently. Survive for those you love.

The knee can be "locked-out" the same way an elbow can. Either by hand or by foot (see Figure 21).

From drunken-style kung-fu comes a simple technique for locking-out a knee and taking down an aggressor that is so simple and so effective, that *even a small child can use it* against a full grown adult abductor. American students refer to it as the "Wolverine" (see Figure 27). Teach it to your children.

Figure 28. "Hair-Twist Takedown."

a. Having successfully closed with an attacker, Palm-strike into his jaw, pushing his head around, while . . .

b. . . . simultaneously grabbing a hold of his hair and pulling his head around.

c. Having secured this double grip on your attacker, suddenly step back and/or pivot away from him, dumping him to the ground (review Figure 13, "Pivoting").

Another simple takedown technique also comes to us from Li Po's drunken style called the "Hair-Twist" (see Figure 28) and requires no strength to perform because it relies on pivoting (Figure 13) to unbalance an attacker:

FIGHTING BACK

Having learned an appreciation for the various personal body weapons available to you at any given time, for use in any given situation, you will now learn specific applications of these tactics, tools, and techniques.

First off, no self-defense instructor can—or should—give you specific responses to specific threat situations. That's because all situations are different. You need to learn to think on your feet, before you end up on your ass.

Whereas everything works, everything doesn't work every time. This applies as well to martial arts in general, and the techniques in this book in particular. This is why, as practical as possible given your lifestyle, you need to practice the mental and physical exercises you've learned in this book; perhaps augmenting that knowledge by enrolling in a course of self-defense study taught by a qualified instructor—someone not just teaching "ancient Chinese secrets" but teaching a little common sense as well.

There's nothing wrong with learning self-defense from a perfect human specimen: 240-pounds of lean, mean ex-Marine. But how many of us are perfect human specimens?

One of the first things you learned in this book was keeping it real—being real with yourself, so as to realistically assess—and survive—a dangerous situation.

The following examples of specific attacks and possible defensive counters are just that, examples of possible defenses. Don't lock yourself in to only one defense scenario. Don't tell yourself, "If the bully does this, I'll do this. And then when he responds by doing this, I'll counter with this . . ."

War on the battlefield, with troops and tanks and such might be compared to chess, but a no-holds-barred street assault-slash-fight for survival would be more appropriately compared to two hungry dogs fighting over a bone!

Sure there's strategy involved in surviving any dangerous street fight—most of that prefight strategy: take care of your business during daylight hours, don't pick up the hitchhikers in the hockey mask, and so on. And practical tactical considerations: He who runs away today lives another day!

But, by and large, when attacked without warning, by the time you realize what's happening your body is already fighting for its life, while the stunned overanalytic part of your brain is still screaming, "My God! What's happening!?!" At times like that—and unfortunately there will be times like that—only the combination of your present desperation plus your prior preparation will see you safely through the ordeal.

So get your mind right—desperation. And put some practice—preparation—into learning the following defenses to the most common attacks you're likely to run into out there on those mean streets.

Defense Against a Punch

Job One: Get out of the way! Keep distance and objects (blockers) between you and your bully.

There are ten directions you can move to avoid a punch, corresponding to the eight compass points, plus "up" (jumping up, out of the way), and "down" (ducking). Theoretically, you could keep backing up, ducking, and dodging punches all day and night, until your bully gets too tired to continue. Realistic in some situations, not practical in most, though it did seem to work a lot of the time for Caine of *Kung-fu!*

Ducking and dodging is a good delaying tactic only when you think someone will be coming to your rescue. Otherwise, you should consider taking more proactive action.

First, don't allow the puncher to "box" you up, and remember your "Spear-stepping." (Figures 10, 11, and 12)

Having avoided the point of his "spear," you are now in position to counterattack into his centerline: striking into his groin with your reverse Sword-hand or "Turtle's Head," perhaps "reopening negotiations" by seizing a Tiger-claw grip on his testicles! Or you can strike up into his chin and face with your Rising palm/Tiger-claw strikes. (Figure 20) Pick up a pencil, pen, or other pointed object and stab it into his fist each time he punches. Use your "Short-wing" elbow to block-strike into his punching arm, damaging his arm and allowing you time to counterattack. This technique comes from Cao Cao's iron wall kung-fu:

Figure 29. "Iron Wall Block-Strike."

a. Intending to attack you with "The ol' One-two," your attacker throws his initial leading arm punch . . .

b. Immediately counter by attacking into his punching arm with a "Short-wing" elbow block-strike.

c. When (if!) your attacker follows through with his second arm punch, suddenly reverse the direction of your elbow to first block-strike into his second punching arm before then seizing hold of it.

d. Having successfully seized a hold on his attacking arm, use your other arm as a fulcrum to strike into the exposed elbow of his trapped arm—either applying an AK-2 Arm-bar lock or else breaking his arm at the elbow. Remember the "never hold" rule.

e. Augment your AK-2 Arm-bar by pivoting away from your trapped attacker while maintaining your Arm-bar (review Figure 13).

Just because you can't out punch your bully doesn't mean you can't use Musashi's strategy of "Cutting at the Edges," damaging his punching equipment.

Remember: There are no blocks, only strikes. So don't "block" his punching arm—strike into it. Take away his attack tools and he will have nothing with which to build his victory.

Defense Against a Kick

As already mentioned, the two most likely kicks you will run into will be a straight "Front Snap-Kick" and a forward "Round-Kick" (aka "Round-house"). Use the same pen-pencil stabbing defense you used against your

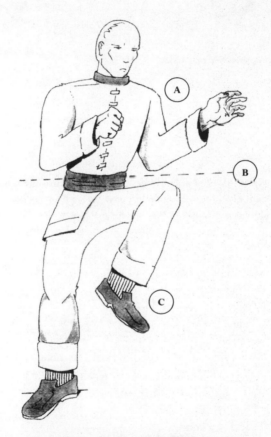

Figure 30. The Waist Rule.

a. Defend attacks directed at targets above your waist with your hands, forearms, and elbows.
b. Defend kicks and other attacks (e.g., grabbing lunges) targeting your lower body and legs with your own legs.
c. You can also use your blocking legs to "jam" an attacker's forward momentum and, when in close, use your legs to prevent him from kicking and kneeing you. See Figure 21.

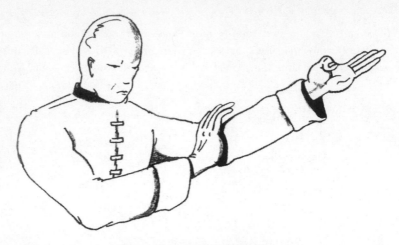

Figure 31. Augmented Blocking.

Augment your blocking arm by "reinforcing" it with your other arm. For
example, when blocking with your left arm, shore it up by placing your right
palm on the inside of the blocking arm (*see also* Figure 22).

bully's punching hand on his legs and feet when he tries to kick above your
waist.

When it comes to blocking in general and blocking kicks in particular,
martial artists have an axiom known as the "Waist Rule," which states, "If it's
below your waist, block with your legs. If it's above your waist, block with
your hands." What this means is that low kicks are defended against by either
turning the leg (to deflect a kick), or else you raise your leg to block against
a kick aimed at your knees or thigh (see Figure 30).

Use the Chinese-Cross Kick from Figure 21 to "jam" (stifle) his kick
before it gets off the ground.

Of course, the best way to "block" a kick or sweep to your lower legs is
by lifting your leg out of the way. Not only does this save you being hit (and
possibly knocked to the ground) but his missing can also throw him off balance—something you should be ready to take advantage of.

Correspondingly, always block strikes to your trunk and head with your
arms and elbows.

When you use your arms to block, remember "One in, one out. One

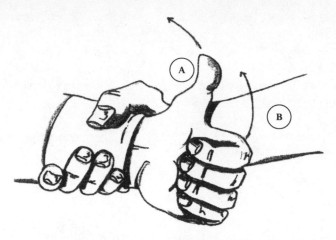

Figure 32. "Hitchhiker Wrist Escape."

a. As soon as your attacker grabs your wrist, immediately stick your thumb up in the air and "follow" it, pulling your wrist back and out of your attacker's grip.

b. Variation: Having used this "Hitchhiker" move to escape your attacker's grip, you can now easily seize control of his wrist by simply draping your freed hand over top his wrist. This puts you in position to follow through with a multitude of techniques, including placing him in an AK-1 Wrist-lock (Figure 25). *See also* Figures 26 and 33.

Note: This "Hitchhiker" wrist escape takes advantage of the fact that an attacker's grip is weakest at the thumb. When performed correctly, this technique requires little or no strength to perform and can easily be used by young children to escape an adult abductor.

up, one down," "There are no blocks, only *no-blocks,"* and, as much as possible, use one arm to augment (support) the other blocking arm, as shown in Figure 31.

For defensive blocking against being stomped while on the ground, review "Ground Technique," Figure 16.

Defense Against a Wrist Grab

A person's grip is weakest at the thumb. Therefore, when someone seizes your wrist, point your thumb up (like a hitchhiker—see Figure 32) and *follow that thumb*. Even a child can escape from an abductor's grasp using this technique. Take time to teach this to your children.

Notice how this "Thumb Escape" puts your hand in perfect position for then reversing the hold by placing your bully into a Wrist-lock and, there, into an AK-2 Arm-bar, giving you a double lock on your bully (review Figures 25 and 26).

Figure 33. "Trapped Wrist Escape Follow Through."

a. Having reversed your attacker's wrist hold (Figure 32), and/or having otherwise secured a grip on his wrist . . .

b. Suddenly step back and down (deep back stance), unbalancing him, "leading" him to the ground.

Note: This technique can also be augmented by first applying an AK-1 wrist lock prior to taking your attacker to the ground.

Kid tip: Even a child can use an AK-2 Arm-bar maneuver on a larger adult. When his wrist has been seized by an adult, the child uses the handlebars of his bicycle, the open window of his would-be abductor's car, a fence, telephone pole, or signpost to lock-out the predator's reaching arm.

Should you meet resistance to this (or any) self-defense escape, augment your AK-1 and AK-2 technique by unbalancing your attacker. Use the Cross-Kick from Figure 21 again, striking into his knee, both locking his leg

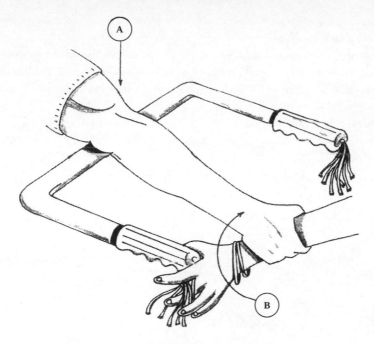

Figure 34. "AK-2 Arm-Bar Variation: Child's Escape."

a. A child can easily employ an "AK-2 Arm-bar to escape a would-be abductor by using the handlebars of his bike as the fulcrum.

b. Having slammed his attcker's arm down onto the handlebars fulcrum, the child can then escape using the "Hitchhiker" wrist escape in Figure 32.

Note: This same technique can be used with an open car window, a signpost, etc. as a fulcrum.

out (preventing him recovering his balance) and making him instinctually loosen his grip because his immediate priority is not falling, as opposed to holding on to you.

Defense Against a Lapel Grab

Your bully seizes a hold on the front of your shirt or your lapel, and as he draws back his other hand to punch you:

Immediately countergrab a hold on his gripping hand while your free arm simultaneously uses the iron wall elbow block-strike (Figure 29) to deflect his punch.

Immediately upon deflecting the punch, your blocking arm continues across your chest and jams its thumb—hard!—into the back of the bully's gripping hand. Immediately dig the rest of your fingers into the pad of his gripping hand.

Now, as you take a step back and down (i.e., lower your weight without bending forward), twist his now trapped hand into a Wrist-lock. By taking another step back, you will "lead" your bully face-first into the ground.

It's okay to use both hands to reinforce this Wrist-lock.

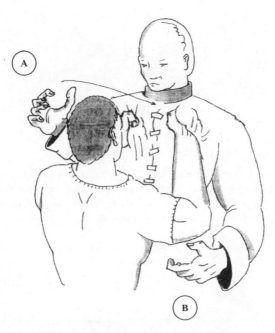

Figure 35. "Double-Hand Grab-Choke Escape."

    a. Having been seized by an attacker who is using both his hands to grab your lapels or who is attempting to choke you, immediately cross your hand over his near hand to seize a hold on his far hand and apply an AK-1 Wrist-lock (see Figure 25).

    b. Augment and follow through by applying an AK-2 Arm-bar/break.

Note: This technique can also easily be used as a counter to a single-handed choke.

Variation: Pinned with your back against a wall, and unable to take a step back and down, forcefully thrust a Spear-hand strike toward his eyes and/or throat, eliciting a flinch reaction, distracting him long enough for you to apply your Wrist-lock with your other hand.

Defense Against a Choke

Choke holds have four variations: front and back, one-handed, and double-handed.

Defense Against a Front Choke

Respond to a front single-handed choke using the same technique you did for defeating your bully's lapel grab. (See Figure 25.) This technique can also be used to counter a two-handed front choke, although two other defenses are also effective:

The first, when a bully is attempting to choke you with both hands, is to strike up between his arms with a punch or a Spear-hand directly to his throat. The second is the Two-Handed Tiger-claw rake, taken straight from the hu-gui fighting form. (See Figure 22 and the hu-gui fighting form in the appendix of this book.)

However, if your arms are shorter than your attacker's, then you can use the "Snake Crosses Log" technique:

FYI: This technique can also be used when you are pinned to the ground with an attacker sitting on your chest trying to choke the life out of you. Review Illustration 16.

Defense Against a Rear Choke

For a choke from behind, use your rear elbow strikes (to ribs, solar plexus, neck, face, and temple) as well as backward head butts to make him loosen his grip.

When occupied with strangling your upper body, an attacker often neglects protecting his own lower body. Therefore, attack his groin with backward Hammer-fist, Sword-hand blows, and Tiger-claw grabs. Stomp backward into his knees and down onto his instep.

If your attacker attempts to lift you off your feet while strangling you from behind go with the flow. By adding your push to his pull, you can propel yourself up and back, toppling both yourself and your attacker to the

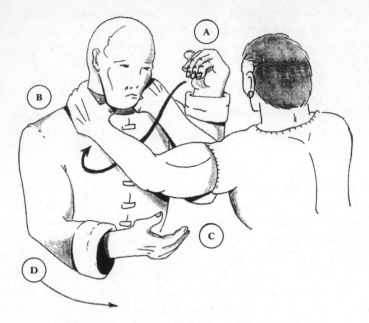

Figure 36. "Snake-Crosses-Log Choke Escape."

a. As your attacker attempts to choke you with both hands, slide your hand over his arm closest to your hand and then under his other arm (like a serpent slithering over one log under the next).

b. Now "lever" your arm down at the elbow and up at the forearm, forcing his arms to cross one another . . .

c. Simultaneously pivot away from your attacker.

    At the very least, this maneuver will force your attacker to let go his hold on you. If your attacker stubbornly tries to maintain his grip on you, the combination of your twisting his arms and pivotiong away will throw him to the floor.

d. Augment this move by striking into your attacker with your free hand, for example, striking into his elbow in preparation for an AK-2 Arm-bar/break.

Note: An elderly person can use this same technique by substituting his walking cane (threading it over one arm, under the other, then twising it) in place of his arm.

ground. You can also "kick off" from a wall, tree, and so on to unexpectedly push both you and your bully off balance.

Because you "see" this move coming, you will be able to brace yourself for the impact of hitting the ground while he will take the brunt of the impact, perhaps knocking the wind from him, and/or otherwise disorienting him.

When lifted off your feet, you can also lock your legs around his legs (close to his knees), unbalancing him and causing you both to fall to the ground.

Being choked and not being able to breathe is a frightening prospect, akin to drowning in water, which elicits the same panic reactions from the body. Even professional fighters sometimes panic when their oxygen is cut off. You can clearly see this by how quickly highly trained MMA (Mixed Martial Arts) fighters "tap out" once their opponent succeeds in placing them in a solid choke hold.

When—carefully—practicing your choke escape technique with a friend, try this: Right before starting, forcefully exhale all the air from your lungs. Then try to perform your escape maneuver before drawing in a fresh breath. There is a big difference in struggling with an attacker when you have two full lungs of air (giving you two to three minutes leeway) versus having had the wind knocked out of you and having to fight with no oxygen left in your body (thirty seconds to "lights out!").

Challenge: Think you're in good "fighting shape"? Exhale all the breath in your body and try throwing punches for thirty seconds.

Defense Against a Weapon

The trusted and time-tested martial arts rule for confronting an assailant with a weapon is: "Fight the man, don't fight the weapon." Whereas you can't break the steel that a knife or gun is made of, you can break the all-too flesh-and-blood hand that holds these weapons.

Most people untrained in the martial arts in general, and weapons in particular, have an inflated fear of exactly what weapons are actually capable of, and much of this misinformed fear is fueled by "if it bleeds it leads" media reports, by movies, and increasingly by violent video game portrayals.

Part of your realistic self-defense training must involve a discussion of unarmed defense against weapons, ideally with you learning how to use those weapons yourself. This is only our being realistically prepared for what's out there.

Not only is it possible you will find yourself one day in a dark alley facing such weapons, but there is also the possibility that, in such a kill-or-be-killed situation, you might succeed in wresting an assailant's weapon away from him . . . and then use it on him!

You will also want to be able to identify weapons—revolver or automatic, shotgun versus AK-47—so as to better inform law enforcement personnel what kind(s) of weapons your attacker is carrying.

First off, when faced with an armed attacker wanting your money or car—give him your money or car. Property is not worth dying over. Not even your wedding ring. (I'm sure your better half would much rather have you come home safe and sound without your wedding band than to have to identify your battered and bullet-riddled corpse by your wedding band?)

Of course, it's a different story when the bully isn't after your lunch money, instead he's after you. Beyond those thugs and crack-heads who just want your money, there's a bevy of bizarre psychopaths and predators who are out for flesh and blood—literally.

The number-one rule when an assailant pulls a weapon on you is don't go anywhere with an attacker—it's called a "secondary crime site," and that's always where the hikers stumble across the "partially decomposed body." If a thug wants your money or car, he wants the goods ASAP, and he wants to leave the scene of the crime ASAP. If your assailant hesitates, lingers, tries to order you into the back room "to tie you up," or tries to force you to get into a vehicle, you're likely facing a psycho who has more than money on his mind.

Never, ever go anywhere with such a thug. He's just trying to get you into a more convenient spot where he can rape, torture, and ultimately kill you.

Escape at all cost. There are many examples of hostages escaping from such psychos by jumping out second-story windows, by diving through plate-glass windows, jumping from fast-moving vehicles, even deliberately crashing their cars. Do whatever you think necessary to survive. You can recover from cuts, scrapes, and broken bones, but you can't from death.

Gunmen whose sole intent is to rob a store might take the time to lock workers in a walk-in freezer before fleeing. Seldom will robbers take the time to herd those workers into a back room to bound and gag them, unless they have decided to leave no witnesses. Having bound and gagged their victims, it's a simple matter for those gunmen to kill each and every one of those now helpless victims. We read about it all the time.

FYI: Gunmen who take the time to hide their identities (ski mask, etc.) are less likely to feel the need to kill witnesses. Consequently, "robbers" who storm in without masks, who show no concern about witnesses seeing their faces, may have already decided to leave no witnesses.

The same goes for a crazed gunman wielding an automatic weapon forcing his way into a school and ordering all the students to cram themselves together in one corner of the room or to lay face down on the floor. It doesn't matter if it's a modern classroom at Columbine or Virginia Tech, or a quaint one-room Amish schoolhouse in Pennsylvania . . . once a crazed gunman succeeds in getting all his ducks in a row—literally!—it's a shooting gallery.

That's why you never go anywhere with a predator, not even into the back room. Once that predator herds you into that back room or locks you in the trunk of the car, that's all she wrote.

As we've maintained throughout this book, to fight back or not to fight back, that is the question. Each of us have to make that choice when the time comes—and we pray that time never comes. If your decision is to fight back—Flight 93!—then it's a good idea to arm yourself with knowledge of what different types of weapons are out there and what they can and cannot do.

Defense Against a Gun

Believe it or not, the odds are in your favor when confronted by a gunman. Gunmen, especially those after your money, don't want to shoot you, they just want to scare you into giving them your money. Give them your money.

First, the odds are he won't shoot, and even if he does shoot, he'll hesitate for a couple seconds—hesitation on his part helps you.

Most street thugs get their firearms "training" from playing *Grand Theft Auto* videogames. That's why, in all those convenience store surveillance videos you see the robbers holding their pistols high-up, sideways, with their wrists bent—exactly like they do on those "gansta" music videos.

That doesn't mean such young thugs aren't dangerous. They are dangerous . . . *and they are stupid,* which makes them twice as dangerous. Give them the money and, like the rabid dogs they are, don't look them directly in the eye—they take that as a challenge. Would we could convince them that getting a GED was a challenge! End of editorial.

Second, if your thug does shoot, the odds are he'll miss you, even if he's spraying bullets all over the place. It's especially hard to hit a moving target.

Some experts tell you to run in a zigzag pattern in order to make it harder for a gunman to zero in on you. My thought on the matter is that zigzagging slows you down and your efforts would be better spent getting as far away from the gunman as possible as soon as possible.

Third, if he does luck out and hit you, the odds are he won't hit anything vital. You'd be surprised how many places you can get hit by a bullet and survive. Barring massive blood loss, only a shot directly to the brain, to your heart, or considerable damage to your spine or internal organs will result in immediate death. A bullet in the arm, leg, even the lung is survivable.

Finally, even if he succeeds in hitting you, the odds are help will arrive in time to save you. 9-1-1, EMT, they save more than they lose.

So the odds are in your favor. But each person must decide for himself.

And there's time and circumstance to consider: If a masked gunman walks into a convenience store or bank, the odds are he's there to get some money. If an unmasked gunman suddenly barges into your school classroom, the odds are he's not there to rob everybody.

When forced to counterattack a gunman, always keep a "blocker" between you and the gunman as you rush toward him. This can be something as large as a table (wielded by two or more people); a chair, held so the seat absorbs or deflects, or at least slows any bullets fired in your direction; a metal or even plastic tray; even a large book can deflect or absorb a bullet meant for you.*

When defending against a gun, it matters whether it's a long-barreled gun (rifle or shotgun) or a handgun.

Long Guns If your assailant is wielding a long gun, notice whether or not

---

*A bullet slows to one degree or another anytime it has to pass through any object. Even passing through thick layers of clothing can help slow a bullet, causing it to do less damage upon impact with your body.

it has a magazine clip (where the bullets are stored) projecting midway down its length, most often directly in front of the trigger. This is a good indication he has a "fully automatic" or a "machine-gun" long gun capable of literally spraying the room with bullets, killing dozens within seconds, before he has to reload. If you survive his initial "emptying" of this clip, you may be able to escape or rush him while he is changing clips. Other long guns, bolt-action rifles, and most shotguns have to be "levered" (recocked) after each shot, precious seconds you can use to escape or rush the gunman.

Handguns. Handguns come in revolver and automatic versions. A revolver looks like one of those guns you see in cowboy movies, with a revolving

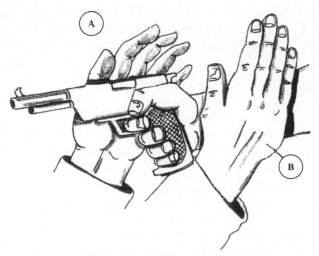

Figure 37. "Defense Against a Gun."

a. Having closed with your pistol-wielding attacker, Spearpoint-step out of the direct line of fire and trap your attacker's gunhand between your two hands by pressing inward on the back of his hand (or by twisting the gunbarrel) in toward his centerline while . . .

b. Simultaneously your other hand presses against the inside of his gunhand wrist, helping to turn the gun in toward his centerline.

c. Having safely and successfully turned his gunhand in toward his centerline, you are now in position to apply an AK-1 Wrist-lock and/or AK-2 Arm-bar/break (review Figures 25 and 26, and 33–36).

cylinder (usually containing six bullets) fired by squeezing the trigger each time. When wrestling a revolver away from a gunman, prevent his gun from firing by jamming your hand over the hammer (situated just above where he is gripping the pistol).

Automatic pistols can hold twice as many bullets as a revolver. These bullets are held in a magazine clip situated in the handle of the firearm. Semiautomatic pistols fire only when the trigger is squeezed. Fully automatic handguns can empty their clip (like a machine gun) anytime the trigger is held down. As with automatic rifles, escape or rush and overpower a gunman carrying an automatic pistol as he is putting a fresh clip into his weapon. Placing a firm grip on the "slide" that runs across the top of an automatic pistol can prevent it from firing.

When forced to wrestle with a handgun-wielding gunman, use movement similar to your Wrist-lock, by levering the handgun inward toward the gunman's body. You will be aided in this by the fact that the gunman's finger will be trapped in the trigger guard and, in not wanting to let go of his weapon, the gunman will, in effect, be forcing his own hand into a painful Wrist-lock position.

If you cannot lever the handgun inward toward the gunman's body, try to keep the gun pointed toward the ceiling, as there is less chance of an accidental discharge shooting you in the lower body or accidentally hitting another innocent victim.

While your attacker's hands are occupied (over his head) fighting you for the weapon, strike with knees to his exposed groin and/or stomps to his instep.

Likewise, having closed with a gunman in order to wrestle a long gun from him, having seized a hold on the barrel and stock, lever the rifle toward the ceiling so as to minimize the chances of an accidental discharge. Again, the gunman's finger being trapped in the trigger guard and the fact that he will not want to relinquish his hold on the rifle aid you in your task.

As with your overhead handgun, counterstrike into your attacker's lower body with knees to the groin, stomps to his feet, and Roundhouse sweeps to his legs.

Defense Against a Knife

Knives are often used to threaten people—and they are threatening! At least to the untrained. When a predator puts a knife to your throat and orders you to go with him he either doesn't want to kill you and may be more intent on rape, or else he wants to get you to a more secluded site where he can then kill you at his convenience.

If he wants your money, he'll take your money and flee. If he wants you, no amount of money is going to save your life. How many times do we have to tell you: "Never go anywhere with an attacker." We can't emphasize that enough. Granted, being cut or stabbed is frightening, but it is survivable.

Knives and other bladed weapons come at you in two ways: either your attacker is thrusting forward—trying to stab you—or else he is swinging the cutting edge back and forth in front of him.

The vital areas you need to protect against stabbing attacks are your eyes, neck, chest, and abdomen. Against a cutting attack: your neck, throat, and lower abdomen.

Getting cut or stabbed in the arm is going to hurt like hell, but it's not going to kill you unless you hang around long enough to bleed to death, and then only in the unlikely event that your attacker has cut one of your major arteries. Severed fingers can be reattached, a life cut short can't.

The blocks and strategic positioning you've learned (and practiced) already will guard you through these attacks. Tried-and-true martial arts wisdom tells us that "If a man can't hit you with his hand, he can't cut you with his knife."

Recall earlier in this book how you learned to better predict which way an unarmed attacker was going to come at you by noticing his stance and how he held his hands. The same system applies to a knife-wielding attacker.

A knife-wielding attacker holds his weapon in either an "outside grip" or an "inside grip."

An outside grip keeps the point of his weapon pointing up, out from his hand on the thumb side. When using this grip, an attacker generally swings his knife back and forth, trying to cut rather than stab. However, using this grip, he can also stab upward (usually targeting your gut and, rarer, your throat).

An inside grip reverses the grip of the outside grip, with the point of the knife (ice pick, etc.) extending down from the other side of the palm. Aggressors using this grip often hide their blade till the last instant by holding it flush with their forearm. Remember, if an attacker is intent on killing you, you'll probably never see the knife coming—either he'll keep it hidden to the last instant, or else he'll attack you from behind (Omar, 2001). This inside grip is used for stabbing down at the victim, usually targeting the neck, back, upper chest, and, to a lesser extent, the face.

Once you've mastered your block/no-block technique, so long as an attacker can't hit you with his hand, he won't be able to hit you with a knife.

Protect yourself from a knife-wielding bully by picking up any environmental weapon you can scavenge. Keep the knife-wielding attacker as far away as possible. keep blocking objects between you and your attacker as much as possible. Use an umbrella, golf club, or hefty stick to prod your attacker away and/or knock his weapon from his hand and/or pummel him.

You'll especially want to protect your leading hand by wearing thick gloves or else by covering your hand with a shoe or other protection. Likewise, wrap a jacket or thick towel around your forearm. Wrap your arm but leave your hands free to grab hold and counterstrike your attacker.

Having closed with a knife-wielding attacker, seize a hold on his knife arm and counter with your AK-1 and AK-2 maneuvers (see Figures 25 and 26).

As when grappling with a gunman, lever the knife inward toward your attacker's centerline (review Figure 32). You can also use kicks: Your Chinese-Cross Kick (Figure 21), your Front Snap-Kick (Figure 23), and your Roundhouse sweeping-in kick (Figure 24). Beware of his stabbing into your kicking legs.

Remember that *you're not fighting the weapon, you're fighting the man.* All too often people become distracted by the weapon. Don't forget: While you're staring at that knife in his hand, your bully can still kick you in the nuts.

Likewise, don't be intimidated by the size of an attacker's knife. Larger knives (like a sword or machete) are actually easier to defend against (because they are harder and slower for your assailant to swing) than are smaller knives (which are harder to see and to wrest away from him).

A blade-wielding attacker will come at you either stabbing inward at you, targeting your abdomen and face, sometimes stabbing downward from overhead. Or else he will attack you by cutting back and forth in a swinging motion, almost always cutting at your abdomen.

When unable to keep distance between you and a knife-wielding attacker, use your Spearpoint-stepping to get inside a stabbing attack (Figure 12), where you can then counter with no-blocks and strikes (Figures 14 and 20).

Figure 38. Defense Against a Bludgeon.

Finding yourself attacked by a bludgeon-wielding attacker, jump back, allowing the attacker to complete his full swing, then suddenly closing with him before he has a chance to retract his swing.

a. As he completes the full arc of his swing, neither of his arms will be a danger to you.

Close quickly to jam his return swing as you counterstrike into his centerline (e.g., knee to the groin).

b. At full swing, his weight will be fully committed.

c. At full swing, he may already be partially off balance by the force of his swing.

d. Variation: Use this same strategy when your attacker raises his club over his head to strike, closing and countering into his fully exposed centerline as he draws his arms up to their highest point.

Defense Against a Bludgeon

> *"Speak softly and carry a big stick . . . to make him SCREAM*
> *LOUDLY!"*
> —Duke Hohvart

An attacker wielding a bludgeon, for example, a baseball bat, attacks in the same way a knife attacker does: either by swinging the bludgeon back and forth in front of his body, or else by striking down from overhead.

When unable to get out of the way of a descending bludgeon attack, use an environmental weapons "blocker" (tray, large book, stout stick held horizontal) to take the brunt of the impact of the bludgeon striking (See Figure 18).

Barring that, when forced to block with your arm, always block at an angle so as to deflect most of the impact. (Review Figure 3.) Immediately after deflecting such a blow, close with your attacker, before he can raise his bludgeon for another blow. Use your Spearpoint stepping to avoid the descending blow and to get in close to your attacker.

When confronting an attacker swinging a bludgeon back and forth (like a baseball swing), wait until the bludgeon passes by you and then close with your attacker before he has time to bring the bat back from his wide swing.

Not only will this timely maneuver allow you to close with your attacker without getting hit but also it will allow you to close with him *when he is most vulnerable:* he is in an even stance, so he's unable to kick; both his hands are occupied holding the bat; and his arms are both turned to one side.

For additional self-defense techniques, see—and practice!—the hu-gui tiger in the appendix.

6

"Just Walk Away" . . . *and Why Sometimes You Can't*

"No plausible scenario was made for how this horror could have been prevented once he began that morning."
—**Virginia Tech president Charles Steger in Kurz and Smith (2007)**

From the playground to the battleground, by their seeming random acts of violence, bullies are the bane of our existence, turning a leisurely walk home into running a gauntlet.

Sometimes, we wish we could just walk away from trouble, from troubling times, from our personal bullies, and from international bullies that—if the media is to be believed—seem to be getting the upper hand, by taking more and more ground everyday.

In the aftermath of tragedies such as Columbine and Virginia Tech, we do want we can to pick up the pieces, to try to make sense of it all. Mostly, we just try to make sense of it all. And we help out where we can, each in our own way.

In September 2007, the Dave Matthews Band headlined a benefit concert in Blacksburg for the families of the victims of the Virginia Tech massacre. Thanks Dave.

Some help with inspirational music, others have only prayers to offer. Still others try to reassure us with the facts that the odds are still on our side.

In an effort to alleviate some of our anxiety, James Alan Fox, a professor of criminal justice at Northeastern University, points out that incidents like the Virginia Tech massacre are actually few and far between.

A coauthor (with Jack Levin and Kenna Quinet) of *The Will to Kill: Making Sense of Senseless Murder* (2008), Fox explains that with over twenty million college students in the United States, the chances of being murdered on campus are about as likely as being fatally struck by lightning. Between 2001 to 2005 just seventy-six homicides were reported on college campuses in the United States:

> "When compared with virtually any metropolitan area, a student's chances of dying on homicide actually decrease once he or she steps on campus." (2007)

And, of the homicides that do take place on campus, the majority were acquaintance killings or drug deals gone bad, as opposed to a blood-crazed madman. Scant comfort to those who lose children to any cause.

Professor Fox concludes with the respectful observation that bulletproof backpacks, excessive attention to emergency response systems, and the like only serve as constant reminders of vulnerability, reinforcing the overblown image we have of students as targets.

Thanks for the statistics, Professor Fox . . . but sometimes a little paranoia is a good thing—sharpening the senses, helping us focus; perhaps even—indulge me as I wax philosophical—encouraging us to take time to stop and smell the roses, before a momentary lapse of attention on our part and/or the mounting madness collecting in another troubled soul's mind forces us to smell a spray of funeral flowers instead.

So with all due respect to the dear professor, I think I'm still going to buy my kid one of those instructional videos demonstrating how students can "outsmart a bullet" by running from side to side in a zigzag pattern. (Even though I'm still personally convinced the way to go is a straight line—as far away as possible, as fast as possible!) Oh yeah, and one of those new bulletproof backpacks, too.

Still others encourage us to take more preventative (preemptive) actions to safeguard ourselves and our children against the bullies of the world. Specifically, that we need to become more alert to the warning signs given off by troubled youth and that we need to take those signs more seriously in order to better prevent troubled youth from growing up to be troubled adults . . . assuming they make it that far.

Rachel Johnson (2007) has the foresight to point out what is obvious to many, and hard to swallow for others: that what we need to be concentrating on are those very red flags that everyone seems to remember in hindsight, as the body bags are being carried out.

Says Johnson about gunman Cho and the tragedy at Virginia Tech:

> "There were so many warning signs, from the scary stories he wrote in English class to the way he interacted with everyone around him. [He] was dealing with so much more than just typical, daily issues, and he tried to make that obvious through his actions. How could he not have been confronted after he wrote the gruesome story about killing his classmates?
>
> "The Columbine High School shooting was a similar situation and unfortunately is a precedent for the Virginia Tech shootings. The Columbine shooters were troubled young men whose actions and attitudes cried out for someone to simply notice them.
>
> "Cho was no different. He was trying to be radical so that finally someone would take notice of him. Unfortunately, his actions and behavior were disregarded, and he finally got the attention that he was looking for only after a massacre.
>
> "Let this be a lesson to all to take the time to listen to one another and pay attention to warning signs." (2007:10A)

Many agree with Johnson. For example, a report issued in August 2007 criticized the Virginia Tech University for missing many signs Cho was a threat:

> "[I]if only the University had recognized Cho's long record of mental instability and monitored him more closely." ("Least Risky Path Raises Risk," *USA TODAY,* September 4, 2007)

Yet, can we realistically expect a full psychological screening before a person is allowed to enter college? Ideal, but hardly realistic.

The psychologist Erich Fromm observed in *Escape from Freedom* (1941) that, given the choice between freedom or security, the human animal will choose security every time. Thus, while civil libertarians are quick to point out the potential dangers of curtailing an individual's right to privacy, others feel that they are getting a bargain, trading a little privacy for peace of mind: "Privacy laws might need adapting so that universities know in advance who will need special help." Personal safety versus safeguarding our civil liberties? Hopefully, we will be able to find a compromise somewhere between "screening" on the one hand, and "screaming" on the other!

When tragedies such as Columbine and Virginia Tech land on the doorstep of our consciousness, no one knows the cause, but everyone has a boogeyman. Everyone has their favorite demon. But for every sacred demon, there's a sacred cow.

Our nomination for Best Supporting Villain might be the general erosion of "traditional family values" and the undermining of "parental authority," but we must tread lightly lest we find ourselves accused of goose-stepping all over our child's inalienable rights to "life, liberty, and the pursuit of happiness." (I guess it would be a moot point to point out that "life" is the first right listed and that the rest become kinda moot unless we succeed in keeping our children alive!)

However, we may be convinced that violent music lyrics and even more violent video games are the culprit, but we dare not stand accused of advocating censorship in any shape or form.

And heaven help us if we happen to think the ready availability of thirty-round-clip assault weapons make it just a wee-bit easier to mow down thirty students in thirty seconds than does easy access to a crossbow. Heaven help us because Charlton Heston certainly isn't going to!

Indeed, one man's demon is another man's sacred cow.

Still, in our rush to find answers—any answer!—to "Make sure something like this never happens again," we must be cautious not to make the same "mistake" bullies are infamous for making, that of erring on the side of "overkill" to solve real or imagined problems. What was it Nietzsche said? Beware of fighting dragons lest you find yourself becoming a dragon.

Thus we read about the mother in Florida hauled into court because she forced her daughter to fight back against a school bully. Or the cautionary tale of overreaction coming out of Colorado Springs, where the Discovery Canyon Campus elementary school banned playing the game of tag after some children complained they were harassed or chased against their will *(USA TODAY,* August 30, 2007:5A).

We must always be careful not to throw the very babies we are trying to save out with the bullying bathwater. We must never punish all for the madness of a few.

Would that we could just walk away from such decisions. Let someone else make the hard decisions . . .

So if just walking away isn't the answer, what is?

Increased awareness. First, increasing awareness in our personal lives, then learning to translate that personal awareness into more community-wide awareness, encouraging others—by example—to do the same.

And, yes, the Chinese have a saying for this too:

> "A peaceful man makes for a peaceful family. Peaceful families make for a peaceful village. Peaceful villages make for a peaceful land. Peaceful lands make for a peace world."

Change the word "peaceful" for "aware" and we might be on to something.

Take heart. Embrace hope. There have been improvements in our overall awareness of, and thus effectiveness in, dealing with bullies at all levels of society, be those bullies in the classroom, the bedroom, or the boardroom. Admittedly, such progress comes in spurts, with peaks and valleys of attention given the problem, a problem all too often suddenly—abrupt and bloody!—jerked back to the forefront of our consciousness by yet another tragedy.

IMPROVEMENTS IN THE BEDROOM

Over the years, we've seen an increase in both the availability and effectiveness of our overall relationship abuse Sheltering system, making it more likely an abused spouse or girlfriend will walk away (run!) from an abusive relationship.

Somewhere along the way we finally realized we could make it easier for a battered woman to break free, to take the kids and run, when she knows she and the kids have somewhere to run to.

Here again awareness is the key: Helping those women (and in some cases, men) become more aware that they do have choices and helping them realize that they are strong enough to make those choices. Fortunately, where a battered woman might not listen to the police or to PSA's telling them to get out of an abusive relationship, thank God they'll listen to Oprah! Thanks, Oprah.

One of the most important factors helping eliminate relationship bullying is the willingness of others to intervene, to get involved. The bystander effect be damned yet again!

But all agree that a woman's best defense is her growing awareness of her rightful place in the universe, with all rights and privileges therein. Rights and privileges worth fighting for. Any other alternative is unacceptable.

It's either increase a woman's awareness, while increasing our willingness to help, or else give every bride a can of gasoline along with the bridal bouquet.

IMPROVEMENTS IN THE BOARDROOM

Companies, and their employees, are finally increasing their awareness of the causes, conditions, and cost of sexual harassment and other forms of bullying in the workplace.

Workplace dissatisfaction need not fester until it erupts into internecine litigation or explodes into gunfire. All too often we've seen the explosive results of unacknowledged egos and unchecked emotion.

Companies can no longer accept (read: "afford") the explicit or implicit indifference and/or complicity of supervisors and superiors when it comes to workplace bullying.

Despite this, according to the *Los Angeles Times,* the number of "bullying bosses" may be on the rise due to staff shortages, requiring companies to rely more and more on bottom line–oriented managers with less and less people skills.

But help is on the way in the form of a bill recently proposed in New Jersey that will allow bullied workers to claim $25,000 in damages if an employer, either explicitly or by their indifference, creates "an abusive work environment."

New York, Vermont, Washington, and California are all following suit (or is that filing suit?), with newly proposed "sue-the-boss" legislation of their own. (Bacon et al., 2007:3A)

IMPROVEMENTS IN THE CLASSROOM

Increased awareness, and timely action, work in classroom bullying situations—from the recess scuffle to confrontations with potentially more deadly consequences.

For example, in Joplin, Missouri, a court ruled in July 2007 that a fourteen-year-old boy should be tried as an adult on four felony counts stemming from his firing an assault weapon at Memorial Middle School. Luckily, the school didn't live up to its name, as the boy, thirteen at the time, was over-powered after his gun jammed as he was attempting to shoot the principal *(USA TODAY,* September 13, 2007:7A).

We all need to lose our "After-the-fact, after the body-bags" attitude, in favor of putting our back and greenbacks into early intervention by preventing bully babies from becoming bully boys from becoming bully gunmen. An ounce of prevention is surely worth a pint of blood.

We all need to admit that bullies start young. Therefore, it's only logical to put comprehensive understanding and concentrated effort into catching such bullies early on, catching the playground bully before he grows into the bullying teen, who "takes" a wife to become the bullying husband, or else goes off to college where he becomes Cho.

In Cheyenne, Wyoming, an on-going statewide education effort was begun in 2007 that stresses positive youth development and combats bullying. Efforts include a group of country music stars participating in a radio program aimed at eliminating bullying in schools by helping bullied children cope without resorting to violence. The one-hour radio program, hosted by the country legend Charlie Daniels, is being made available to stations nationwide *(USA TODAY,* September 20, 2007:4A).

So what about the budding bullies we don't identify in preschool, in grade school, or in high school? What about those who make it all the way undetected, unsuspected—onto vulnerable college campuses?

Increased security gives comfort to some.

A 1996 report found that 81 percent of public universities already had armed police agencies on campus. Predictably, after the April 16, 2007, Virginia Tech shooting many colleges are rethinking an armed police presence on campus. (Johnson, 2007:A1)

And at Virginia Tech itself?

- Dorms previously locked only at night are now locked twenty-four hours a day.
- Dorms are now accessible only to student residents with an electronic pass.
- Older dorm locks have been replaced with exit bars that cannot be chained shut (as gunman Cho did during his rampage).
- Students can now register for the new emergency notification system.

Dozens of other universities have installed similar emergency message texting systems that can send thousands of alerts to cell phones and e-mail accounts within seconds. *(USA TODAY,* August 17, 2007:4A)

One such system received its baptism under fire in September 2007, when two students were shot at the University of Delaware at Dover.

But while we can applaud attempts at such hi-tech solutions (e.g., better tracking and control of mental patients, better surveillance, and more timely electronic notification), in the end our best hope to prevent such tragedies may simply come down to increasing our awareness and our willingness to become involved, our reactions, and hopefully preactions we take to stand up to bullying in all its forms.

What's that old saying? "The more you sweat in times of peace . . . the less you bleed in times of war."

If we are to catch bullies young, we must first admit where we went—and still are going—wrong. We have helped create, and continue to perpetuate, an atmosphere of bullying, either through our actions or via our inaction.

Like all animals, bullies breed where they feed. We create a culture of bullying through not speaking out against sports icons who spit in referees' faces and who feel free to assault spectators. We create, and continue to perpetuate, a culture of bullying through violent and misogynistic music videos that glorify an "in-your-face" lifestyle. After all, isn't that what the playground bully does? What your bullying boss does? What the abusive husband does? Get "in-your-face"?

We are all guilty of not speaking up when confronted by this "in-your-face," spit at the world, hit at the world attitude. We are afraid we'll be labeled "old," "out of tune with the times," "sexist," even "racist." It seems they have us bullied.

"It's just young people expressing themselves" is the excuse. And that's just what it is: an excuse. But those aren't "kids" on those music videos. Those are grown men—grown in body at least. "Grown" men and women, idolized sports figures and entertainers who command your children's undivided attention for hours every day.

How much time a day of "undivided attention" do you get with your kids? When's the last time your kid wore your picture, name, or logo on his ball cap, shoes, T-shirt, or the ass of his pants?

You're a careful, caring parent. You take time out to warn your child about the dangers of the world. He hears your message once . . . maybe twice. But he listens to their message hundreds of times, over and over. And their message is mixed with seductive imagery, maybe "get-free-stuff" offers. What chance has a parent got? They are bullying your children away from you.

Frustrating, yes. But you can't walk away from your responsibilities as a parent. You have to deal with the world before it deals with you . . . and your children.

Any way you look at it, it all comes down to the most basic—most primal—of all our instincts: flight or fight, a decision human beings must make everyday, all day, from the playground to the battleground. And, for those beset by bullies, the playground is the battleground.

Sometimes we flee, to fight another day. Sometimes we fight today. Choice. Sometimes our DNA makes the choice for us. Sometimes life does. Let your conscience be your guide. Your bully doesn't have one.

Walk away from trouble when you can—run when necessary. But walk away only when you can walk away with your dignity, honor, and self-worth intact.

And, as a last resort, walk away . . . after leaving your chastised bully wishing he'd walked away . . . before he made the life-altering mistake of having awakened your sleeping tiger!

CONCLUSION:
"Red Flags or White Flags?"

"It's frustrating to see one shooting after another that could be prevented. Schools have emergency response plans rather than prevention plans."
—Forensic clinical psychologist Dewey Cornell, in Bazar and Bello (2007:4A)

On October 10, 2007, a fourteen-year-old boy named Asa Coon shot four people—two of his fellow students and two of his teachers—at the Success Tech Academy in Cleveland, Ohio, before then turning the gun on himself.

The following day, October 11, a fourteen-year-old boy was taken into custody at his home in a Philadelphia suburb after the police learned he had allegedly been talking about launching a Columbine-type attack on his former high school. Police were alerted by the father of another boy who the arrested boy had tried to recruit into his plan.

Searching the boy's bedroom, the police discovered a cache of weapons, including a 9mm automatic assault rifle, knives, swords, and several home-made bombs. Police also confiscated books on bomb making, what has been described as "violence-filled notebooks," and videos of the 1999 Columbine attack. (Dale, 2007:4A)

The tragedy in Cleveland and the near-tragedy in Philadelphia—barely twenty-four hours apart—have at least two very important points in common, aside from the coincidental age of the boys involved.

First, bullying has been cited as both fuse and catalyst in both instances.

Second, in both cases there were early warning signs—red flags, if you will. In the Cleveland incident, those warnings were not heeded. Conversely, the Philadelphia incident had a better outcome only because the early warning signs were noticed by alert individuals, the proper authorities notified, and prompt action taken.

BULLYING

Asa Coon was often taunted by fellow students for his Goth style of dress: dark eye makeup, hair dyed black, black nail polish, spiked armbands, dog-collar necklaces, and black clothing, including the kind of black trench coat made infamous by the Columbine shooters who had dubbed themselves the "trench coat Mafia." Coon was also known to have "frequent angry exchanges with students." (Bazar and Bello, 2007:4A)

At least one neighbor of Coon's believes it was just such "badgering" (i.e., bullying) that caused Coon to snap: "People picking on him pushed him over the edge." (ibid. 4A)

Likewise, that fourteen-year-old Philadelphia boy was described as "a home-schooled teenager who felt bullied" and "a kid who thought that he was bullied previously and he was going to exact his revenge." (Dale, 2007:4A)

PRIOR WARNINGS

A week before Coon went on his rampage, he had threatened to blow up the school and stab students. (Bazar and Bello, 2007:4A) According to one student who knew Coon, "He threatened to stab everybody. . . . We didn't think nothing of it." Another student recalled Coon threatening, "I got something for you all." (Cauchon and Gomez, 2007:3A)

Yet, these warnings were not passed along to the proper Cleveland authorities.

And while many argue fervently for increased security in schools, with more metal detectors, surveillance cameras, and security guards, the sad fact is none of these, not even a generous combination of these, is foolproof.

When such troubled students decide to die—and to take others with them—like the "suicide bombers" they are, little can be done to "talk them out of it" once they've strapped on their weapons. Neither is an increased police presence necessarily a deterrent.

Packing two handguns, two boxes of ammunition, and two knives, Coon was still able to walk right past a security guard (the school had no walk-through metal detectors, by the way). And, ironically, the shooting happened across the street from the FBI office in downtown Cleveland.

This is why an early warning system beats a retaliatory strike any day.

In Philly, this kind of early warning system did work, someone did follow "the 3 R's" to recognize, report, and respond in a timely fashion.

To "the 3 R's" we should add a fourth: require, as in require that reports of threatening talk and actions be immediately investigated.

In the same way it is now mandatory for doctors, teachers, and other professionals to report suspected child abuse—or themselves be held as accessories after the fact—so to, it should be mandatory for anyone—especially those in authority—to report any suspicious and threatening activity.

I know what you're thinking: What if I'm wrong in my suspicions?

True, to be wrong and to act is to be embarrassed. But to be right—and fail to act—is to be dead!

Like disgruntled workers, troubled teens who plan deadly "suicide" attacks often warn of their intentions. That's why we all need to start paying closer attention to threatening behavior and talk. A good child psychologist would probably tell us the reason teens (and perhaps adults) give off warning signs is because, deep down, there is a still "good" part of them that wants help, that wants to be stopped.

Perhaps.

While none of us want to be guilty of stifling a child's development, or of sterotyping kids, let's be adult about this; certain "lifestyle" behavior patterns (Goth, for instance, with their fascination for the "dark side" of the human psyche) seem all too easily to go hand-in-hand with—if not openly promote—dark and destructive thoughts and actions.

And while a certain amount of experimentation with difference is acceptable—even to be expected—from young people with empowerment issues, desperately trying to find where they fit in in the world, when difference becomes deviance becomes deadly, then it concerns us all.

So let's risk a little political incorrectness when there's a danger that a "lifestyle" may becomes a death style! And let's start listening to the experts.

For example, the respected criminologist Jack Levin of Boston's Northeastern University believes every school needs to have a twofold program to stop bullying and to overcome the mind-set that reporting threats is "snitching."

In other words, we need to encourage the prompt reporting of "minor" bullying incidents, before we have to encourage the reporting of more potentially deadly retaliatory actions stemming from that bullying.

Levin is insightful—and "hip" enough—to point out that nobody likes a person who "rats," but that schools (and parents) have a responsibility to provide an environment where students who hear threats feel safe enough to tell trusted teachers and counselors. At the very least, students should be able to report threats anonymously. (Bazar and Bello, 2007:4A)

In the end, as parents, we must all learn to be more alert to these red flags, while simultaneously demanding that those whose salaries are squeezed out of our tax dollars become both diligent in their attention toward our children, as well as timely in their response to the merest whiff of threat.

When it comes to our children, we must learn to spot the red flags, because raising the white flag is not an option we—or our children—can live with.

APPENDIX:
Hu-gui Tiger Practice Fighting Form

Performance of this practice fighting form (kata) on a regular basis will not only strengthen you physically but will also help you further focus, and then free up your mind and body from fear:

"Discipline of the body awakens the strength of the mind and spirit. Strength of the body builds confidence of mind and spirit." (Only, 2007)

Mastering this easy-to-learn kata will also give you hundreds more martial arts techniques that you can easily apply to modern-day bullying and self-defense situations.

For a more advanced analysis of tiger-style kung-fu in general, and of this fighting form in particular, see Haha Lung's *Cao Dai Kung-fu* (2002) and *Lost Fighting Arts of Vietnam* (2006).

1. Standing facing "North," your hands at your sides, feet together, bring both hands up from your sides to form a Closed Fists (knuckles forward) X-Block (right hand in front of left). Snapping open your fingers, turn your palms forward to form Twin Tiger-claws. (See Figure 31.)

2. Forcefully separating your Twin Tiger-claws, circle your arms widely outward and down until they cross at your navel. As your arms arc out and down, bend slightly at the knee. Retain an upright posture throughout. (See Figures 18 and 20.)

3. As your Tiger-claws cross at your navel, rise out of your squat and step your right foot out into a right heel stance (East), simultaneously perform a right, face-level decending Tiger-claw strike (East).

Note: A "heel stance" is identical to back stance, except that weight is on the heel only.

Figure 39. "Heel Stance."

4. Repeat Heel stance/Tiger-claw strike from Movement #3, West.
5. Shifting East into a left back stance, perform a right Palm-up Block. (Inverted version of Illustration 14's Shuo-uke No-Block.)
6. Shifting your weight forward into a right forward stance, perform a right decending Tiger-claw strike followed immediately by a left descending Tiger-claw strike from the same stance. This is a Double Tiger-claw strike in rapid succession.

7. Pull your rear left foot to your leading right leg's knee to form a right "Crane Stance." Simultaneously perform a right high-level Vertical-fist strike East.

Note: Some fighting cadre replace the "Crane Stance" at this point with a "Cat Stance."

Figure 40. "Northern Crane Stance."

8. Repeat Movements #5–7, mirror image, West/left.
9. Stepping your left foot behind your right foot, perform a Tiger-squat (North). Simultaneously strike North with a right low-level inverted Tiger-claw strike (targeting groin) while your left hand forms a Palm-outward Tiger-claw guarding your forehead.

Figure 41. "Tiger Squat."

10.   Pivoting 180 degrees as you rise from your Tiger-squat into a left forward stance (North), strike down with a left descending Elbow strike that "collapses" into a left descending Tiger-claw strike (North) followed immediately by a right descending Tiger-claw strike (Noth), all in rapid succession.

Note: Your right Tiger-claw strike continues through its exaggerated arc, opening to loudly slap your left thigh. Traditionally, yell a loud "kat" as you slap.

11.   Stepping forward into a right forward stance (North), perform a right high-level Back-fist strike followed immediately by a left mid-level Vertical-fist from the same stance.

12.   Placing your left foot behind right, perform a Tiger-squat (East). Simultaneously your right arm performs a high-level Rising-block (i.e.

left Tiger-claw guards forehead), while your left hand strikes (East) with a low-level left Palm-thrust. (See Figure 3.)

13. Your left foot steps West into an even "HORSE STANCE." Right forearm crosses left to form a low-level X-Block.

14. Repeat Movement #12 West/left, and then repeat Movement #13, stepping back (East) into a Horse Stance. End with low-level right-over-left X-Block.

15. Still in your Horse Stance facing North, raise your X-Block to face-level and snap them open into Tiger-claws. (Identical hand position in Movement #1.)

16. Right knee suddenly drops to floor as you perform an inverted right Tiger-claw strike (North) and your left Tiger-claw guards forehead. (Identical hand position to Movement #9.)

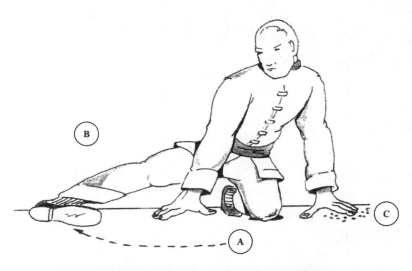

Figure 42. "Iron Broom Sweeping Technique."

a. As your attacker rushes toward you, drop to one knee with both your hands on the ground for balance, your extended leg making a wide half-circle arc on the ground as it glides across the ground heel first to sweep your attacker's leg(s) out from under him.

b. Variation: From this balanced-on-knee position you can also reverse the direction of your kicking-sweep to that of a Roundhouse Kick-sweep (see Figure 24).

c. Any time your hand touches the ground, fill it.

Figure 43. "Two-Point Kick."

a. Facing forward (N), your attacker rushes at you from your right
   side (W) . . .
b. Twisting away from your attacker, suddenly place your right hand
   on the ground (E) . . .
c. Counting the momentum created by placing your hand on the
   ground, swing your left leg up and around (W) in a Reverse
   Roundhouse Kick (aka "Hook Kick"), targeting your attacker's
   head or torso.
d. Land with a hand, and follow through the momentum of your
   Heel Kick by landing and striking with a powerful Hammer-fist or
   similar descending hand strike.
e. Always fill your hand when your hand touches the ground.
   Seizing up a small rock will help reinforce your striking hand as
   you follow through with your Heel Kick.

17. Balanced on your right knee, turn to face South and sweep your left leg outward (South) while simultaneously reverse the positions of your Tiger-claws (left strikes South, right guards forehead). This Leg-Sweep is called the "Iron Broom."

18. Still squatting, pull your left leg in as you simultaneously perform a left Cross-body Block North and a scooping upwards right Tiger-claw (targeting the groin) South.

19. Shifting your weight forward onto your left leg, rise quickly to perform a high-level right Back-fist strike that hides your immediate follow-up strike with a foot strike following immediately behind a "Shadowhand" move.

20. As your right foot lands in a right forward stance (South), perform a high-level left inverted Tiger-claw strike (South).

21. Stepping forward into a left forward stance (South), perform a high-level right inverted Tiger-claw strike. (A mirror image of Movement #20.)

22. Stepping forward into a right forward stance (South), perform a high-level left inverted Tiger-claw strike (South). (Identical to Movement #19.)

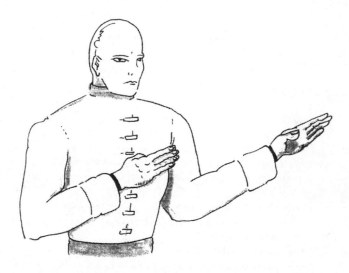

Figure 44. "Double Sword-Hands."

23. Bending forward, place your right hand on the floor (East), pick up your left/rear foot and, pivoting right (West), perform a high-level reverse Roundhouse "Heel Kick" West.

24. Placing your left kicking foot down into a right back stance (West), perform a midlevel double Sword-hand Block.

25. Sliding both feet one step to the right (East) into a left back stance (East), perform a midlevel double Sword-hand Block. (This is the mirror image of Movement #24.)

26. Pulling your right foot to left foot (feet together facing North), cross your forearms to form a chest-level Closed-fists X-Block, right-over-left. (This is the same position as Movement #1.)

27. Glance left, glance right. Open your palms, drop them to your sides.

AUTHORITIES

Adams, Andrea. *Bullying at Work*. London: Virago Press, 1992.

Babbit, Irving, trans. *The Sayings of Buddha (The Dhammapada)*. New York: New Directions Books, 1936.

Bacon, John, et al. "Problems with Bully Bosses? Sue 'Em!" *USA TODAY*, September 22, 2007:3A.

Bazar, Emily, and Marisol Bello. "Lesson of Shootings: Schools Act Too Late." *USA Today*, October 12, 2007.

Beardon, Keith. "100 Mighty Sex Facts." *FHM Magazine*, September 2001:122.

Bing, Stanley. *Crazy Bosses*. New York: Collins Publishing, 2007.

Buscaglia, Leo. *The Way of the Bull*. New York: Fawcett Crest, Ballantine Books, 1973.

Castellitto, Linda M. "Crazy Bosses Can Be Worked Around." *USA TODAY*, May 21, 2007:58.

Cauchon, Dennis, and Alan Gomez. "Teen Shoots 4 at School in Cleveland." *USA Today*, October 1, 2007.

Crowley, Michael. *"No Mercy, Kid!"* Readers Digest, May, 2007.

Cruise, Jorge. "Kickstart Your Heart." *USA Today Weekend*, August 17–19, 2007:4.

Dale, Mary Claire. "Philly Teen Arrested with Cache of Weapons." *USA Today*, October 12, 2007.

Deans, Bob. "Captain John Smith." *Time*, May 7, 2007:61.

Fox, James Alan. "Q: Are College Campuses Safe? A: Yes." *USA Today*, July 18, 2007.

—, Jack Lewis, and Kenna Quinet. *The Will to Kill: Making Sense of Senseless Murder.* Boston: Pearson/Allyn, 2008.

Gibbs, Nancy. "Darkness Falls: One Troubled Student Rains down Death on a Quiet Campus." Time, April 30, 2007:36–52.

Gilbert, Allen, ed. *The Letters of Machiavelli.* Chicago: University of Chicago Press, 1961.

Gold, Stephanie. "A Higher Road to Relaxation." *Psychology Today,* July–August 2007.

Goleman, Daniel. *Emotional Intelligence.* New York: Bantam Books, 1995.

Haden Elgin, Suzette. *Success with the Gentle Art of Verbal Self-Defense.* New York: Prentice-Hall, 1989.

Higgs, Robert. *"Bullying: What Have I Ever Done to You?"* http://loveourchildren usa.org, May 17, 2007.

Johnson, Kevin. "Universities Rethink Unarmed Police." *USA Today,* September 20, 2007.

Johnson, Rachel. "Lesson from Va. Tech: Take Warning Signs Seriously." *USA Today,* September 12, 2007.

Kurz Jr., Hank, and Vicki Smith. "Va. Tech President Defends Himself." *Associated Press,* August 30, 2007.

Levinson, D., and K. Christensen, eds. *Encyclopedia of Sport: From Ancient Times to the Present.* New York: ABC-CLIO, 1996.

Liddy, G. Gordon. *Will.* New York: St. Martin's Press, 1997.

Limes-Dougan, Bonnie, and Janet Kistner. "Physically Abused Preschoolers' Response to Peers' Distress." *Developmental Psychology,* vol. 26, 1990.

Lung, Haha. *The Ancient Art of Strangulation.* Boulder, CO: Paladin Press, 1995.

—*Ninja Craft.* Sharon Center, OH: Alpha Publications, 1997a.

—*Assassin! Secrets of the Cult of the Assassins.* Boulder, CO: Paladin Press, 1997b.

—*Knights of Darkness: Secrets of the World's Deadliest Night-Fighters.* Boulder, CO: Paladin Press, 1998.

—*Cao Dai Kung-fu.* Port Townsend, WA: Loompanics Unlimited, 2002.

—*Assassin!* New York: Citadel Press, 2004a.

—*Knights of Darkness.* New York: Citadel Press, 2004b.

—*Lost Fighting Arts of Vietnam.* New York: Citadel Press, 2006a.

—*Mind Control.* New York: Citadel Press, 2006b.

—*Total Mind Penetration.* New York: Citadel Press, 2007.

—*Koppo-Jitsu: The Forbidden Art of Bone-Breaking.* Publication pending.

—*The 99 Truths: Hannibal's Black Art of War.* Publication pending.

—, and Christopher B. Prowant. Black Science: Ancient and *Modern Ninja Mind Manipulation.* Boulder, CO: Paladin Press, 2001.

—*Mind Manipulation: Ancient and Modern Ninja Techniques.* New York: Citadel Press, 2002a

AUTHORITIES

—*Shadowhand: History and Secrets of Ninja Taisavaki.* Boulder, CO: Paladin Press, 2002b.

—*Theatre of Hell: Dr. Lung's Complete Guide to Torture.* Port Townsend, WA: Loompanics Unlimited, 2003.

—*Ninja Shadowhand: The Art of Invisibility.* New York: Citadel Press, 2004.

—, and Eric Tucker. *The Nine Halls of Death: Ninja Secrets of Mind Mastery.* New York: Citadel Press, 2007b.

Lyman, Stanford M., and Marvin B. Scott. *A Sociology of the Absurd.* 2nd ed. New York: General Hall, 1989.

Main, Mary, and Carol George. "Responses of Abused and Disadvantaged Toddlers to Distress in Age Mates: A Study in the Day-Care Setting." *Developmental Psychology,* vol. 21, no. 3, 1985.

Martin, Michael, and Cynthia Waltman-Greenwood. *Solve Your Child's School-Related Problems.* New York: HarperPerennial, 1995.

Meadows, Robert J. *Understanding Violence and Victimization.* 3rd ed. Upper Saddle River, NJ, Prentice Hall, 2004.

Musashi, Miyamoto. *A Book of Five Rings (Go Rin No Sho).* Misc. translations.

Myers, David G. *Exploring Psychology.* 6th ed. New York: Worth Publishers, 2005.

Naito, Hatsuho. *Thunder Gods: The Kamikaze Pilots Tell Their Story.* Trans. Mayumi Ichikawa. Tokyo, New York: Kodansha International, 1989.

Omar, Ralf Dean. *"Ninja Death Touch: The Fact and the Fiction."* *Blackbelt*, September 1989.

—*Death on Your Doorstep: 101 Weapons in the Home.* Sharon Center, OH: Alpha Publications, 1994.

—*Prison Killing Techniques: Blade, Bludgeon and Bomb.* Port Townsend, WA: Loompanics Unlimited, 2001.

—*Blood on the Sidewalk: 101 Weapons on the Street.* Publication pending.

—*Direct Action: Take Back the Streets!* Publication pending.

Only, Joshua. *Wormwood: The Terrible Truth about Islam.* Spirit Lake, ID: Only Publications, 2007.

Seagrave, Sterling. *The Soong Dynasty.* New York: Harper and Row, 1985.

Skinner, Dirk. *Street Ninja: Ancient Secrets for Mastering Today's Mean Streets.* New York: Barricade Books, 1995.

Sun Tzu. *The Art of War (Ping-fa).* Misc. translations.

Thomas, Alexander, et al. "Longitudinal Study of Negative Emotional States and Adjustments from Early Childhood through Adolescence." *Child Development,* vol. 59, September 1988.

233

Tokitsu, Kenji. *Miyamoto Musashi: His Life and Writings.* Boston, London: Shambhala, 2004.

Waller, James. *Becoming Evil: How Ordinary People Commit Genocide and Mass Killing.* New York: Oxford University Press, 2002.

Weber, Max. *The Theory of Social and Economic Organization.* New York: The Free Press, 1947.

Wright, Lesley, and Marti Smye. *Corporate Abuse.* New York: Macmillan, 1996.

Zimbardo, Philip. "Pathology of Imprisonment." *Transaction/Society,* April 1972.